THE IRON FIST AND
THE VELVET GLOVE

THE IRON FIST AND THE VELVET GLOVE
an analysis of the U.S. police

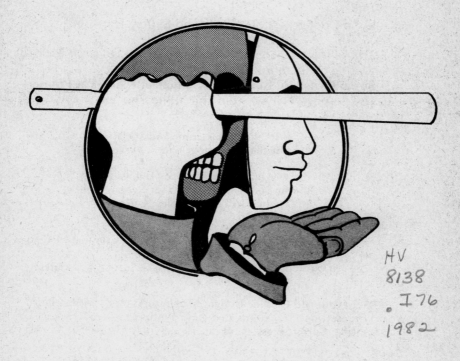

Institute for the Study of Labor
and Economic Crisis

This book was collectively written by:
Tony Platt, Jon Frappier, Gerda Ray, Richard Schauffler,
Larry Trujillo (Staff and Associates of the Institute for the
Study of Labor and Economic Crisis)
and
Lynn Cooper, Elliott Currie and Sidney Harring

The following people contributed to the research for and
writing of the book:
Susie Bernstein, Bill Bigelow, Michael Klare, Pat Poyner,
Joy Scruggs, Nancy Stein and Millie Thayer

Published by Crime and Social
Justice Associates, San Francisco

Originally produced and published
by the Staff of the Center for Research on
Criminal Justice, Berkeley, California

Layout and Graphic Design: Elizabeth Sutherland Martínez
Typesetting: Archetype, Berkeley; Synthex Press, San Francisco
Printing: Garrett Press, San Francisco; Synthex Press, San Francisco
ISBN: 1-917404-02-5
Library of Congress Catalog Card Number 82-060574

The correct ISBN for the 3rd edition of
The Iron Fist and the Velvet Glove is:
0-935206-02-7

Address all orders to:
Synthesis Publications
P.O. Box 40099
San Francisco, CA 94140

KM
11-10-83

TABLE OF CONTENTS

FOREWORD TO THE THIRD EDITION

This is the third printing of *The Iron Fist and the Velvet Glove*. It was first published in 1975 by the Center for Research on Criminal Justice. After the first edition of 10,000 copies sold out, the book was extensively revised and reprinted in 1977 (see the preface to the second edition for an explanation of the revisions). In 1978 the work begun by the Center for Research on Criminal Justice was continued by the Institute for the Study of Labor and Economic Crisis (ISLEC) in San Francisco. ISLEC is an independent, progressive institute, established in 1977, which does research on criminal justice and other important national and international policy issues. Most of ISLEC's research in the criminal justice area is published in its journal, *Crime and Social Justice*, edited by Tony Platt and Paul Takagi. Since the second edition of another 10,000 copies of *The Iron Fist and the Velvet Glove* was sold out by 1981, and since the book is still very much in demand, ISLEC has decided to publish this third edition.

We think that the general analysis and framework of this book still provide a persuasive explanation of the role and contradictions of the police in the United States in the 1980s. While there have been some important new developments in policing since this book was written in 1977 (for example, the dismantling of the Law Enforcement Assistance Administration, the unshackling of the FBI and CIA, the increasing use of "deadly force," etc.), the main trends that we identified five years ago still prevail.

In fact, our analysis and predictions have been very much confirmed by the events of the last few years. What we called the "military-corporate" model of policing—with its emphasis on technology, efficiency and repression from a managerial perspective—has become the exemplary professional standard for the police. Since 1977, especially under Reagan, there has been an expansion of the criminal justice apparatus and a decisive shift to the right in criminal justice policies. This is reflected in the unprecedented increase in the penal population, in the growth of "law and order" legislation, in the grossly disproportionate imprisonment of minorities, and in the resurgence of political witch-hunting that is reminiscent of McCarthyism but potentially far more insidious and dangerous. These repressive policies of "law and order," which not too long ago appeared to be monopolized by right-wing political organizations and fringe groups, are rapidly becoming the conventional wisdom in the White House, Congress, state legislatures, and academia.

Now, more than ever before, we need to understand the police and repressive apparatus because we are living in a period which, to quote Marlene Dixon, "may prove to be the opening of an era of emergent neofascism. . . . So it has come to pass that the outward face of the United States, the face of the imperialists, the face of CIA, Special Forces, the face of transna-

3

tional capital, that face has now turned inward to confront the masses of the people of the United States. It is the *implosion* of Empire, it is the very beginning of an era in which the people of the United States will begin to see the democratic veils stripped away from the face of American power; they will begin to experience what has been the fate of the colony" (*Contemporary Marxism*, 4).

We encourage the reader to supplement and update *The Iron Fist and the Velvet Glove* by consulting the following select publications, as well as many other specialized articles and books that have been published since 1977. In order to understand the important interconnections between the police, the criminal justice apparatus, and the state in these dangerous times of economic and political crisis, we refer the reader to the journal *Crime and Social Justice*, especially No. 15 on "Law and Order in the 1980s" and No. 17 on "Meeting the Challenge of the 1980s," and to the journal *Contemporary Marxism*, especially No. 4 which addresses the "World Capitalist Crisis and the Rise of the Right." Both are journals of ISLEC and can be ordered from Synthesis Publications, P.O. Box 40099, San Francisco, California 94140.

In the last five years, there has been a steady growth in the criminal justice apparatus, in the number of police personnel, and in criminal justice budgets. Between 1977 and 1978, for example, criminal justice expenditures in the U.S. increased by 12% to over $24 billion; of this, about $13 billion was allocated to the police. For various documents on budgets and personnel, consult the publications of the U.S. Department of Justice's Bureau of Justice Statistics, especially the *Sourcebook of Criminal Justice Statistics – 1980*, edited by Michael Hindelang, Michael Gottfredson, and Timothy Flanagan, published in 1981.

In the last few years, we have learned a great deal about the organization and operations of the political police and intelligence apparatus. With the help of the Freedom of Information Act and documents provided by the Rockefeller Commission Report on CIA activities in the U.S. (1975) and the Church Committee Report on domestic intelligence (1976), there has been increased scholarly interest in political surveillance and political repression. We strongly recommend that the reader first consult Frank Donner's definitive and comprehensive book, *The Age of Surveillance: The Aims and Methods of America's Political Intelligence System* (New York: Vintage Books, 1981). For a useful historical survey, see Robert Goldstein's *Political Repression in Modern America: From 1870 to the Present* (New York: Schenkman, 1978). The following books also contain important information: David Wise, *The American Police State: The Government Against the People* (New York: Vintage Books, 1978); Morton Halperin et al., *The Lawless State: The Crimes of the U.S. Intelligence Agencies* (New York: Penguin, 1976); and Richard Morgan, *Domestic Intelligence: Monitoring Dissent in America* (Austin, Texas: University of Texas Press, 1980). For a comprehensive, annotated bibliography (albeit somewhat out of date), we refer the reader to the "materials list" on "Surveillance and Harassment for Political Reasons by U.S. Government Agencies," published by the Campaign for Political Rights in its December, 1978, issue of *Organizing Notes*. For comparative purposes, we recommend Tony Bunyan, *The History and Practice of the Political Police in Britain* (London: Quartet Books, 1977) and the English journal, *State Research*, which publishes carefully researched information and commentaries on political policing in Europe.

We welcome your comments on *The Iron Fist and the Velvet Glove*. Please address any correspondence to the Institute for the Study of Labor and Economic Crisis, 608 Taraval Street, San Francisco, California 94116.

Tony Platt
ISLEC, San Francisco
May, 1982

PREFACE

The idea for this pamphlet grew out of the political work of the Union of Radical Criminologists and the North American Congress on Latin America (NACLA) in Berkeley, California. The rapidly escalating police apparatus and the frequency of police repression, as well as the lack of a systematic radical analysis of the police, prompted us to combine our collective efforts to write this book. Out of this union was born the autonomous Center for Research on Criminal Justice. We wrote this book, not as a definitive statement on the police, but as an exploratory attempt to critically assess their function in the United States. The book is aimed at all people concerned with making fundamental changes in the police apparatus and the society as a whole.

More than anything, this book has served as a process of educating ourselves. When we began over a year ago, none of us realized the depth and breadth this project would take on. From the preliminary delegations of research responsibilities to the critical reading and political discussions of the first drafts, we began to realize the difficulties involved in our work. Part of the difficulty came from the lack of a general analysis of the police on the part of the Left and part came from our realization of the inadequacies of our own analysis as members of the Left specifically concerned with the criminal justice system. Soon meetings became regular and more disciplined. Rewrites were due in the office several days before the meetings and people were encouraged to respond to them with written criticisms. In the process of collectively attempting to understand the complexities of the role of the police in the U.S. we often became frustrated and discouraged, while at other times we felt real insight, progress and accomplishment in our work. As the process continued we began to share a common vision and sense of purpose in our work—a bond we feel makes the analysis flow from beginning to end. Moreover, the process helped us to analyze and develop our own political consciousness and share that growth with each other.

We are concerned with developing a theoretical analysis that can provide people with adequate knowledge and insight from which concrete political action can be mounted. In this spirit we conclude the book with some general guidelines, that flow from our analysis, of ways to organize and link the demand for control of the police to the demand for control over all aspects of our lives. In this way we feel our work contributes to the call for a radical transformation of present social conditions in the U.S. and towards a greater humanity.

Many people have influenced this book. We would like to acknowledge and sincerely thank the following who aided, supported and contributed to our work:
Florence Anamoto, Karen Bailey, Jim Chanin, Denise Drachnik, David Jackson, Paul Jacobs, Claude Marks, Patty Miller, Larry Moorehead, Alphonso Pinkney, Gerda Ray, Lou Sempliner, Paul Takagi Marilyn Katz, Bob Wells

In deciding to print a second, revised version of *The Iron Fist and the Velvet Glove*, we were guided by two things. First, the response to the original edition was encouraging and gratifying.

Within a year, we had sold out our first printing—and the feedback we received from people using the book across the country, in classes and in local organizing, convinced us that another printing would be helpful and well received. In addition, we welcomed the chance to expand and strengthen the book in several ways. The book as a whole has been re-organized for better clarity and readability. We have expanded and thoroughly rewritten several sections—especially those dealing with the history and development of the police—and we have updated the book to take account of new developments, particularly the increasing militancy of police organizations, the impact of the current fiscal crisis on police strategy, and new trends in political surveillance. Finally, we have re-thought and rewritten the sections dealing with our view of the functions of the police (*Introduction*) and of strategies for change (*Conclusion*); and added new material in the section on *Documents*.

We feel that these changes reflect our own growing understanding of the role of the police in the United States today, and we hope readers, both old and new, will find them useful in their own work. As always, we don't regard the *Iron Fist* as an academic exercise, but as a way of providing the kind of analysis that can help guide effective political action. We're grateful for the positive response so far, and we greatly appreciate the helpful comments and suggestions we've received from many people and hope they continue. We want to particularly thank Mark Levine and John Pallas for their valuable help on this project.

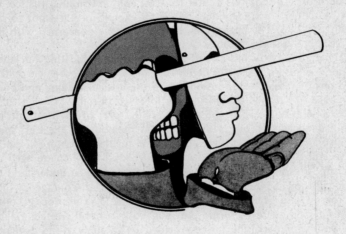

I INTRODUCTION

There must be something in the very core of a social system which increases its wealth without diminishing its misery, and increases in crime even more rapidly than in numbers.
Karl Marx
New York Daily Tribune
September 16, 1859

WHY THIS BOOK?

During the past ten years, the police have taken on an unprecedented importance in the U.S. In the past, the police forces in this country were, for the most part, fragmented and scattered in many different levels and jurisdictions, uncoordinated with each other, without central planning or comprehensive strategies. Relatively little money was spent on strengthening local police forces and little attention was given to developing new concepts and techniques of police practice. In the 1960's all this began to change.

First, there has been a rapid growth in the sheer number of police in this country and in the funds generated to support them. Government spending on the criminal justice system in general has been steadily increasing for the last two decades, and very dramatically in the past ten years. In 1955, criminal justice expenditures at all levels of government—local, state, and Federal—amounted to about one-half of 1 percent of the U.S. Gross National Product; by 1971, it had risen to about 1 percent, and the rate of increase since 1966 was about five times as great as it was in the previous decade. From 1971-1974 alone, spending on criminal justice jumped over 42 percent, from $10½ billion to about $15 billion. Of this money, over $8½ billion—about 57 percent—was spent on the police in 1974,[1] eight times what was spent on the police, at all levels of government, ten years earlier.[2] The total number of police in the United States went up by about 75,000 between 1971-1974, from 575,000 to 653,000.[3]

At the present rate of increase, there will be about 900,000 police in the United States in 1984. While many areas of public spending have been sharply cut back in the economic crisis of the 1970's, police protection remains one of the fastest-growing parts of the public sector. In some cities and states, the recent growth of the police has been even more spectacular. In Colorado, spending on the police jumped 80 percent between 1971-1974.[4] The Los Angeles police force doubled in size in the ten years between 1964-1974, while Chicago's force increased by about two-thirds.[5]

Even more significant than the general increase in the size and fiscal importance of the police is the growing centralization and sophistication of the police system—and the criminal justice system generally—over the last few years. As the chart below shows, most spending on criminal justice still comes from the local level—but the share of the states and especially of the Federal government is rising fast. Federal spending on criminal justice shot up by 62 percent between 1971-1974, and on police in particular by about 52 percent.[6] For the first time in U.S. history, the Federal government has become deeply involved in the police system, mainly through the creation of the massive Federal Law Enforcement Assistance Administration (LEAA), devoted primarily to standardizing and centralizing the police and other criminal justice agencies, and to funding the development of new and increasingly sophisticated police strategies. At the same time, the 1960's saw the rise of a whole "police-industrial complex," a rapidly growing industry that took technical developments originally created for overseas warfare or for the space program and, backed by government funds, applied them to the problems of domestic "order" in the United States.

In addition to the rise of new, sophisticated technologies, another striking development in the U.S. police apparatus during the sixties was the growth of new strategies of community

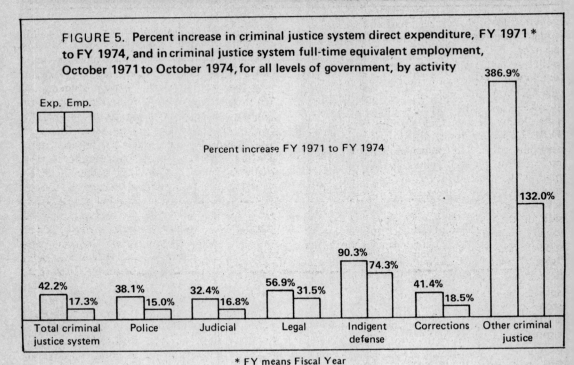

FIGURE 5. Percent increase in criminal justice system direct expenditure, FY 1971 * to FY 1974, and in criminal justice system full-time equivalent employment, October 1971 to October 1974, for all levels of government, by activity

* FY means Fiscal Year

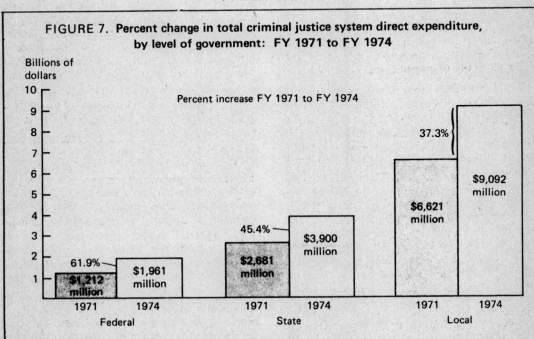

FIGURE 7. Percent change in total criminal justice system direct expenditure, by level of government: FY 1971 to FY 1974

penetration and "citizen participation" that sought to integrate people into the process of policing and to secure the legitimacy of the police system itself. Along with this has been a dramatic increase in the money and attention given to various kinds of "police education" programs and other efforts designed to give a new "professional" look to the police. The Federal government in the early 1970's began spending about $20 million annually on police education in the universities, colleges, and even high schools, and today over 750 colleges and universities offer degrees or courses in "police science" or "criminal justice."[7] On the other side of the coin, the police have developed a variety of new "tough" specialized units— special anti-riot and tactical patrol forces, "special weapons" teams, and highly sophisticated intelligence units. And the growth and spread of the U.S. police apparatus has not stopped at the national boundaries; since the sixties, the United States has been actively exporting its police concepts, technologies, and personnel to the far corners of the American empire. Finally, the government effort to beef up and streamline the police system has been matched by an equally dramatic increase in the number of private police, security guards, and private corporations engaged in producing and selling all kinds of complicated security hardware and services.

The new emphasis on the police is also reflected in popular culture in the United States. Today there are so many television shows dealing with the police that it is hard to keep up with them, and movies with some kind of police theme dominate the neighborhood theaters (see box).

What happened to cause this sudden growth in the size and significance of the police? Most importantly, the 1960's and early '70's have been a time of great crisis for American capitalism—not the first crisis the U.S. capitalist system has undergone, but one of the most severe. The crisis has had many different aspects, economic, social, and political, but in terms of the growth of the police, the most important is the erosion of the popular acceptance of the corporate system and of the political power that supports it, both at home and abroad. During the last ten years, this crisis in legitimacy has been manifested in many ways—not only in the widespread resistance and rebellion in the Third World,* student, and White working-class communities, but in the rapidly and steadily rising rates of street crime. The combined rates of the seven "serious" crimes as defined by the F.B.I. (murder, rape, robbery, burglary, aggravated assault, larceny, and auto theft) rose by 158 percent between 1960 and 1971.[8] Crime became a central preoccupation and fear for many people during this period, and emerged as a crucial political issue of the sixties. It became especially critical in the "inner cities," where by the early seventies one person in every five was being victimized by some form of serious crime each year.[7]

The new emphasis on strengthening and streamlining the police is one of the most important responses of the American government to the widespread challenge to its legitimacy. It goes along with other, similar attempts to refurbish the "correctional" system, to harness the public schools more tightly to corporate values and interests, and to rationalize the "mental health" and welfare systems in the face of the growing disintegration of the "consensus" that was supposed to exist in the U.S. in the 1940's and '50's. How successful the state[10] is in developing such means of integration and repression will depend on how effectively we are able to resist that development.

THE ROLE OF THE POLICE

Why are we so concerned about the growth of the police in the first place? Why don't we welcome it as a step toward a safer and more decent society?

The answer lies in our basic view of the functions that the police perform in the U.S. today, and have performed throughout U.S.

* Throughout this book, we use the term "Third World" to refer to Blacks, Chicanos, Puerto Ricans, other Spanish-Americans, Asian-Americans and Native Americans, within the United States, as well as people of color overseas.

TV POLICE PROGRAMS (1974-75)

Anyone who watches TV knows that police-type programs dominate the screen. Each season new police series are aired and re-runs are picked up by other networks. The powerful medium of television is attempting to change the reputation the police have as being brutal, racist, corrupt and the protectors of wealthy and powerful interests. Television tries to legitimize the police by distorting on the screen what the police practice daily.

Three major themes run through many of the police programs: (1) The war against organized crime is a very popular theme. Most people want the mafia stopped and feel the police should get the job done. But the impression TV programs give is that large resources are put into the fight against organized crime. Not only is this a distortion, but the widespread corruption within many metropolitan police departments is partly due to friendly relations with organized crime. (2) After the TV police have established themselves as mafia fighters, the programs often deal with the more sensitive issue of radicalism. Whether infiltrating a radical political organization, suppressing a protest or neutralizing a terrorist group,

the program portrays the police as protectors of property and life against the unprincipled fanatics. The programs do not discuss the conditions which give rise to organized opposition nor does the viewer get an honest picture of how the police operate in various communities. In the 1950's the enemy was communism and today it is terrorism. (3) The police programs cannot totally deny their bad image, so many of them will address the problem of brutality, corruption or racism, but *only* as it is manifested by one deviant police officer who is then relieved of his duty. This is intended to convince the viewer that the rest of the police force is free from these problems and is capable of cleaning its own house.

The following chart includes the twenty police programs aired on the three major networks (ABC, CBS and NBC). The chart does not include the numerous programs of private detectives who are often ex-police officers and who work closely with the police. Examples are Mannix, Harry-O, Barnaby Jones and Cannon. Also not included in the chart are re-runs like FBI, Mod Squad and Mission Impossible. Watch for yourself.

TITLE (NETWORK)	CHARACTER(S)
Get Christie Love (ABC)	Black undercover policewoman
Caribe (ABC)	"Association of American States" crimefighters
Kodiak (ABC)	Alaska State Patrol troopers
Baretta (ABC)	New York City undercover cop
Barney Miller (ABC)	New York City Police Captain
Nakia (ABC)	A Native American New Mexico deputy sheriff
Rookies (ABC)	Los Angeles rookies on the beat
Streets of SF (ABC)	Two San Francisco detectives
SWAT (ABC)	Los Angeles Police Department's Special Weapons and Tactics Unit
Hawaii Five-0 (CBS)	Hawaii State Police Detectives
Kojak (CBS)	New York City Police homicide detective
Adam—12 (NBC)	Two Los Angeles cops on the beat
Emergency (NBC)	Los Angeles Police emergency unit
Ironside (NBC)	Wheelchaired police investigator
Columbo (NBC)	Los Angeles police detective
McCloud (NBC)	Taos, N.M. sheriff
McMillan and Wife (NBC)	Police commissioner
Police Story (NBC)	Los Angeles Police Department in operation
Police Woman (NBC)	A white undercover policewoman in Los Angeles
Sierra (NBC)	Police in the high Sierras

Weekly production costs average about $200,000 for an hour program.

history. Although the actual role of the police at any given time—like the role of the state in general in advanced capitalist societies—is complex and should not be oversimplified, it is clear that the police have *primarily* served to enforce the class, racial, sexual, and cultural oppression that has been an integral part of the development of capitalism in the U.S.[11] As long as this function remains, any strengthening of the powers of the police, any movement toward greater efficiency or sophistication in their methods, must be seen as inherently contrary to the interests and needs of the majority of people in this country, and in other countries where the U.S. police system penetrates.

Our position is very different from that of most people who write about the police. Whether "liberal" or "conservative," most commentators on the police share a common assumption: they all take the existence of the police for granted. They assume that any modern society necessarily has to have a large and ever-present body of people whose purpose is to use coercion and force on other people. "Conservatives" usually point to such things as the decline in respect for authority, the breakdown of traditional values or of family discipline, as the source of the need for the police, who are seen as a "thin blue line" holding back the forces of evil and destruction that lurk just beneath the surface of civilization. This view is often found within police departments (and was promoted for decades by the F.B.I. under J. Edgar Hoover) and in many popular movie and T.V. portrayals of the police. A more "liberal" approach—increasingly evident among academic and professional police reformers—sees the need for police in the growing complexity and diversity of modern urban society. Liberal commentators often point to social and economic conditions—especially poverty and unemployment—as factors underlying the crime and social disorder that make the police necessary. But these conditions are usually accepted, in the liberal view, as either inevitable or as problems that can only be solved in the "long run." In the meantime, we have to accept the basic role of the police for the indefinite future, although we can do something about correcting police abuses and inefficiency. A classic

example of this kind of thinking can be found in the (1967) Report of the President's Crime Commission, a standard source for modern liberal platitudes about the police. The Commission recognized that "the police did not create and cannot resolve the social conditions that stimulate crime," and went so far as to acknowledge that "the economy is not geared to provide (criminals) with jobs." But the Commission did not go on to examine in detail the particular conditions that cause crime, or how these conditions are related to the most basic structures of the U.S. economy.[12] It did not ask, for example, why the economy has not been able to provide enough jobs throughout the entire twentieth century. The larger social and economic issues were raised, but then conveniently dropped, and the rest of the Report deals with ways of improving the functional capacity of the criminal justice system.

To accept the basic role of the police in this way is to accept the system of social, political, and economic relations that role supports. Behind both the liberal and conservative views of the police there is a basic pessimism about the possibilities for human liberation and co-operation, a pessimism that we do not share. We believe that a society that must be held together by constant force or the threat of force is an oppressive society, and we do not believe that oppression is inevitable. Around us there are examples of societies that have done much to eliminate the sources of exploitation and suffering that generate crime. A main premise of our approach to the police, then, is that we believe things *can* be different; that we can build a society without grinding poverty, ill-health, mutual exploitation and fear—and, therefore, without a vast, repressive police apparatus.

How do the present police enforce the oppressive social and personal relations of capitalist society? There are two different, but related ways in which this is accomplished.
(1) The laws that define what is and what is not "crime"—and thus what is or is not a concern of the police—have been primarily defined in U.S. history by and for the people who benefit most from the capitalist system;

11

(2) Even within the inherently one-sided system of laws the police have been used *selectively*, enforcing *some* of the laws against *some* kinds of people, while allowing other laws to fall into disuse and letting other kinds of law-breakers go free, or nearly free.

(1) The Definition of Crime

The most violent and socially harmful acts in the history of the U.S. have been carried out by the government and the wealthy rulers of the corporate economy. Whether measured in human lives or dollars, these acts constitute the most severe crimes of all, though they are not labelled as such in the criminal codes. The overwhelming number of killings in the 1960's were committed by the U.S. armed forces in Southeast Asia. The largest thefts in U.S. history were carried out by the U.S. government against the lands of Mexicans and the various Native American tribes. The most brutal kidnapping since Blacks were forced into slavery was carried out by the U.S. government, against the Japanese-Americans in the 1940's, when they were stripped of their belongings and held in camps during World War II.[13] Perhaps most importantly, the process of getting rich off the labor of other people, far from being considered a crime, is the basis of normal economic life in the U.S., and people who do it successfully have great prestige and power.

Historically, the *main* function of the police has been to protect the property and well-being of those who benefit most from an economy based on the extraction of private profit. The police were created primarily in response to rioting and disorder directed against oppressive working and living conditions in the emerging industrial cities (see below, sections II and III for history). They were used consistently to put down striking workers in the industrial conflicts of the late 19th and early 20th centuries. The police did not shoot or beat the corporate executives of Carnegie Steel, the Pullman Company, or the Pennsylvania Railroad who subjected their workers to long hours, physical danger, and low pay; instead, they shot and beat the workers who protested against that exploitation. In the 1960's, the

police did not arrest the men who planned and directed the U.S. aggression in Southeast Asia; they arrested the people who protested against that aggression. And in the ghetto revolts of Harlem, Watts, and Newark, the police did not use tear gas and shotguns on slumlords or on merchants who sold shoddy and overpriced goods; they used them on the Black people who rebelled against that victimization.

All of this is often conveniently forgotten in discussions of the police. It adds up to the simple fact that the police were not created to serve "society" or "the people," but to serve *some* parts of society and *some* people at the expense of others. Sometimes, this means that things like racism, sexism, economic exploitation, or military aggression are defined as worthy rather than criminal. In other cases, something more subtle happens. Many of the most socially and personally damaging acts that *are* forbidden in U.S. law are handled as "civil" rather than "criminal" issues. This is often true, for example, for such things as denying people jobs on the grounds of sex or race, or violating safety or anti-pollution regulations. Generally, the executives of corporations and other institutions that violate these laws are not visited by armed police, handcuffed and thrown in patrol wagons, and taken to jail. Instead, a long, drawn out, and expensive process of litigation takes place, during which "business as usual" goes on as before. This distinction, like the basic definition of crime, is not natural or inevitable, but reflects the social priorities and sources of political power in a society built on private profit.

(2) Selective Enforcement

Even when the actions of the wealthy and powerful are defined as criminal and detected, the penalties they face are usually relatively mild and rarely applied in practice. Offenses such as embezzlement, fraud, tax fraud, and forgery resulted in a loss of $1.73 billion in 1965. In the same year, robbery, burglary, auto theft, and larceny resulted in a loss of $690 million—less than half as much. Although the "crime in the suites" represented much more stolen wealth, it was much less severely punished. Less than 20 percent of those convicted of tax fraud in 1969 (which averaged $190,000) served prison terms, and these terms averaged only 9 months. At the same time, over 90 percent of those convicted of robbery were sentenced to prison, where they served an average of 52 months.[14]

Alongside this systematic leniency toward white-collar or corporate offenders, there is considerable evidence showing that underneath the formal structure of the criminal law there is an unofficial but systematic pattern of selective use of the police to coerce and intimidate oppressed people. Studies of police street practices consistently show that the police use their discretion to arrest more often against working-class people than others. For example, middle-class youth are much more likely to be let off with a reprimand for many kinds of crimes, while working-class youth are far more likely to be formally arrested and charged, for the same kinds of offenses.[15] More dramatically, it has been shown that the police systematically use their ultimate weapon, deadly force, much more against Third World people than against Whites. A recent study found that between 1960 and 1968, 51 percent of the people killed by police were Black—in a country where Blacks make up something over 10 percent of the population.[16] The police response to the crime of rape is another example of this pattern, for although rape—unlike most expressions of sexism—is considered in law as a serious

crime, it is typically dealt with in ways that serve to degrade and further victimize women and to enforce oppressive and stereotypical conceptions of women's role.[17] In these and other ways too numerous to mention here, the routine operation of the police creates an informal system of criminal law that, even more than the formal one, is designed to support the fundamentally oppressive social relations of capitalism. It should be emphasized that this is not just a question of easily correctible police "abuses." The selective use of the police has been a systematic and constant feature of the whole pattern of "social control" in the U.S., and its consistency shows how tightly it is tied in to the repressive needs of the system as a whole.

DEALING WITH CRIME

Even though we believe that the most dangerous criminals sit in corporate and government offices, we recognize that the more conventional kinds of crime—"street crimes"—are a real and frightening problem which must be confronted. The Left in the United States has neglected, with few notable exceptions, to deal with the problem of street crime as the serious social problem that it is. In the United States people are faced every day with the danger of theft or personal violence. According to the 1974 FBI Uniform Crime Reports,[18] there were just under one million violent crimes (murder, forcible rape, robbery and aggravated assault) and over nine million property crimes (burglary, larceny theft and motor-vehicle theft) reported to law enforcement officials.

We know, however, that many, if not most, crimes are not even reported to police. This is confirmed by a recent series of "victimization" studies which are based on systematic interviews with representative samples of the urban population. In these studies, people are asked about the number and types of crimes in which they have been the victim. This provides a much more accurate picture of the extent of crime than the FBI Reports which are primarily based on crimes reported to the police. One such victimization study conducted in 1973

13

showed that less than one out of five people reported to police instances of personal larceny without contact.[19] Some experts estimate that only 10 percent of all rapes are reported,[20] and the reporting rate for wife-beating is even lower. The primary reason for not contacting police is the belief that police cannot do anything.[21] The victims of crime are overwhelmingly poor people, particularly Third World people and those living in urban areas. A LEAA victimization study in 1973 showed that, in all but two of nineteen categories of personal victimization, Blacks and other Third World people with family incomes less than $3,000 were most often victimized.[22] The group with the second highest victimization rate was White people with family incomes under $3,000.[23] Another study using the same nineteen categories showed that in every category unemployed people were more likely to be victims of crime in rates two to three times higher than those employed.[24]

While the greatest fear of crime exists in poor and Third World communities because most street crime is committed by the poor against the poor—disproportionately Third World people—the concern with crime as a political issue is concentrated in the middle and upper classes.[25] In 1948, only 4 percent of the population felt crime was their community's worst problem but in 1972 the figure in large cities was 21 percent. The state has used this issue of street crime as a mask to encourage fear and racist attitudes and to divert people's attention away from corporate and government crime. Since street crime is an authentic issue that easily arouses people, the promise to establish law and order and make the streets safe is an appealing one. Because the fear of crime is a demoralizing and oppressive fact of life, many people believe the police should be supported and encouraged since it is theoretically their job to provide protection against this type of crime. In reality, however, the police have been ineffective in dealing with street crimes and do not protect the property or lives of poor and Third World people, as we shall show throughout this book. The solutions proposed by law and order politicians and the state include harsher treatment of criminals,

more police with less legal restrictions and more technological equipment, and a strong moral order based on family and religion; but politicians cannot offer *viable* solutions to crime because they do not discuss the real causes.

The reasons why there is so much street crime in the United States are complex, but they are rooted in the material deprivations, personal alienation and misery that capitalism produces. Under the capitalist system, emphasizing high profits at the expense of people's needs, workers are prevented from developing cooperative social relations that grow in the process of producing needed services and goods with fellow workers. A large part of the alienation and insecurity results from the tenuous position of many individuals in the labor force, to unemployment and underemployment, to dead-end jobs and job instability. Divisively pitting people against each other for scarce jobs is integral to the capitalist system since the fear of unemployment weakens resistance. Third World people are the most victimized by this, feeling it through racism from both the people in the labor market and by the employers' need to keep people divided.[26]

Crime is caused not only by economic policies which result in direct material suffering for millions of people, but also by the individualistic, competitive and cynical values which are endemic to capitalist social relations and ideology. The ideological function of unfulfilling, alienated work is to dehumanize workers; and this condition makes it difficult for workers to discover the socialist alternative. Although street criminals do constitute a real danger to many of us, the basic crime problem originates with the ruling class whose control of and profit from capitalism perpetuates oppressive social relationships.

No "war on crime" can provide a truly enduring solution to the problem of crime unless it directly attacks the sources of that misery and alienation. Strengthening the existing police does not do this; but only helps to strengthen the system that generates crime in the first place. Flooding the society with more and better-equipped police—putting a cop on every corner—could have some effect on the rate of crime. But this kind of "solution" would not touch the underlying roots of crime, and could only be done at tremendous economic, political and social costs.

To deal with crime by strengthening the police is to accept the inevitability of crime and the permanence of the oppressive social system which breeds it. We believe that the real solution to ending street crime is in the struggle for a society that can meet people's basic needs. We have a right to live in a society where labor without profit and equitable social relationships can set the conditions for eradicating crime. In socialist societies many kinds of crime—including theft, drug use, and crimes of personal violence—have strikingly decreased, although crime has not altogether disappeared in them. Crime is likely to decrease even more in these societies, as the traces of earlier, oppressive relationships are gradually destroyed. In China, for example, the notorious drug traffic, which before 1949 was perhaps the most serious and widespread crime problem, had been virtually eliminated by 1952. This was made possible by the introduction of severe penal sanctions against large-scale manufacturers and distributors, amnesty and government support for drug users (including stipends and free treatment centers), and a massive public education campaign in which tens of thousands of people participated. Once the profitable basis of drugs was removed, it was then possible to wage a political struggle against the exploitative social relations which sustained its use.[27]

To understand the specific pattern of crime in any particular capitalist system, we must examine the concrete historical conditions and development of each society. The United States has much higher rates of crime than all other "developed" capitalist countries, for example Sweden, Switzerland, or England. In the United States, the historical patterns of racism help to explain the specific types and amount of crime. U.S. capitalist development has depended heavily on the super-exploitation of Third World people. The resulting special oppression of Third World people contributes to higher rates of U.S. street crime. However, the oppression itself which is characterized also by higher rates of disease, infant mortality, unemploy-

ment, etc. is the more fundamental and harmful crime.

While the long-term struggle for socialism is waged, people have a right and need to make political and economic demands on the state. The rich can afford private police and security systems to protect their interests; working people have to fight for the right to a decent standard of living and to exercise our constitutional freedoms. We think that it is crucial for crime control programs to be linked with an analysis of the political economy. To do less than this is to feed into corporate reforms and to give people the illusion that exploitation can be conquered under capitalism. These struggles for immediate demands should not be minimized, partly because they serve to expose the hypocrisy of bourgeois democracy and partly because they provide important support for the institutions and rights that the working class has gained. In the closing section of this book, we will return to examine this issue of the relationship between the struggle for immediate reforms and the long-range struggle for socialism.

FRAMEWORK FOR ANALYSIS

Up to now, there has been insufficient analysis of changes in the police system to provide a basis for effective understanding and resistance. For the most part, analysis of the new developments in the police has been made by liberal commentators. But the liberal analysis of the police, as we have suggested and will show in detail later, is basically misleading and mystifying, and more often than not has served as a main means of ideological justification for the growth and power of the new police forces.

The starting point for any analysis of the police is the nature of the state. The Marxist analysis, developed most thoroughly by Lenin in *State and Revolution*,[28] has seen the police in capitalist society as one part—along with the military and the penal system—of the apparatus of state force and violence, which directly serves the interests of the capitalist class. The capitalist state serves to facilitate the accumulation of capital in the hands of this ruling class. It helps to concentrate profits in the hands of

15

the rich in a number of ways: by directly financing a number of key industries, by regulating destructive competition, by purchasing and absorbing surplus production, by maintaining a large segment of the working class through various social welfare expenditures, and by preserving the stability of the existing social order and existing class relations. All social institutions combine to serve various aspects of this capital accumulation function. The police, however, serve as the front line mechanism of repression. As such, the central function of the police is to control the working class. This class control takes a number of forms, ranging from strikebreaking, to helping divide Third World and White workers, to infiltrating working class political activities, to repressing working class culture and recreational activities.

Third World communities, which include the most exploited sectors of the working class, have historically experienced the most severe forms of repression. In addition to being victimized by the class-related functions of the criminal justice system, they are further oppressed by its racist double standards and practices. This accounts for the disproportionate repre-

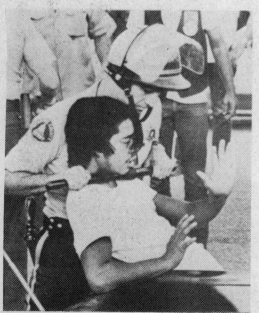

16

sentation of Blacks, Chicanos, Puerto Ricans, Native Americans, and Asians in arrest statistics as well as in the jails and prisons.

Overtly repressive police action (the *Iron Fist*) functions within a liberal democratic framework because the ruling class in an advanced capitalist society generally finds democracy as the best state form. This framework provides a greater potential for cooptation of the working class and for mystification of power relationships. The capitalist state places a great emphasis on the legitimation of state power.[29] Powerful ideology-producing institutions—such as the educational system, the mass media and organized religion—mystify the nature of state power. It is presented as being separate and above class conflict and representing the interests of all segments of the population, rather than an instrument of control for the ruling class. Social welfare institutions (social security, unemployment compensation, welfare) work to reinforce this mystification by ameliorating some of the most exploitative aspects of capitalism, chiefly poverty and unemployment. The extent of this amelioration depends on the balance of class power at a given time: during the 1930's, the government devoted a major proportion of its resources to public welfare expenditures, while during the 1970's these expenditures are proportionately much lower.[30]

The police institution masks its central class control function behind various kinds of public service—helping people in trouble, solving a few dangerous crimes, directing traffic and providing public information. These and other "community relations" activities constitute the *Velvet Glove* side of police work. It is important to see both sides as integrally intertwined. The legitimating functions provided by the public service programs of the police enables them to increase the level of violent repression. Moreover, the mystification of the class control nature of policing, and the mass dissemination of ruling class ideological justification of the police, such as "law and order" rhetoric, is in itself repressive, and serves important class control functions. In order to work effectively against the complex forms of police repression of the 1970's, we need to begin to answer the following questions:

(a) How, specifically, have the police changed and developed in response to changes in the nature of U.S. capitalism and in its governmental machinery?

(b) What specific kinds of strategies are now being developed by the police?

(c) What internal contradictions are there *within* the police forces—the possible sources of conflict, dissent, and resistance among the police themselves?

(d) What are the implications of all these issues for our own strategies of resistance and change?

The purpose of this book is to begin that kind of analysis (although we regard it as *only* a beginning) and to back it up with some specific data on the modern U.S. police. We hope that this will be useful in giving some understanding and sense of direction to people who are, or will be, involved in political action around the police, to people who face police repression in their own lives, and to everyone interested in understanding how the police work in capitalist society. If you are doing such work, we would like to communicate with you. We want to emphasize that we do not see this book as a *definitive* work on the police, but rather as a resource that others can use to build on in doing further work.

OVERVIEW OF BOOK

The seven remaining sections of this book can be divided into four general topics. In sections II and III, we provide an extensive historical analysis of the origins and role of the police in the U.S., beginning with the crudest forms of policing—such as slave patrols and the watch system—and tracing their development into the modern urban department. While the *form* of policing has changed considerably over time, depending on changes in the mode of production from an agricultural to industrial economy, the class control functions of the police in capitalist society have always remained paramount. We focus especially on the movement to modernize and professionalize the police during the Progressive era, since it was during this period that the state apparatus was expanded and became more sophisticated. This

is followed by an overview of developments in policing through the 1960's and a more detailed analysis of the Federal Law Enforcement Assistance Administration, which is increasingly becoming the major source of subsidies and planning for the criminal justice system. This part of the book concludes with information about and an analysis of militancy within police departments, its roots and contemporary form, especially focusing on its implications for understanding the internal dynamics of the police apparatus.

The major part of the book, sections IV, V and VI, analyzes recent strategies and developments within the modern police system. Sections IV and V examine the major ideological and strategic directions that city police forces have been taking since the 1960's, focusing on the development of new technologies and paramilitary police units, and the rise of the "police-industrial" complex on the one hand, and on the other the emergence of new strategies of community pacification. These

sections include a closer look at specific aspects of the iron fist (such as SWAT and political surveillance) and the velvet glove (such as women police and team policing). Section VI examines two aspects of the continuing expansion and diversification of the repressive apparatus—first, the export of U.S. police training and techniques to repressive regimes, especially in the Third World, in an effort to achieve political stability for multinational corporations; and secondly, the booming business in private police at home.

Section VII examines the most recent developments in the police, especially the impact of the fiscal crisis, summarizes the experience of organizations and popular movements in their struggles against the police (including a critique of the limitations of liberal reformism), and discusses the implications for organizing in the future. Finally, the last section of the book contains an extensive bibliography, listing books, journals, and other materials, as well as a research guide to government documents and other sources of information. Section VIII also includes select documents and a list of organizations working against police repression.

1. U.S. Department of Justice, Law Enforcement Assistance Administration, *Trends in Expenditure and Employment Data for the Criminal Justice System, 1971-1974*, Washington, D.C., U.S. Government Printing Office, 1976, pp. 2-3.
2. Center for National Security Studies, *Law and Disorder IV*, Washington, D.C., Center for National Security Studies, 1976, p. 3.
3. U.S. Department of Justice, op. cit., p. 18.
4. Ibid., p. 32.
5. Center for National Security Studies, op. cit., p. 3.
6. U.S. Department of Justice, op. cit., p. 11, 8 respectively.
7. Richard Quinney, *Critique of Legal Order*, Boston, Little, Brown, and Co., 1973, p. 74.
8. LEAA, *Sourcebook of Criminal Justice Statistics*, Washington, D.C., Government Printing Office, 1973, p. 198.
9. National Advisory Commission on Criminal Justice Standards and Goals, *A National Strategy to Reduce Crime*, Washington, D.C., Government Printing Office, 1973, p. 19.
10. Our use of the word "state" may be unclear to some readers. By "state," we refer to the whole range of political institutions—including not only the courts, military and police but also such things as the schools and the welfare system—through which the structure of the capitalist system is maintained.
11. There is presently a considerable amount of debate among radical theorists about the exact way the state functions in modern capitalist societies. For a good description of the issues involved, see David Gold et al., "Recent Developments in Marxist Theories of the Capitalist State," *Monthly Review*, October-November 1975, Vol. 27, Nos. 5 and 6, pp. 29-43, 36-51.
12. President's Crime Commission, *The Challenge of Crime in a Free Society*, Washington, D.C., Government Printing Office, 1967, p. 1.
13. This is a somewhat modified version of the statement in American Friends Service Committee, *Struggle for Justice*, New York, Hill and Wang, 1970, p. 11.
14. Erik Wright, *The Politics of Punishment*, New York, Harper and Row, 1973, pp. 28-30.
15. For some studies, see any criminology text, for example, Richard Quinney, *The Social Reality of Crime*, Boston, Little, Brown, and Co. 1970.
16. Paul Takagi, "A Garrison State in 'Democratic' Society," *Crime and Social Justice*, 1, Spring-Summer, 1974, p. 29.
17. For an analysis of stereotypical responses to rape, see Julia R. Schwendinger and Herman Schwendinger, "Rape Myths: In Legal, Theoretical, and Everyday Practice," *Crime and Social Justice*, 1, Spring-Summer 1974.
18. Federal Bureau of Investigation, *Uniform Crime Reports*, U.S. Government Printing Office, 1974, p. 11.
19. Michael J. Hindelang et al., *Sourcebook of Criminal Justice Statistics—1974*, U.S. Government Printing Office, p. 233.
20. This is an unofficial estimate by Bay Area Women Against Rape in Berkeley, California.
21. Hindelang, op. cit., p. 242.
22. Ibid., p. 236.
23. Ibid., p. 237.
24. John E. Conklin, *The Impact of Crime*, Macmillan, 1975, p. 26.
25. Hindelang, op. cit., p. 171.
26. For a more extensive discussion of this issue, see Editorial, "The Politics of Street Crime," *Crime and Social Justice*, No. 5, Spring-Summer 1976, pp. 1-4.
27. Annette T. Rubinstein, "How China Got Rid of Opium," *Monthly Review*, October 1973, Vol. 25, No. 5, pp. 58-63.
28. Lenin's classic work, written at the time of the Russian Revolution, is available in many editions.
29. Ralph Miliband, *The State in Capitalist Society*, New York, Basic Books, 1969.
30. Frances Fox Piven and Richard A. Cloward, *Regulating the Poor: The Functions of Public Welfare*, New York, Random House, 1971.

II. ORIGINS AND DEVELOPMENT OF THE POLICE

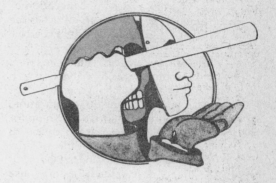

INTRODUCTION

Most accounts of the origins of the U.S. police look back to the first organized day and night police of New York in 1845. Liberal police historians have seized on that date as a starting point for a line of analysis which sees the development of the police as a natural by-product of the increasing crime and social complexity of urban and industrial life. This argument flows from a basic misconception of the police function, a view which mystifies the role of the police as part of the state's coercive apparatus.

The study of the police requires a much broader and more complex analysis of the historical processes which generated the modern police apparatus and its organization, practices and functions. While it is common for analyses of the police to pay lip service to history, most current work on the modern police is ahistorical in that no understanding of the *process* of the development of the police over time is presented. We see the analysis of the current police institution as embodying a few key themes that recur throughout the history of the police, often in the same form, but sometimes in a succession of new forms.

The class control function is always the most essential function that the police serve in a capitalist society, although they serve other functions as well. Since the democratic state requires some legitimacy, the police must also make some attempt to serve popular needs, as long as these needs are not inconsistent with the class-control function. A number of themes can be seen in an historical analysis of the performance of various police functions. *First,* the police always operate as part of a much larger class control apparatus which includes the military, the National Guard, a number of public agencies that perform police functions, private police, and finally direct ruling class vigilante action. *Second,* there is always substantial resistance to the police because class conflict by definition involves resistance. *Third,* the form of the police apparatus adapts to meet changes in the mode of production—the police in an industrial society will operate differently

than the police in an agricultural slave economy. *Fourth,* changes in the mode of production and other social changes occur ahead of the police institution because economic development frequently outstrips the political forms that support it. Therefore, there are always ruling class "reform" impulses aimed at changing the police to conform to the emerging needs of new social relations. *Fifth,* there is a continuous line of efforts aimed at making the police more efficient, more businesslike, and more centrally controlled. These efforts are closely intertwined with reform movements, and are important elements in legitimating the repressive function of the police.

1. THE FIRST POLICE

The earliest form of the modern American police lies in the Southern slave patrols which predate New York's 1845 accomplishment by almost half a century. Black slavery was the dominant mode of production in the ante-bellum South, and the largest 2-3 percent of the planters ruled the legislatures of each of the Southern states. These legislatures established slave codes, starting with South Carolina's 1712 copy of the Barbados statute. The slave codes which provided for the brutal slave patrols, both protected the planters' property rights in human beings and held the slaves, despite their chattel status, legally responsible for misdemeanors and felonies.[1]

The plantation slave patrols, often consisting of three armed men on horseback covering a "beat" of 15 square miles, were charged with maintaining discipline, catching runaway slaves and preventing slave insurrection. In pursuing this duty, they routinely invaded slave quarters and whipped and terrorized Blacks caught without passes after curfew. They also helped enforce the laws against slave literacy, trade and gambling. Although the law called on all White males to perform patrol service, the large planters usually paid fines or hired substitutes, leaving patrolling to the landless or small landholding Whites. These Whites hated the planters, who controlled the best land and access to markets, almost as much as the slaves, but whatever the object of their anger, the slaves were its most frequent target. The slaves in turn resisted the patrollers with warning systems and ambushes.

When slave rebellion reached its peak in full scale insurrections, the largest of which involved 300-500 slaves marching on New Orleans in 1811, the slave patrols were supplemented by the state militia and regular army. In addition, the regularly established sheriffs, constabulary and justices of the peace were routinely called upon to help capture runaway slaves.

Policing, then, in its earliest years, developed as a planter class strategy of race and class control, designed both to keep the Black slaves in subjugation and to exacerbate the contradictions between Black slaves and poor Whites. The patrols did not operate with bureaucratic routine and tended to lapse between outbreaks of slave revolt. They lasted, however, until the Civil War. In many respects, the post-Reconstruction Black laws reestablished the police practices of the slave codes, while nominally changing "slave patrols" to "police departments."

MILITIAS AND THE WATCH SYSTEM

In the North and West, the police institution evolved in response to a different set of race and class contradictions. For the English, Scotch-Irish and German settlers who built the port cities and pushed agricultural settlement westward along the river valleys and across the Appalachians, the Native Americans who inhabited the desired land posed the first "police" problem. Many settlers relied on their own initiative and force of arms to rob the land and, where they built cities, like Philadelphia, they organized militia companies to fight against the Indians as well as perform other functions.

Within their own communities, the colonists established no professional police forces. Unlike the English, who by the eighteenth century had been disarmed by law, the American settlers were armed and ready to gather upon the magistrate's call as a *posse commitatus* (literally, "power of the community") to pursue

fleeing felons. In small New England towns, settlement laws which excluded landless new arrivals and a church hierarchy which regulated the moral and land dealings of inhabitants, substituted for a police force.

In the large cities, such as Philadelphia, New York, Boston, Baltimore and Charleston, the growing bourgeoisie of merchants, lawyers and political leaders established night watches, paid for by the city, to guard their warehouses and homes. Recruited from the sector of the population least involved in productive labor, these watchmen were poorly paid, almost completely unsupervised and notorious for falling asleep or being drunk on the job. Eighteenth century American cities were not free from crime, and riots to lower food prices, tear down whorehouses and prevent British impressment were common.[2] There was, however, no popular demand for improved policing, in part because the majority of citizens perceived any form of standing army as a harbinger of the exploitation and oppression they had migrated so far to escape.

The militia, made up of local men, was called out to suppress some of the large scale disorders, but their loyalties and good sense precluded action whenever a large segment of the population was involved in the disorder. Often they were not even called, for members of the elite themselves sometimes supported and led riots. These riots, which frequently involved property damage but rarely loss of life,

21

were an accepted form of democratic political action in eighteenth and early nineteenth century America. In the case of anti-impressment riots in particular, the merchants also had a direct economic and political stake in keeping the seamen out of the British fleet and free to man the ships of the burgeoning American merchant marine. Nor did John Hancock complain when the Boston militia refused to act against the Stamp Act rioters in 1765, an example followed in almost all of the colonies. If a riot was localized and opposed by the ruling class, however, as was the case with the democratic and land hungry North Carolina Regulators in 1771, the governor could call out the militia of surrounding counties.

After defeating British troops and German mercenaries in the American Revolution, the white settlers were no more eager for a police force than they had been before. The writing of the Constitution, in secret and over vigorous opposition within many states, however, set legal guidelines for increasing and centralizing state power at both the national and state levels. The regular army and state militias were beefed up with relative ease, but cities found it harder to overcome the resistance to despotic government and increased taxes which stood in the way of regular police. Many state constitu-

tions limited the size of city watches; and petty local political infighting over police patronage and graft precluded bureaucratic organization of the police.

The most widespread criticism of the watch system, however, was the same as that of the police forces which succeeded them: they did nothing to prevent crime. When not asleep or drunk, they stood guard duty in selected spots, but despite a steady increase in numbers they did little to stop the crimes of exploitation and personal violence which came to characterize the expanding mercantile centers. By the 1830's and 1840's, much of the urban seacoast population was composed of Irish and Germans who had been encouraged to immigrate as a result of food shortages and political repression. Once in the United States, they were channeled into low paying industrial work and poorly housed in expensive but squalid slums.

The watch and police did nothing to protect the immigrants from their con men and labor contractors, but they came out in force, with the aid of the militia and nativist vigilantes, to break strikes and suppress hunger riots. They also enforced anti-immigrant ordinances on liquor, gambling and Sunday closing. The immigrant communities struggled to gain some influence over the police in their wards through

1. "Berweiser" 2. George upp. 3. James Smith, Captain of the Guard, he takes the Rounds

the Patrol in the year 1803. A Guard appointed to go the rounds and preserve order. the Countersion was Louisiana. Benjamin Weiser, was hale it. he forget the countersign, and said. lose a penny.

the normal political channels of bribery and balloting, and they also, on occasion, actually fought against the police to press their political demands.

When White working people, spurred on by merchants tied to the Southern planter class, took on the Blacks and abolitionists, the police stood by. In New York City, over two thousand uniformed militia, together with a large body of citizens organized as constables, did nothing for three days in 1844 while a White mob rioted against Blacks, badly damaging the Episcopal African church, and pulling down and looting the homes of many Blacks and abolitionists.[3]

The urban elites were dissatisfied with the watch system, but not primarily because of its failure to prevent crime or suppress disorder. There is some evidence that the level of urban crime and disorder after 1830 was not higher than that of the eighteenth century and, in any case, the bourgeoisie was coming increasingly to see crime as a necessary cost, borne mostly by the working class, of their growing economic and political empire. As Josiah Quincy, the mayor of Boston, put it in 1822:

> Poverty, vice and crime, in the degree in which they are witnessed in our day, are, in fact, in some measure the necessary consequences of the social state. Just in proportion as the higher and happier parts of the machine of society are elevated and enlarged, those parts, which are, by necessity or accident, beneath and below, become sunken and depressed.[4]

2. GROWTH OF POLICE *

The bureaucratically organized and partially trained police forces, first established in New York in 1845, differed from their predecessors primarily in their greater size, higher level of armament, and other institutional forms. They represent, however, more of a continuity in ruling class efforts to control the working class than a break with past practices, as some historians of the police have argued.

* For historical continuity, there is no page break between Ch. 1 and Ch. 2. Footnotes for Ch. 1 are at the end of Ch. 2. Elsewhere, footnotes are at the end of each chapter.

By instituting regular salaries to replace the fee-for-service watch system, the urban elites were able to lessen some of the competition among policemen and exert a slightly greater degree of control and discipline over a force which still owed its everyday allegiance to ward politicians. Police uniforms and para-military organization represented attempts to differentiate the police from the rest of the population, to instill military discipline, and to further divide the police from the working class. The coordinated and centralized police organization, which replaced distinct day and night forces, was an early step in the direction of professionalization, a process that continued throughout police history. This early effort to organize the police institution, the first of many ruling class reform efforts, was widely adopted by cities across the United States: Chicago in 1851, New Orleans and Cincinnati in 1852, Philadelphia in 1855, Newark and Baltimore in 1857, Detroit in 1865. Dozens of small to middle-sized cities also emulated this model.[5]

POLICING THE WORKING CLASS

The process of industrialization beginning in the 1830's, and expanding rapidly after the Civil War, greatly intensified class conflict in the United States and transformed the police institution. Manufacturers took the classic laissez-faire position that workers were commodities to be purchased for the cheapest price the market offered. They engaged in a wide range of activities aimed at depressing the cost of labor, including union busting, increasing the supply of labor through immigration, mobilizing different segments of the work-force against each other, and lowering the skill levels required of workers. Wages were depressed to the point that entire families had to work twelve to sixteen hour days to support themselves at a minimum level: dilapidated housing and three starchy meals a day.

Workers did not accept such exploitative conditions without resistance. This took its most organized form in labor strikes which directly threatened the high profit levels that employers maintained through the exploitation

23

of workers. But resistance took dozens of other forms as well: labor organizing, food riots, machine breaking, organized protests of all kinds, and radical political organizing. Resistance which threatened the property "rights" of the manufacturers and their political allies was treated as "crime" because of ruling class domination of the state and its law-making and law-enforcing apparatus.

The police institution was molded into a large-scale class control force in the face of substantial working class resistance. While most existing departments were small and poorly organized in the years immediately following the Civil War, the immediate control and functions of the police were a matter of purely local political control. Where employers were in a position to exercise political domination over industrial centers, they were free to use their political power to "reform" the police institution, i.e., to organize large-scale, anti-labor police forces to replace small, inefficient forces.

The active resistance of the working class to the class control activities of the police is the unwritten side of police history. Traditional police historians who seek to explain the rise of the police in terms of their "public service" functions obviously cannot deal with the contradiction of a major segment of the public in open opposition. The evidence is clear that workers fought the creation of the police and the imposition of police control of their activities. This open class conflict occurred on a wide range of fronts.

The working class in Lynn, Massachusetts, three times organized politically to defeat Republican, shoe-manufacturer mayors, largely over the issue of the strike-breaking function of the police. The initial reorganization of the police had been resisted along the same class lines. In Buffalo, where the workers lacked the political power to defeat the Mayor, delegations of workers protested the use of the police to protect "scabs." Twice in 1894, for example, the Central Labor Union adopted resolutions condemning the police for forbidding labor meetings, and for jailing unemployed workers as "tramps."[6]

There were also untold thousands of in-

stances of forcible popular resistance to police oppression. These included both acts of neighborhood solidarity to protect working class recreational pursuits as well as mass political organizing to oppose police protection of scabs and manufacturers' property at the expense of workers' livelihood. In hundreds of strikes, workers turned out prepared to resist rather than let scabs claim their jobs. Although the most famous of these strikes are well known— Homestead, Pennsylvania, 1892; Ludlow, Colorado, 1914; Pullman, Illinois, 1894—this kind of self-defense activity occurred on a smaller scale much more frequently. Poorly organized or locally organized workers' protests, however, were no match for the manufacturer-controlled repressive apparatus of the state.[7]

The reorganization of police forces in industrial cities of the Northeast to effectively deal with the workers' challenge to capitalist social relations depended upon both local industrial development and patterns of political control. The police department in Lynn, Massachusetts, was built from a small, inefficient force into a model labor control force during the 1860's, while the city was under the tight control of the shoe manufacturers and many workers were off fighting the Civil War. The Buffalo police were reorganized into a labor control force by the city's well integrated manufacturing and commercial elite over a ten year period between 1884 and 1894. This period coincided with the development of the first strong city wide labor organization, the influx of large numbers of Polish and Italian laborers, and the emergence of large-scale labor unrest. The ruling class assumed the responsibility for the direct day to day operation of the police by appointing manufacturers and businessmen to the important offices of Police Commissioner and Superintendent of Police. The entire Buffalo force was then reorganized from an inefficient, uncoordinated street patrol force into a large-scale, para-military force. This transformed every aspect of the police department: the patrol wagon and signal box system were added, representing the most advanced rapid communication and response system then avail-

J. O. Regan Co.

ble; the size of the force was increased four times while the population only doubled; the police force was reorganized into military units and drilled regularly in infantry tactics; control was centralized at downtown headquarters; and officers were assigned to precincts along lines that tended to aggravate ethnic hostilities. In 1895, a "school of instruction" was added for new officers and for older ones if, in the judgement of the Superintendent, they were not sufficiently familiar with police duties. Several moderate anti-corruption drives were also conducted during this period with a view to improving the efficiency of the force. Clear antecedents of progressive reform date from the 1880's and earlier, and served similar functions, although the police were not yet highly rationalized.

Although these changes served a variety of functions after their implementation, the central motivation for this transformation was the emergence of a politically organized working class. Strikes or strike threats were a regular occurrence. At their first sign, a unit of police appeared at the scene and invariably cooperated with management. The police typically set up headquarters *inside* the strike-bound company and freely used whatever force they thought necessary to keep the company open for "business as usual."

While working class strikes represented the most directly threatening "criminal" behavior in that strikes mounted an immediate political and economic threat to the class interests of the manufacturers, the class control function of the police was critical in a number of other areas as well. Political protests of all kinds against the capitalist system were defined as appropriate objects of police repression. Socialists were arrested for making speeches, and socialist and labor union meetings were forbidden—even in private halls.

Day-to-day police patrol practices focused on the control and "resocialization" of the urban working class, particularly immigrants who were suspected of having imported un-American political ideology and social values which "caused" strikes, crime, and labor unions. Ethnic slurs of all kinds were used to describe the immigrant working class in the most demeaning terms, and to justify police repression. A major focus of these police control efforts was upon working class leisure activities, particularly the saloon, which served as a combination living-room, entertainment parlor, and meeting hall. This class control effort was viewed as an essential element of a total effort to impose "industrial discipline" on workers and their families, for working class leisure-time activities stood in the way of the creation of a docile labor force. In the words of one manufacturer, "Tonight's drinker and debaucher is tomorrow a striker for higher wages." Arrests for "public disorder" became a major weapon of class oppression permitting the indiscriminate arrest, jailing, and fining of workers for behavior that went unpunished among the ruling class and their allies.[8]

While the policing of the industrial working class reached its highest form at an early stage in the manufacturing centers of the Northeast—the area east of the Mississippi River and north of the Ohio River—the same forms of repression were reproduced in the West and South as industrialization developed. Denver, Los Angeles, San Francisco, Seattle, New Orleans and Atlanta developed strong anti-labor police institutions by 1900.

The police in the South and border states readily replaced the slave patrols in the violent repression of the Black working class. The control of exploited Black labor was a major impetus behind the development of modern police forces in Atlanta, Charleston and New Orleans. This does not mean that Southern police forces adopted the same "modern" methods along with their newly reorganized and improved police. An Atlanta Police Commissioner, in 1881, was reported urging his men to "kill every damned nigger you have a row with." Lynchings all over the South and in border states met with police indifference; and, on some occasions, police officers were openly involved in the killing of Black people.[9]

In the Southwest, the early police were developed in connection with the subordination of Mexicans and Native Americans as colonized peoples within the U.S. Such special agencies as the Texas Rangers (organized in 1835) were among the first advanced police organizations in the U.S. Walter Prescott Webb, an historian, describes the Texas Rangers as follows:

> When we see him [the Texas Ranger] at his daily task of maintaining law, restoring order, and promoting peace—even though his methods be vigorous—we see him in his proper setting, a man standing alone between a society and its enemies. ... It has been his duty to meet the outlaw breed of three races, the Indian warrior, Mexican bandit, and American desperado, on the enemy's ground and deliver each safely within the jail door or the cemetery gate. It is recorded that he has sent many to both places.[10]

A view of the underside of the history of this period shows that a double standard of justice existed—one for the Native Americans and Mexicans and one for the Anglo Americans. The primary function of the Texas Rangers was to protect the property and wealth of the emerging capitalist class. In fact the Rangers were sometimes called "rinches de la Kineña" (Rangers of the King Ranch) because of their personal use by Richard King and other "cattle barons." The standard operating procedure in dealing with the oppressed was to "shoot first and ask questions later."[11]

POLICE AS WORKERS?

A central contradiction in the organization of the police for the control of the working class is the class origins of individual police officers. The large number of instances of police refusal to engage in anti-worker strike-breaking activity provides ample evidence that this contradiction requires analysis. Those who argue, however, that the working class origins of individual police officers made the police useless as a strike control force are in error. It is more accurate to identify this class identification as a serious problem in the organization of the police as a class control institution. A

26

Texas Rangers, Company "D," with Mexican prisoner

number of measures taken to neutralize the working class solidarity between police and workers proved highly effective.

Ethnic divisions were exploited by the ruling class in order to impede working class solidarity in the factories and mines. This was true in organizing the police as well. Officers were most often from an earlier immigration than most members of the working class, so that American-born police officers controlled Irish workers, Irish officers controlled Polish and Italian workers. Police officers were frequently paid at twice or more the rate of laborers allowing them to move into more comfortable neighborhoods and fostering a class identification with the urban elites. Large scale bribery and corruption, where it existed, further moved many police officers into the petit-bourgeoisie, making them small scale entrepreneurs.

These material bribes to insure the loyalty of the police were matched by ideological and organizational efforts. There was developed at an early stage an ideology of police work that emphasized order-maintenance, discipline, and adherence to a "neutral" code of laws. This ideology was effectively enough inculcated to permit vicious acts of violence in the name of a "law and order" framed and dominated by the ruling class. Where ideology left off as an effective measure in controlling the class loyalties of the police, discipline took over. Entire departments were drilled together in military tactics, and the most sensitive strike control work was done in these units rather than along traditional precinct lines. Military organization and discipline went a long way in controlling the activities of individual officers in strike situations. Strong discipline is a passable substitute for ideological motivation under many conditions.

THE NETWORK OF REPRESSION

The police have always functioned as a part of a much larger class control apparatus in which different armed forces are co-ordinated to reinforce each other in a variety of ways. Some historians of the police have taken the view that the rise of the National Guard and the private police proves that municipal police forces were ineffective for strike control purposes because of their working class sympathies. While this was occasionally the case, such an analysis misrepresents the mutually reinforcing nature of the relationship. Even where the police did an effective job and remained loyal to the manufacturers, a massive strike lasting a long period of time severely over-taxed local resources. Outside of major manufacturing centers, small towns and mining centers could not be expected to maintain a police force larger than necessary to control or regulate working class leisure activities. Finally, the period after the Civil War was marked by major efforts to centralize a number of important police functions under national or state-wide ruling class control.

The militia preceded the development of the police in colonial times. Companies were commonly privately organized which made them effective for anti-labor activity. It also meant, however, that they were not particularly well trained, and many companies were made up of workers. The Great Railroad Strike of 1877 led both to an increased impetus to organize militia companies among sectors of the population "loyal" to the ruling class—primarily clerks, small businessmen, and professionals—and to the decline of private militia companies, which had proven poorly disciplined and inefficient in fighting strikers.

The place of the militia by the 1890's was taken by the National Guard, a highly rationalized, well trained, centralized force controlled by the Governor and co-ordinated with the Army. Annual training at a state camp, weekly drill, Army tactics and state-wide coordination greatly improved on the militia, while at the same time the National Guard retained the militia's most salient advantage—it was at the service of the local ruling class. This was achieved through the political appointment of "gentlemen" soldiers as Generals and the provision that a local mayor or judge could order the Guard out. Both the National Guard and the Militia most often worked with the police, rather than in place of them. Police officers were frequently assigned to work with Guard patrols and Guardsmen were often deputized so that they could make arrests.[12]

Vigilantism also has figured prominently in the development of the coercive apparatus in the United States. The predominant historical myth sees vigilantes as essentially "rednecks"—working class and powerless individuals who create a "law and order" problem by taking the law into their own hands and lynching "criminals," particularly Blacks. This model is inadequate and ignores the integral role that vigilante action has played within the ruling class imposed legal order. The wealthiest and best educated segments of the community organized and participated in the anti-abolitionist and anti-Black riots of the 1840's, anti-labor actions of the post-Civil War period, the wave of lynchings between the Civil War and World War I, and the anti-Socialist repression of 1919.

Vigilante action has often been merged with "legitimate" police institutions. William Scranton put down the railroad strike of 1877 in Scranton, Pennsylvania, by turning out in the middle of town with fifty armed friends and shooting down workers marching on the business district. After the strike, this group was organized into a private militia company. Businessmen were often deputized to engage in anti-labor activity. The San Francisco Vigilance Committee, a ruling class "law and order" group, led to the organization of a more "modern" police force—after they had lynched all of the people they wanted to get rid of. Southern lynchings of Blacks often involved the tacit consent or encouragement of the community elites who recognized the class control functions of encouraging working class Whites to kill working class Blacks.[13]

Private police function in a number of ways that are closely linked to vigilante actions. Instead of personally engaging in violent and illegal suppression of the working class, the rich hire private police to do the work for them. Private police, like the militia, predate the public police, dating well back into the seventeenth century in the United States. The development of a national private police network, pioneered by Alan Pinkerton, greatly expanded as a result of the heightened class conflict accompanying industrialization. The great advantage of using private police was the heightened level of violent repression that such

28

forces employed. Although the police, Army, and National Guard all engaged in a massive amount of violence against the working class, the private police consistently engaged in the most brutal forms of repression. The ruling class did not balk at the hiring of professional "thugs" and "goons" from New York and Chicago to beat up and shoot workers. In addition to increasing the level of violence, the employers' money provided for extra services that the police could not provide: the private police frequently had to guard scabs to keep them from escaping, operate machinery, and perform a wide variety of other tasks. The private police are not properly seen as alternatives to the official police because they were a regular feature of the same class control apparatus. In Pennsylvania, they were given full police

Below: Militia kill 25 strikers in Great Railroad Strike of 1877

power as the infamous Coal and Iron Police. More often, they were deputized for the duration of strikes, or for permanent guard duty at factories and mines, and given full police power. Where they were not legally deputized, they often exercised *de facto* police power because the local police refused to interfere with them.

The police can only be understood as a major component of a much more pervasive state coordinated class control apparatus. Clearly, on a day-to-day level it is the most important in most situations but the important functions served by the other units of the system should never be underestimated.[14]

This political economic analysis of the devel-opment of the police in the United States has stressed continuities rather than breaks with the past. The organization of the police must be seen as a process deeply rooted in changing capitalist productive and social relations. The central function of the police is class control, and this fact is critical to an understanding of the nature of the capitalist state. Historical studies of the Progressive era, considered next, tend to see the period as a break from the earlier, more repressive corporate state. Our analysis will show that while some important new forms were developed to make the police more efficient, the process that we have defined continues through the Progressive period and right up to present efforts at police reform.

1. Howell M. Henry, *The Police Control of Slaves in South Carolina*, Westport, Connecticut, Greenwood Press, 1971; Eugene Genovese, *Roll, Jordan, Roll*, New York, Pantheon, 1974; Herbert Aptheker, *American Negro Slave Revolts*, New York, International Publishers, 1943.
2. Selden Bacon, "The Early Development of American Municipal Police," unpublished Ph.D. dissertation, Yale University, 1939; John K. Alexander, "Poverty, Fear, and Continuity: An Analysis of the Poor in 18th Century Philadelphia," in Allen Davis and Mark Haller, *The Peoples of Philadelphia*, Philadelphia, Temple University Press, 1973; Jesse Lemisch, "Jack Tar in the Streets: Merchant Seamen in the Politics of Revolutionary America," *William and Mary Quarterly*, XXIV, 3, 1966; Elisha P. Douglass, *Rebels and Democrats*, Chicago, Quadrangle, 1965.
3. David Montgomery, "The Shuttle and the Cross: Weavers and Artisans in the Kensington Riots of 1844," *Journal of Social History*, 5, 4, 1972; Michael Feldberg, *The Riots of 1844*, Westport, Connecticut, Greenwood Press, 1975; Joel Tyler Headley, *The Great Riots of New York, 1712-1873*, Indianapolis, Bobbs-Merrill, 1970.
4. Josiah Quincy, *Poverty, Vice and Crime*, Boston, 1822.
5. Roger Lane, *Policing the City: Boston 1822-1885*, Cambridge, Harvard University Press, 1967; James Richardson, *The New York Police: Colonial Times to 1901*, New York, Oxford University Press, 1971; John Flinn and John Wilkie, *Our Police: A History of the Chicago Police*, New York, Arno Press, 1971.
6. Alan Dawley, *Class and Community: The Industrial Revolution in Lynn, Massachusetts*, Cambridge, Harvard University Press, 1975; Sidney L. Harring, "The Buffalo Police: Labor Unrest, Political Power and the Creation of the Police Institution," *Crime and Social Justice*, 4, 1975.
7. Richard O. Boyer and Herbert M. Morais, *Labor's Untold Story*, New York, United Electrical Workers, 1971; Herbert Gutman, *Work, Society, and Culture in Industrial America*, New York, Knopf, 1975.
8. Paul Faler, "Cultural Aspects of the Industrial Revolution: Lynn, Massachusetts Shoemakers and Industrial Morality, 1826-1860," *Labor History*, 15, 3, 1974; David Brody, *Steelworkers in America: The Non-Union Era*, New York, Harper and Row, 1969.
9. Eugene Watts, "The Police in Atlanta: 1890-1905," *Journal of Southern History*, 1972; Allen Grimshaw, *Racial Violence in the United States*, Chicago, Aldine, 1969.
10. Walter Prescott Webb, *The Texas Rangers*, Boston, Houghton Mifflin Company, 1835, p. ix.
11. For a critical discussion of the Texas Rangers see Rodolfo Acuna, *Occupied America: The Chicano's Struggle Toward Liberation*, San Francisco, Canfield Press, 1972, Américo Paredes, *With a Pistol in His Hand*, Austin, University of Texas Press, 1958, and Carey McWilliams, *North from Mexico*, New York, Greenwood Press, 1968.
12. Martha Derthick, *The National Guard in Politics*, Cambridge, Harvard University Press, 1965; Charles Peckham, "The Ohio National Guard and its Police Duties, 1894," *Ohio History*, 1974.
13. Richard Maxwell Brown, *Strain of Violence: Historical Studies of American Violence and Vigilantism*, New York, Oxford University Press, 1974; Arthur Raper, *Tragedy of Lynching*, Chapel Hill, University of North Carolina Press, 1933.
14. Jeremiah Shalloo, *Private Police*, Philadelphia, The American Academy of Political and Social Science, 1933; Edward Levinson, *I Break Strikes*, New York, Arno Press, 1969; Rhonda Jeffries-Jones, "Violence in American History: Plug Uglies in the Progressive Era," *Perspectives in American History*, 8, 1973.

III. PROFESSIONALIZING
THE POLICE

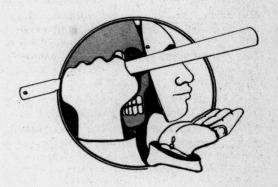

3. THE POLICE AND THE PROGRESSIVE MOVEMENT

INTRODUCTION

In the first two decades of the 20th century, the U.S. was swept by several different movements for reform. Some of these movements, such as the Socialist Party or the Industrial Workers of the World, were movements from below, representing the demands of working people for a fundamental change in social and economic institutions. But there was also a strong movement for reform from above—a movement led by business and professional people, which was aimed at stabilizing the existing political and economic system, rather than changing it into something basically different. This is usually referred to as the "Progressive Movement," and the whole period is often called the "Progressive era."

The Progressive movement combined a criticism of the corruption and inefficiency of many social institutions in the U.S. with an acceptance of the American capitalist system as a whole. Progressives in business and industry, for example, developed the concepts of "scientific management" that enabled managers to get more efficient performance from workers through such things as time-and-motion studies. Progressives in education developed intelligence testing and other means of "efficiently" channeling and tracking young people into appropriate slots in the economy. In the prison system, Progressive reformers created elaborate classifications of different kinds of criminals and of the different kinds of "treatment" that they required. All of these reforms were designed to make these institutions work more smoothly and effectively in an increasingly centralized and tightly-knit economy. Another institution that the Progressives were concerned with was the police, and the reforms they made or suggested have had a lasting influence on later developments in policing.

By the beginning of the 20th century, many Progressives in business, government, and the universities were becoming strongly critical of the police. They regarded most police departments as corrupt and ineffective, subservient to local politics and totally incapable of providing the level of protection they felt a highly interdependent business society required. A main stimulus for their dissatisfaction with the performance of the police was the apparently rising rate of crimes against property—particularly serious crimes such as bank robbery—and another was the rapid growth of organized radicalism among working-class people. The traditional police forces, according to the Progressives, were not only failing to put a stop to rampant crime and political agitation, but were actually aggravating them through the use of misguided and outmoded strategies.

These concerns sparked a movement for police "reform" that was expressed in several ways during the period from about 1910 to the early 1930's. Several local and national commissions were created that dealt either wholly or partly with police problems. Studies of the police were commissioned in Chicago, Cleveland, Los Angeles, and many other cities. The Chicago Crime Commission, formed in 1919, was the forerunner of many of these. Created through the efforts of the Chicago Association of Commerce, the Crime Commission was headed by an impressive list of local notables in business, education, and civic reform. It defined itself very explicitly in business terms:

> It is not a reform organization. It is not a debating society. It is a business proposition created because of the conditions which it faces and is determined to accomplish results by methods which it · is believed will be welcomed by capable public officials willing to do their duty.[1]

Similarly, the Los Angeles Crime Commission was put together by business and insurance leaders after property crime rates had become so high that insurance companies were threatening to withdraw theft coverage from local businesses.[2] In 1931, these concerns reached the national level. Herbert Hoover's National Commission on Law Observance and Enforcement (the Wickersham Commission) brought together a massive amount of research and opinion that foreshadowed the later national commissions of the 1960's and '70's. The Commissioners pointed out that the "general failure of the police" to deal effectively with recent crimes had led to a loss of public confidence and had created a situation in which the respectable citizen was "helpless in the hands of the criminal ·class"; they argued that a "corporate business of any magnitude" that operated on such slipshod principles would soon be bankrupt.[3] Similar warnings and condemnations were issued by several Progressive police administrators who emerged during this period, including Arthur Woods of New York City and August Vollmer of Berkeley, and by a new breed of academic police experts, among whom Raymond Fosdick, whose main work was done under the auspices of the Rockefeller-sponsored "Bureau of Social Hygiene" at Columbia University, was the most influential.

Together, these theorists and working police administrators developed a coherent ideology and a set of police strategies that have remained—with some modifications—as the dominant orthodoxy in more "advanced" police circles.

POLICING AS "SOCIAL ENGINEERING"

The Progressive reformers saw criminal justice as a problem of "social engineering." They believed the U.S. presented unprecedented problems of social control in the 20th century that required much more sophisticated responses than those that had sufficed in the 19th century. The reformers particularly singled out rapid industrialization and the extreme class differentiation that accompanied it as a main source of problems for the criminal justice system, as well as what they called the "heterogeneity" of the American population and the lack of a strong tradition of obedience to constituted authority. A key idea in the Progressives' approach, which has remained as

an integral part of much modern police ideology, was that since modern society was "complex" or "diversified" it required more restraint and regulation.[4] Most Progressive reformers argued that in the simpler and more homogeneous society of 18th and 19th century America there was little need for an elaborate

apparatus of justice or an extensive police. But the more "diversified" society of the 20th century created a much greater potential for conflict and disorder. The point was not to *change* that society fundamentally, but to use the criminal justice system (as well as the schools, social work, and so on) to "harmonize" and "adjust" these potential conflicts within the existing system. A powerful and effective police was an essential part of this. As August Vollmer put it,

Friction between classes and between races, and between those of differing political, social, or religious beliefs, seems to be a universal law. As long as this is true, there will be need for police to preserve order, protect lives and property, and finally, to preserve the integrity of state and nation. Whatever else may be said of the American police, this fact should be more widely known; namely, that without the police and the police organizations, with all their many defects, anarchy would be rife in this country, and the civilization now existing on this hemisphere would perish. The American

WHOLESALE.

N.Y. CITY TREASURY.

RETAIL.

BAKERY

police are justified, if for no other reason than because in their hands rests in large measure the preservation of the nation.[5]

The main criticism the Progressives leveled at the conventional police was that instead of providing the harmonizing function that modern society required, they more often aggravated conflict through corruption, brutality and general incompetence. Many Progressive reformers thought that police "lawlessness" was a major threat to the legitimacy of the capitalist system itself. Jerome Hopkins, a Progressive lawyer who popularized the Wickersham's Commission's findings in a sensational book titled *Our Lawless Police*, expressed this dramatically:

> *We have a strange country, with a heterogeneous population. It is extremely vital to our national future, perhaps to national survival, that a loyal attitude be inculcated in our semi-alien groups toward our fundamental and peculiar national institutions. Anarchy for the coming years is being bred today by the lawless practices that have entered the enforcement of the law.*[6]

Lawless policing, according to the Progressives, "permits the delinquent classes to understand that our institutions are hypocritical, that there is no law or real justice in the land"; as a result, "it breeds vengeful reprisal against the police, the law, and society itself."[7] Harsh and unsympathetic policing, especially of working-class immigrants, could "work more potently to breed discontent and anarchy than all the exhortation, and invocations, and denunciations of soap-box corner orators."[8] The main

34

concern of the Progressive police reformers was to transform the police into an agency that would help to secure the loyalty of the potentially "delinquent classes" at the same time that it efficiently contained their disruptive behavior and kept the lid on their protests against the existing distribution of power and privilege in U.S. society.

A PREVENTIVE POLICE

A second basic premise of Progressive criminal justice reform was that efficient social control meant that crime had to be *prevented* from happening, rather than combatted after it had already occurred. "Preventive justice," wrote the Progressive legal theorist Roscoe Pound, "is no less important than preventive medicine."[9] Progressive writers often talked about police work as a kind of public health operation, "draining the swamps and morasses" that bred crime, the "secret sources of infection which lie hidden in the dark places of city life."[10]

The emphasis on prevention was related to the Progressives' concern for understanding the causes of crime. As the Wickersham Commission put it, the criminal was no longer seen as "a rascal with the heart of a devil," but as someone who "through heredity, environment or training has become a misfit intellectually or morally."[11] The Progressives saw crime as the result of a variety of physical, psychological, and environmental factors, and they argued that the police had to pay more attention to all of these possible causes. According to Fosdick,

or example,

The average police department is still too much merely an agency of law enforcement, divorced from responsibility for the causes of crime. Its energies are consumed in defensive measures, in efforts to correct the manifestations of crime rather than attack its roots. So long as this is the case, the policeman will continue to represent, as he does in so many places at present, the city's bewildered and futile attempt to beat back the spasmodic outcroppings of disorder which are continually in process of manufacture in the inner currents of city life.[12]

The police were seen as especially important agents of preventive control because of their unique ability to provide surveillance and control of the environmental sources of crime —by which the Progressives usually meant the local community or neighborhood. Social scientists, especially during the 1920's and early '30's, increasingly held that crime was concentrated in specific "delinquency areas" within the cities—areas characterized by poverty, high rates of immigration, poor housing, and so on. Needless to say, for the Progressives, the control of the "environmental causes" of crime did not imply making the basic political and economic changes that would eliminate poverty and poor living conditions in the first place. Instead, the prevention of crime meant linking up the criminal justice system with the schools, the family, and other institutions that affected the lives of people considered likely to become criminal. In practice, then, the apparently "humane" emphasis on the environmental causes of crime became the political reality of increased control over aspects of the lives of many people—especially poor people—that previously had been relatively neglected.

SPECIFIC THEMES

Changing the police from an ineffective and alienating force into an efficient instrument of preventive control meant, according to the Progressives, that the police had to take on some new functions, abandon old ones, and undergo important changes in organization and personnel. Specifically, the Progressives' main strategies included the following:

(1) Centralization.

All of the Progressives believed that a critical problem with the traditional police was that they were both too dispersed in local departments, and too close to the local communities —in the sense of being at the mercy of local "politics." They constantly promoted schemes for centralizing and coordinating police decision-making and activities. These ranged from demands for metropolitan policing in large urban areas, to the creation of state-wide police coordinating agencies (August Vollmer proposed that California create a "Ministry of Justice" to handle all police activities),[13] to some kind of national police or national police clearing-house. (The impetus for the develop-

ment. of the F.B.I. in 1908 came from this perspective.) In addition, within individual police departments, the Progressives wanted to centralize as much authority as possible in the highest levels of police administration—the chief or commissioner—and to remove police functions as much as possible from the electoral process. This trend was supported by an ideology that held that police work was a "neutral" function, benefiting all classes in the

35

community, and that decisions about police practices were therefore "technical" questions, "above politics." [14]

The Progressives realized that the American public was traditionally wary of concentrating the power of the police in this way, and they spent much time criticizing the "dangerous tendency" among many people to take "the democratic theory of government too far" in limiting the discretion and power of police executives. The Progressives insisted that the attempt to avoid police repression by subjecting the police to local politics had served only to place the police forces in the hands of the "most notorious and frequently the most dangerous persons in their communities." [15]

(2) Professionalism.

"Upgrading" the quality of police personnel was another main theme in the Progressives' program. The idea was to sift out incompetent, unskilled, or unstable cops and replace them with skilled, educated, and highly sophisticated officers. They complained that traditional police work had been viewed as something anyone could do, and as a result most forces were filled with an "inferior grade" of policemen who were put on the street without any significant training. The Progressives argued that policing was a *science* requiring specialized skills, high intelligence, and intensive training. Probably the most important application of this idea was the development of systematic programs for police education and training. The first specialized police school was founded in Berkeley under August Vollmer in 1908; it taught various courses in social science and criminology as well as standard police practices. New York City developed an influential program of intensive training under the Progressive commissioner Arthur Woods in 1914.

A main function of the ideology of professionalization was to change the class composition and community ties of the police. The Wickersham Commission, for example, presented a number of studies showing that about 75% of rank and file patrolmen on several forces had been recruited from the ranks of unskilled laborers or from "farmers, laborers,

36

railroad men, chauffeurs, and the like." The Commission concluded:

Not that these men should be weeded out on account of their occupation, but there is a strong presumption that they are wanting in the qualities necessary for first-class policemanship. [16]

The Commission similarly called for the abolition of all community residence requirements for the police, on the ground that abolishing them would help solve the problem of a "dearth of available timber" as well as "break down the political grasp on the force." [17] Through such measures, the Progressives hoped to minimize the traditional problem of police loyalty, and to develop a force that would be more predictably responsive to the needs of the wealthy and "respectable."

(3) Technology.

The Progressives aimed to replace the traditional police reliance on fear and brute force with an increased use of technology. During the 19th century, they argued, the police had become identified in the public mind as a club-swinging, brutal organization at the service of special interests. But the use of force, except as a last resort, was counterproductive; a police strategy based on "overpowering" the criminal, Jerome Hopkins wrote, was

quite as apt to give the overpowered individual the sulky resentment, that confirms the criminal tendency, as it is to inculcate in him the permanent submission and genuine acceptance of society's authority upon which the theory of criminal justice relies. Force itself . . . is probably the poorest weapon in the arsenal of criminology. [18]

According to the Progressives, the use of force was especially dangerous in dealing with mass protest. Progressive police writings were filled with case histories showing how the unwise use of force in strikes and riots had unwittingly aided the cause of radical "elements." The Wickersham Commission concluded that

The handling of groups whose attitude toward the government may differ radically from the average requires a well-advised

technique. Here brawn without brain fails.[19]

Achieving the "permanent submission" the Progressives aimed for seemed more likely to result from the increased efficiency and magnified police presence that would be made possible by skillful use of technology. The 19th century reality of the police force as a scattered group of poorly-equipped individual policemen was to be replaced by the idea of the police force as a tightly organized unit, backed by the most advanced technical equipment, that could provide "an impenetrable cordon around the city."[20] The patrol car, for example, which August Vollmer referred to as a "swift angel of death,"[21] was first used by the Berkeley and Kansas City departments during the Progressive era. Progressives also pioneered in the development of improved police communications, and emphasized the importance of elaborate record-keeping and police statistics; many departments first developed systematic record systems dur-

CAN THE LAW REACH HIM?—THE DWARF AND THE GIANT THIEF

ing the Progressive era. Another innovation was the application of chemical and biological technology to police work, especially in the creation of police laboratories using modern scientific equipment. Again, the Berkeley department, with close ties to the University of California, was one of the earliest to make use of this kind of technical advance.[22]

(4) Specialized "Preventive" Functions.

Since the Progressives believed that merely arresting criminals after they had committed crimes was, as Vollmer put it, "like pouring water into a sieve,"[23] they paid much attention to devising new preventive strategies for the police. These mainly involved two related things: (a) linking up the police with other "social service" institutions, like the schools, the welfare system, and special "clinical" facilities for criminals; (b) developing more effective ways of increasing police contact with potentially "troublesome" groups—such as children, foreigners, and the unemployed.

The most attention was given to preventive work among young people, since it was widely agreed that "the young are plastic, impressionable, yielding, and can usually be influenced to go along in productive paths if taken in hand early enough."[24] The Wickersham Commission, noting that the majority of criminals committed to state and Federal prisons were under 30, stressed the importance of linking the police with community welfare agencies to "reach youthful delinquents before they became hardened repeaters."[25] The Berkeley police department under Vollmer pioneered in the development of "predelinquency" work for police departments. "It behooves the policeman," Vollmer wrote in 1923,

> to concentrate his attention upon the problem child during the predelinquent period. The most fruitful source of information is the school. Hence a friendly relationship should be established with teachers, principals, and superintendents.[26]

Vollmer's program for dealing with the predelinquent involved such things as charting the location and special problems of each "troublesome" child in the city on special police maps:

37

... by the use of colored pins the special type of problem may be indicated. For instance, blue may be used to denote that the child is troublesome; red, immoral; green, pugnacious; yellow, light-fingered; black, habitual truant; white, mentally defective, etc. [27]

In 1919 the Berkeley department initiated a survey study designed to predict delinquency in public school children, and in 1925 set up a special "crime prevention division" whose staff included professional social workers and psychologists. This unit worked very closely with Berkeley's "child guidance clinic":

Many a youngster apparently well started in a career of delinquency has recovered as though by magic after the child-guidance clinic of the Berkeley health center has performed some surgical operation or some medication for glandular imbalance ... or recommended improvements in environment, or assisted the child in overcoming fear. [28]

Along the same lines, the New York poli developed a "Police Psychopathic Laboratory in 1915, complete with a psychiatrist, psychologist and other professionals to exami arrested criminals before their appearance court. The main purpose was to sift out a "feebleminded" criminals for special instit tionalization, on the ground that ordinary j or prison treatment would be useless with su people. [29] The many uses of this kind "preventive" work for the state were summ ized by Vollmer this way:

What service can be more ennobling to th officer, more beneficial to the child an contribute more happiness to the relative and greater industrial efficiency, healthi social conditions, better political order the nation than the rescue of children from life of bars and stripes? [30]

Similarly, the Progressive police reforme tried to establish close ties between the poli and other potentially disruptive groups. Durin 1914-1917, the New York Police operated kind of make-work "employment agency" f people out of work, getting neighborhoods put up small amounts of money to hi unemployed people to clean the streets and o other menial work; they also accumulated small fund, paid for by the police themselve to provide books of tickets that were redeer able for food and fuel at local businesses. [31] Th Progressives also stressed the need for wome police to establish a close relation with poter tial women criminals, especially by "supervi ing dance halls and other recreational estal lishments." [32] A similar principle was th particular ethnic neighborhoods should b patrolled by police from the same ethnic grou The Wickersham Commission, for exampl proposed hiring more foreign-born policeme familiar with the "language, habits, custom and cultural background" of immigrant com munities. [33]

Another aspect of the new preventive stra egy was a strong emphasis on public relation The Progressives wanted to overcome what the regarded as the irrational hostility and suspicio toward the police that had been a tradition feature of American society. The public had t be taught that the police were on their side. As August Vollmer put it,

> *The public must drop its childish attitude of hostility and learn to appreciate this friendly, reassuring helpfulness, unceasing vigilance, and other services that the professionally trained policeman stands ready to give to all the people, high and low, rich and poor.*[34]

The Wickersham Commission argued that the public's attitude toward the police could be improved by "the wise presentation of the case to civics classes in the schools." The Berkeley department was commended for its work in changing public attitudes through "speeches, newspaper articles, and so on."[35] An especially inventive program to change the attitude of poor youths to the police was developed by the New York police under Woods. This was a system of "Junior Police," through which 5,000 boys between eleven and sixteen, in 32 different police precincts in New York, were organized into Junior Police squads, given uniforms and drilled, given lessons in first-aid, safety, the rules of the road, and "law and order" generally, and involved in games and athletic competition. According to Woods, the program was successful:

> *The boy comes to feel that the policeman whom he has considered his natural enemy is really a man whom he can look to for help in doing the things that he most likes to do. We notice a marked falling off in juvenile delinquencies in precincts where there are Junior Police Forces.*[36]

(5) Stripping away useless or alienating functions.

Finally, the Progressives believed that many of the problems of the police were the result of their engaging in functions that had nothing to do with their primary task of maintaining order. The police had become a "catch-all" agency for assorted government functions that no other agency was handling, such as licensing various enterprises, dog-catching, and, most important, enforcing morals laws. The Progressives criticized what they saw as the peculiarly American tendency to criminalize personal be-

havior that offended prevailing standards of morality but was not really dangerous. They argued that it was inherently impossible for the police to enforce things like "laws against kissing, laws against face powder and rouge, laws against earrings, laws fixing the length of women's skirts, laws fixing the size of hatpins."[37] Moreover, trying to enforce these laws often led to widespread police corruption and to the withdrawal of police resources from other more important tasks, and usually created considerable public hostility against the police. The Progressive police reformers, like most of their counterparts today, were much less interested in enforcing traditional middle-class morality than in protecting the most basic social and economic structures of modern capitalism.

THE UNDERSIDE OF THE PROGRESSIVE ERA

While Progressive police reformers focused considerable efforts on restructuring the police into a more efficient and professional class control apparatus, their ideas were introduced into only a few police departments. In general the police institutions of the Progressive era carried on just as they had in the late nineteenth century with an emphasis on the violent repression of the working class movements.

The year 1919 marks a number of critical

events. The end of World War I sparked labor demands for a fair share of the huge wartime profits. A wave of strikes broke out all across the country led by the Seattle General Strike and a strike against the entire steel industry. Thousands of workers were beaten and arrested by local police, the National Guard, private police, and county sheriffs. Industrialists made a full scale attempt to break unions completely and the police were in the forefront of that effort.

In addition to outright attack on strikers, working class political ideology became a particular target. The Socialist Party suffered massive repression in a series of federally coordinated raids on the night of January 2, 1920. In all, 10,000 people were arrested, many of them union organizers. These "Palmer Raids" (named after the U.S. Attorney General who directed them) climaxed a series of Federal, state, local, and vigilante actions against the organized left. Racism reached new heights during the 1918-1919 era as well. There were serious attacks on Blacks by Whites supported by the police in New Orleans, Charleston, Tulsa, Omaha, Washington D.C., Knoxville, Chicago, East St. Louis and other cities.[38]

The 1920's produced the first serious Fed-

eral efforts to build a national police force. Part of this effort came from the involvement of the F.B.I. in attacks on the working class beginning with the Palmer Raids. Indirect coordination by the Federal government was replaced by both the legal basis and institutional capability for direct Federal police actions. The Prohibition experiment further strengthened the Federal police apparatus. Many local governments were not concerned with Prohibition enforcement: Prohibition represented an effort of conservative, rural forces to regulate the recreational activities of the urban immigrant working class. This led to increased reliance on the Federal police and a large force was created expressly for enforcing liquor laws.[39]

The Depression of the 1930's heightened class conflict and led to more instances of bloody repression of the working class. Two workers were killed and hundreds injured in the 1934 General Strike in San Francisco and Oakland. Police violence against working class struggle reached its climax with the murder of ten workers in the "Memorial Day Massacre" in Chicago in 1937 when the police fired point-blank and without warning at a peaceful labor demonstration. Communist-led CIO victories resulted in major gains for work-

ers and in Federal legislation guaranteeing unions the right to organize and requiring collective bargaining. This was followed during the 1940's by the cooptation of trade union officials by the ruling class which recognized that conservative unions could perform certain labor control functions. Progressive elements were later purged from union leadership,[40] repeating the process of 1919.

CONCLUSION

Much of the Progressive program for transforming the police sounds familiar; the ideas and strategies they developed have remained (with important modifications, as we will see below) as the stock-in-trade of "advanced" police thinking. Because of that, it is especially important to understand what the Progressive reform of the police was and was not. It was basically an attempt to streamline police organization and practices in the service of class interests and business values. The Progressives promoted themselves as disinterested reformers whose goal was to turn the police into a technically proficient and politically "neutral" agency of "social service," but their definition of political neutrality and of "social service"

meant stabilizing the existing political and economic structure through efficient "engineering" of social conflict. The two main results of their reform efforts were (1) the development of a conception of police "professionalism" that served to insulate the police from any significant local community influence, and (2) the promotion of new technologies and new strategies to enable the police to exercise a higher level of surveillance and control of oppressed communities. Along with this, they laid the groundwork for an ideology, still with us, stressing that a strong and pervasive police system was an inevitable and desirable feature of modern life. By relying on paramilitary efficiency, technological prowess, community penetration and widespread propaganda in place of the mere force and violence of the past, the Progressives hoped to make an increased level of coercion and domination an accepted, or even welcomed, part of everyday life in the United States.

Progressive reformers envisioned a "velvet glove" strategy for the police: a relatively non-coercive thoroughly professional police force enjoying a high level of legitimacy. These reforms were not widely implemented for a number of reasons, including the resistance of the police rank and file, and the heightened

41

class conflict of the Depression that led to strong working class challenges to the existing social order. Finally, it must be remembered that the Progressives represented only one segment of ruling class ideology. The more conservative elements placed their reliance on the brutal repression that the police had used so effectively up to that point. The Depression and the "New Deal" ultimately led to a victory by ruling class forces prepared to make an accommodation with organized labor which replaced police repression with institutional forms of class control. The central concern of the police was accordingly shifted to non-union, working class Blacks and other Third World people who were less integrated into trade unions.

1. Editorial, "The Chicago Crime Commission," *Journal of Criminal Law and Criminology*, Vol. X, 1919, p. 8.
2. See Gene E. Carte, *August Vollmer and the Rise of Police Professionalism*, unpublished D. Crim. thesis, School of Criminology, University of California, Berkeley, 1973, p. 144.
3. National Commission on Law Observance and Enforcement, Vol. 13, *Police*, Washington, D.C., U.S. Government Printing Office, 1931, p. 1.
4. Roscoe Pound, *Criminal Justice in the American City—A Summary*, Cleveland, Cleveland Foundation, 1922, p. 15.
5. Quoted in Carte, op. cit., p. 181.
6. Jerome Hopkins, *Our Lawless Police*, New York, Viking Press, 1931, p. 361.
7. Ibid., p. 316.
8. Arthur Woods, *Policeman and Public*, New Haven, Yale University Press, 1919, p. 65.
9. Pound, op. cit., p. 51.
10. Raymond Fosdick, *American Police Systems*, New York, The Century Company, 1920, pp. 357, 359.
11. National Commission on Law Observance and Enforcement, op. cit., p. 76-78.
12. Fosdick, op. cit., p. 356.
13. See Carte, op. cit., p. 104.
14. For a good example of this mentality, see Fosdick, op. cit., esp. Chps. 6 and 7.
15. National Commission on Law Observance and Enforcement, op. cit., pp. 50-51.
16. Cf. Ibid., p. 9.
17. Ibid., p. 63.
18. Hopkins, op. cit., p. 317.
19. National Commission on Law Observance and Enforcement, op. cit., p. 137.
20. Ibid., p. 88.
21. August Vollmer, quoted in Jonathan Rubinstein, *City Police*, New York, Farrar, Strauss, and Giroux, 1973.
22. On the special significance of the Berkeley Department in the development of police technology, see Carte, op. cit., passim.
23. August Vollmer, "Aims and Ideals of the Police," *Journal of Criminal Law and Criminology*, Vol. 13, #2, Aug. 1922, p. 254.
24. National Commission on Law Observance and Enforcement, op. cit., p. 113.
25. Ibid., p. 114.
26. August Vollmer, "Predelinquency," *Journal of Criminal Law and Criminology*, Vol. 14, #2, Aug. 1923, pp. 280-283.
27. Ibid., p. 283.
28. National Commission on Law Observance, *Police*, op. cit., p. 120.
29. See Louis E. Bisch, "A Police Psychopathic Laboratory," *Journal of Criminal Law and Criminology*, Vol. 7, #1, May 1916.
30. Vollmer, "Predelinquency," op. cit., p. 283.
31. Fosdick, op. cit., esp. Chaps. 6 and 7.
32. National Commission on Law Observance and Enforcement, op. cit., p. 116.
33. Ibid., p. 7.
34. Vollmer, "Aims and Ideals of the Police," op. cit., p. 237.
35. National Commission on Law Observance and Enforcement, op. cit., p. 136, 120.
36. Quoted in Fosdick, op. cit., p. 369.
37. Ibid., pp. 52-53.
38. David Brody, *Labor in Crisis: The Great Steel Strike of 1919*, Philadelphia, Lippincott, 1965; William Preston, Jr., *Aliens and Dissenters*, Cambridge, Harvard University Press, 1963; Arthur I. Waskow, *From Race Riot to Sit In*, New York, Doubleday, 1966; Richard L. Friedheim, *The Seattle General Strike*, Seattle, University of Washington Press, 1964.
39. Max Lowenthal, *The Federal Bureau of Investigation*, New York, Harcourt, 1950; Andrew Sinclair, *Prohibition: The Era of Excess*, Boston, Little, Brown, 1962.
40. Richard O. Boyer and Herbert Morais, *Labor's Untold Story*, New York, United Electrical Workers, 1971; Jerold Auerbach, *Labor and Liberty: The LaFollette Committee and the New Deal*, Indianapolis, Bobbs-Merrill, 1966; Stanley Aronowitz, *False Promises*, New York, McGraw-Hill, 1974.

4. WORLD WAR II TO THE 1960'S

Although most of the ideas that underlie the recent development of the police have roots going back well into police practices in the nineteenth century, the application of a wide variety of reform strategies in the current period has its origins in the crises of the 1960's. The depression ended in economic expansion brought about by World War II and the subsequent imperialism. During the War, 120,000 West Coast Japanese Americans were locked in concentration camps at the direction of racist politicians and military leaders representing land-hungry business and ranching interests.

The post-war period produced recession which led to heightened class conflict. Massive Black migration from the rural South to the urban North permanently changed the racial and class composition of major cities. The post-war years saw an increase in labor militancy as well: the years 1945-46 saw one of the largest strike waves in American history involving over eight million workers. All told, between 1945 and 1955 there were 43,000 strikes involving 27 million workers.

These labor gains were met with massive repression. Police continued breaking strikes and beating union members, but eventually by sheer force of numbers and political concessions workers were able to win important income gains. The state's repression turned to attacks on working class ideology. The House Un-American Activities Committee and later the Senate's McCarthy Hearings brought the imperialist Cold War home and led to purges of progressive elements from organized labor, government, and the universities. The Smith Act, blatantly aimed at thought control by making it a felony to "advocate" revolution in the United States, led to 110 prosecutions or indictments--about half of these of working class trade union leaders—before it was declared unconstitutional. Abroad, the Cold War myth served the function of legitimating American "police actions" beginning with Korea, and later including Lebanon, Cuba, the Dominican Republic, and Vietnam. These efforts were accompanied by American involvement through technology and "advisors" in the domestic police institutions of dozens of countries (see chapter 15).[1]

Racism, unemployment, and exploitation led to a sharply rising crime rate beginning immediately after World War II. The supposedly complacent Eisenhower years (1952-60) saw nearly a doubling of the crime rate (actually an 85 percent increase) which compares with the 120 percent increase under Kennedy and Johnson (1961-68). The class control function of the police continued to be central to its actions during this period. Police actively participated in race riots directed against Blacks in Detroit (1943) and Chicanos in Los Angeles (1943). Police activity was redirected toward increased patrol of Black communities and the proportion of Blacks locked in prison soared. The pattern of irregular attempts at police "reform"

continued with an emphasis on management training and new forms of technology, especially the radio car. There was a recurrent concern with the police "image," partly resulting from regular corruption scandals. In the early 1960's, Chicago was so shaken by a police burglary scandal that it appointed as Superintendent, O. W. Wilson, a criminology professor who was also an important architect of post-war police professionalism. He placed a major emphasis on changing the police image by such efforts as adopting light blue patrol cars with blue lights instead of the usual red.

STRUGGLES IN THE 1960'S

The decade of the 1960's produced a series of major challenges to the existing capitalist social order that led to a major attempt to redevelop the police into a vastly improved repressive class control apparatus. The main source of this escalation lay in the increasing contradictions of the capitalist system, and in the rise of popular movements challenging the racist, exploitative, and imperialist actions of the corporate state. The enormous gap between the rich and the poor, the misery of poverty in the midst of great wealth and waste on military spending, and the suppression of basic human rights, generated a wave of resistance unprecedented since the organizing years of the labor movement. This was expressed in three ways that are important in terms of understanding the expansion and rationalization of the police in the 1970's.

First, and most important, was the Civil Rights movement demanding equal rights for Blacks, Chicanos and other Third World people, including an end to police brutality. Beginning in 1964, a series of Black rebellions broke out in over 100 cities across America. Police repression reproduced the brutal violence of the worst labor struggles of the late nineteenth and early twentieth century: 43 people were killed in Detroit; 34 in Los Angeles, and 23 in Newark. Many of these killings were essentially lynchings: three Black men were captured and systematically executed by the police in the Algiers Motel in Detroit.[2]

Second, there developed a massive anti-war movement in reaction to U.S. imperialist intervention in Vietnam. Hundreds of campuses were shut down for substantial periods of time, thousands of students were gassed and beaten, and eleven were killed. Hundreds of thousands of citizens marched on Washington demanding an end to the war. Thousands of peaceful demonstrators were illegally locked up by the police. The set-back that U.S. imperialism suffered with the victory of the Vietnamese people was intensified by renewed challenges to U.S. policy in other Third World countries.

Third, high levels of exploitation led to high levels of crime, but unlike the Eisenhower era when a rapid increase in crime passed unnoticed, the 1960's saw crime emerge as a major political issue. Part of the "law and order" and "crime in the streets" issue was simply a respectable way of waging a racist campaign against Blacks, Chicanos and other Third World people. Another part was a demand for stability and increased repression from the conservative sectors of society who saw their class position threatened by political challenges to the existing social order. A growing fear of crime was documented by an actual rise in the level of serious crime. This reflected the social disintegration of the decaying cities abandoned as "unprofitable" by the wealthy corporations. This process was accelerated by the exodus to the suburbs by Whites, either in search of decent housing, or afraid of Blacks or crime.[3]

CORPORATE REFORMS

All these developments led the corporate state to make increased class control demands on the police. The police responded vigorously and violently to the challenge, but failed to live up to expectations. The police response to Black rebellions was inefficient and brutal, their impact on crime was all but invisible, and they failed to blunt the wave of campus rebellions in spite of a number of widely publicized attacks. Furthermore, the police response to these situations frequently exposed them as clumsy and inept. Police and National Guard troops repeatedly shot it out with each other in ghetto riots thinking that they had "snipers" on roofs. On campuses, police were led in wild goose

ases in all directions while actions were
gaged in elsewhere. Teargas canisters were
rown back into the ranks of the police. The
Democratic" Party had its convention inter-
pted both by anti-war protesters, and by the
icago police department's arrests and beat-
3s of television newsmen, delegates, and
fice workers on their way home. All of this
dicated that the police were not only in-
pable of containing the violence and dis-
ection of the sixties, but were actually
ntributing to it and accelerating the decline
the legitimacy of the state. The recognition
t an overtly brutal and ineffective police
uld have serious consequences for the stabil-
 of the system led to an unprecedented
obilization of the energy and resources of
al and Federal governments, universities,
rporate foundations, and "think tanks" in a
ssive effort to devise more subtle and effec-
e strategies and forms of organization for the
ice. Although these reforms raise real criti-
ns of the police system they do not chal-
ge the structure of political and economic
ver that lies behind it, nor do they analyze

the way that the police function to serve the
structure of power and privilege.

The ruling class, recognizing the police function as too important to be left to politicians
and police administrators, directly intervened
to emphasize the need for business-type organization and efficiency in police operations, and
to involve ruling class foundations and policy-
making bodies in the reorganization of the
police institution. A number of blue-ribbon
commissions were created to study the problems of the criminal justice system in general
and the police in particular.[4] During the late
1960's and early '70's, these problems were
investigated by four separate Federal commissions and by several corporate or foundation-
sponsored study groups. These commissions
represent a serious effort to develop rationalized strategies for "crime control" to meet
the needs of the modern corporate system (see
Bibliography, chapter 19). The membership of
the commissions shows how tightly interrelated
the government and the corporations have
become in pursuit of that goal. People such as:
Otis Chandler (publisher of the *Los Angeles*

45

The National Guard at Kent State University

Times and senior vice president of the Times-Mirror Co.), Charles B. Thornton (Chairman of the Board and Chief Executive Officer, Litton Industries, Inc.), Milton S. Eisenhower (Chairman, President Emeritus of Johns Hopkins University, and Director of Baltimore and Ohio Railroad and C and O Railroad), Russell W. Peterson (Chairman of the Board, Textile Research Institute), Donald F. Taylor (President, Merrill Manufacturing Corporation), Wayne E. Thompson (Senior Vice President of Dayton Hudson Corporation), Emilio G. Collado (Executive Vice President of Standard Oil Company, N.J.), and Herman L. Weiss (Vice Chairman of the Board of General Electric Company) have all participated in various commissions.

COMMUNITY RESISTANCE

It was not only the ruling class that took an interest in shaping the police in response to their performance in the 1960's. Working class people organized to oppose police repression, just as they had earlier when the police were actively engaged in suppressing the labor movement (see chapter 3). Beginning in the late 1950's, there was a resurgence of popular militancy, led first by southern Blacks against legal segregation and later by northern Blacks against the fundamentally oppressive conditions

46

of ghetto life. In the South, organizations lik the Deacons for Defense, faced with continu attacks from the Ku Klux Klan and the sympathizers, created counter-police organiz tions and provided armed citizens' patrols the ghetto.[5] In the North, police brutali triggered rebellions in the ghettos of Harlen Watts, Newark, Detroit, and many other citie Though suffering many casualties, Blac fought back and surprised both the police ar more conventional community organizatio with their militancy and courage.

As the political struggles of the 60's inten fied and broadened on many fronts—th women's movement, the anti-war and an imperialist campaigns, and student rebellions attacks on the police increased. These attac included individual acts of rage and frustratio (like Victor Lewis Comacho Rivera, a you Puerto Rican veteran, who was killed in shoot-out in a New York police station 1973[6]), as well as organized guerrilla actio Killings of police officers and attacks on poli and military installations increased in the la decade. According to the F.B.I., 116 la enforcement officers were killed in 1971, 1 in 1972, and 134 in 1973.[7] (It should stressed, however, that killings of police offic did *not* increase as rapidly as did *police* killin of *civilians*.[8])

In addition to militant actions by individuals and underground groups, organized political campaigns were also developed in Black and student communities. In the mid-1960's, the Black Panther Party for Self-Defense was organized in Oakland, where they established a system of armed patrols which followed the police, instructing suspects about their legal rights and preventing brutality.[9] Point No. 7 of the Party's ten point program, created in 1966, stated:

> We want an immediate end to POLICE BRUTALITY and MURDER of black people.
> We believe we can end police brutality in our black community by organizing black self-defense groups that are dedicated to defending our black community from racist police oppression and brutality. [10]

Other Third World organizations, such as the Young Lords in New York, the Community Patrol Corps in Harlem, and Real Alternatives Program in San Francisco, included the right to self-defense as an integral part of their political programs, as did such White working class organizations as Rising Up Angry in Chicago and White Lightning in New York. Among other functions, these groups made an attempt to protect people from crime, force heroin dealers out of the community, and resist police harassment of young people and rent strikers.

These struggles, especially in Third World communities, brought the police under intense scrutiny and generated demands for civilian review boards and other methods of accountability. The first review board was organized in Rochester, New York, followed by New York City and Philadelphia. Despite initial popular support, the boards were either quickly phased out or coopted. The Philadelphia board's experience was typical of many such efforts around the country. With no subpoena power or independent investigative staff, it had to depend on the police for fact-finding and to wait for civilian complaints before it could initiate investigations. With little support from the city administration and open hostility from the local Police Association, it was distrusted by community organizations, was bureaucratically inefficient, and in fact did nothing to minimize police racism.[11] Similarly, in New York in 1966, the Patrolmen's Benevolent Association waged a successful referendum campaign based on fear and racism to defeat the civilian review board[12] (see chapter 6). These counter-attacks against modest attempts to curb arbitrary police power were so successful that by 1976 Berkeley's Police Review Commission (PRC) was perhaps the only remnant of the widespread campaign for civilian review boards. And the PRC, as we discuss later in chapter 17, is not without significant problems.

The resurgent militancy of Third World communities in the United States was related to struggles for national liberation in Africa, Asia, and Latin America. People of color here increasingly identified with the forces of worldwide decolonialization, characterizing their ghettos and barrios as "internal colonies" of the United States. The functions of the police, according to this perspective, are "not to protect the indigenous inhabitants, but to protect the property of the colonizer who lives outside the community and acts to restrain any Black person from breaking out of the colonial wards."[13]

By the late 1960's, these ideas and movements crystallized into a demand for community control of the police. At the same time that the Panthers and other groups were organizing in Third World communities, many student communities were becoming politicized and experienced regular conflict with the police as a result of anti-war demonstrations, college protests, and drug arrests. In student and youth communities such as Berkeley, Madison, Isla Vista, Ann Arbor, the East Village, and Haight-Ashbury, political and neighborhood organizations emerged and began to work for local control.[14] These parallel developments in Third World and student communities culminated in a legislative proposal for community control of the police, developed by the Black Panther Party in 1969 and put into practice through a referendum campaign in Berkeley in 1970-71.

The Berkeley proposal (see chapter 21) called for direct control of the police by locally elected councils in three neighborhood districts (the Black community, the student community, and the upper-middle class Berkeley Hills). Supporters of this legislative amendment to the city charter hoped that it would create new centers of popular power, decentralize governmental decision-making, and reduce the power of the state machinery. The demand for community control, as formulated by the Black Panther Party and tested in practice in Berkeley, was designed to attack not only the professionalism of the police but also the roots of their power. This was to be achieved through legislative reforms that would put the police under popular control, make them racially representative of the communities in which they worked, and replace bureaucratic and militaristic forms of police organization with more democratic forms and a social service orientation. The campaign offered a class and racial perspective on the police which fundamentally differed from typical liberal reforms.

Although about one-third of the electorate voted for the proposal, it was defeated by disunity of Black and White supporters, internal dissent within the campaign organization, inexperience in electoral politics, and the opposition of the police and powerful sectors of the local community to progressive programs.[15] The movement for community control in Berkeley quickly subsided after its electoral defeat. Similar, but less resourceful, campaigns were mounted in Chicago and Milwaukee where they were likewise defeated.[16] The demand for community control, however, is still commonly raised as a slogan in struggles against the police. We shall return later (in chapter 17) to discuss in greater detail the strengths and weaknesses of this approach.

IRON FIST AND VELVET GLOVE

From the 1960's emerged a fairly coherent set of police strategies, which have been more or less steadily implemented and backed by continuing research and governmental funds. In the following sections, we have tried to give a basic picture of the nature and direction of these strategies; their underlying ideological and strategic assumptions, their translation into actual police practice, and their probable impact. Although the new developments in policing are complex and sometimes confusing, we think that it's useful to regard the new approach to the police as having two distinct but closely related sides. One is a "hard" side, based on sophisticated technology and a generally increased capacity to use force; the other is a "soft" side, based on new forms of community pacification and other attempts to "sell" the police to the public. The "hard" side was the first to be seriously developed, but today both sides are usually mixed together, and used interdependently, in the practice of any given police agency: the iron fist in the velvet glove

It's important to recognize that *both* sides of the new police approach are strategies of

repression. Whether they stress the virtues of weapons technology or of "community input," neither of them challenges the structure of privilege and exploitation in the U.S. Both of them serve to support that structure by making the system of repression that serves it more powerful or more palatable or both. Like the similar techniques developed in the sixties to maintain the overseas empire (on which many of the new police techniques were patterned), these new police strategies represent an attempt to streamline and mystify the repressive power of the state, not to minimize it or change its direction. The forms of repression may change, but their functions remain the same. In the late 1960's, the new forms of policing were strongly influenced by the unprecedented involvement of the Federal government on whose behalf the Law Enforcement Assistance Administration has played a decisive role. Before evaluating the repressive functions of the iron fist and the velvet glove, we will first examine the legislative machinery which gives this apparatus ideological guidance and financial backing.

1. Richard Boyer and Herbert Morais, *Labor's Untold Story*, New York, United Electrical Workers, 1971; Roger Daniels, *Concentration Camps USA: Japanese Americans and World War II*, New York, Holt, Rinehart and Winston, 1972; Richard Rovere, *Senator Joe McCarthy*, New York, Harcourt, 1959; Michael Klare, *War Without End*, New York, Random House, 1972.
2. National Advisory Commission on Civil Disorders, *Kerner Report*, Washington, D.C., U.S. Government Printing Office, 1968.
3. Fred Graham, *The Self-Inflicted Wound*, New York, Macmillan, 1970; Robert Cipes, *The Crime War: The Manufactured Crusade*, New York, New American Library, 1968.
4. On the politics of government commissions see Tony Platt, *The Politics of Riot Commissions*, New York, Macmillan, 1971. For one analysis of ruling class shaping of social policy, see G. William Domhoff, "How the Power Elite Shapes Social Legislation," in *The Higher Circles*, New York, Random House, 1970.
5. Harold A. Nelson, "The Defenders: A Case Study of an Informal Police Organization," *Social Problems*, Fall, 1967, pp. 124-147.
6. *New York Times*, July 24 & 25, 1973.
7. *New York Times*, January 13, 1974.
8. Paul Takagi, "A Garrison State in a 'Democratic' Society," *Crime and Social Justice*, 1, Spring-Summer, 1974, pp. 27-33.
9. Philip S. Foner, ed., *The Black Panthers Speak*, New York, Lippincott, 1970.
10. Ibid., p. 3.
11. Gordon E. Misner and Joseph D. Lohman, "Civilian Review Philadelphia," in Leonard Ruchelman, Ed., *Who Rules the Police*, New York, New York University Press, 1973, pp. 46-75.
12. Ed Cray, "The Politics of Blue Power," *The Nation*, April 21, 1969. See also Harold Beral and Marcus Sisk, "The Administration of Complaints by Civilians Against the Police," *Harvard Law Review*, January 1964, pp. 499-519; President's Commission on Law Enforcement and Administration of Justice, *The Police*, Washington, D.C., U.S. Government Printing Office, 1967.
13. Robert Staples, "White Racism, Black Crime and American Justice," Unpublished paper presented at the International Society of Criminology, 1972.
14. Tom Hayden, *Trial*, New York, Holt, Rinehart, and Winston, 1970.
15. This analysis is largely derived from Tom Hayden and Carol Kurtz, "The Lessons of Community Control in Berkeley, 1971," Unpublished paper on file at the Center for Research on Criminal Justice.
16. For details of the Chicago Community Control of Police Conference see *The Black Panther* Intercommunal News Service, Vol. X, No. 4, Saturday, June 9, 1973, p. 3. Also see Northside Campaign For Community Control of the Police, *Community Control*, Vol. 1, Nos. 1, 2, and 3 (August-October, 1973). For details of the Milwaukee campaign see *The Black Panther* Intercommunal News Service, Vol. XII, No. 2, Saturday, August 3, 1974, p. 4. Also, see *The Milwaukee Journal*, July 11, 1974, p. 1.

5. THE LAW ENFORCEMENT ASSISTANCE ADMINISTRATION

The Law Enforcement Assistance Administration (LEAA) provides the organizational basis for putting both sides of the modern police strategy into practice. By 1968 it had become increasingly clear that state and local governments were not able to reduce instability and disruption, and could not restore confidence in the status quo. It was obvious that some sort of national action was required. LEAA was established as the Federal agency to deal with the problem.

LEAA'S ORIGIN AND RESPONSIBILITIES

In the legislation originally establishing LEAA, crime was described as a "national catastrophe." While Congress agreed that crime control was basically a local and state responsibility, these units of government were too decentralized and acted too haphazardly. The Federal government had to assume a role in fighting crime. A "war on crime" was declared, and LEAA was to lead the attack.[1] LEAA was designed to supply Federal money, expertise, and direction for remodeling and refurbishing the coercive apparatus of the criminal justice system.

Since its inception in 1968, LEAA has become one of the fastest growing agencies in the Federal government. The budget has increased from $63 million in 1969 to $1,015 million for fiscal year 1976. Federal expenditures for the criminal justice system only represent a small percentage of state and local budgets for criminal justice operations,[2] but LEAA is a major force for influencing, standardizing, unifying, and coordinating policies and programs for the police, courts, and corrections. Through consolidation of planning and uniformity of operations LEAA has the responsibility of improving and rationalizing the internal security network. LEAA has supplied over $3 billion to fund projects and research, and to purchase equipment and com-

puterized information and intelligence systems for criminal justice agencies.

LEAA attacks the problem of crime mainly as a problem of policing. While the courts and corrections are important, the police, as the first line of national defense, are considered the central force in controlling crime and maintaining stability. Therefore, LEAA spends a majority of its money on advancing the repressive operations of the police.

LEAA money is distributed primarily in three ways: block action grants, discretionary grants, and through the National Institute for Law Enforcement and Criminal Justice (NILECJ). Action grants, allocated through LEAA's regional offices, account for 85 percent of LEAA funding. The remaining 15 percent is distributed directly from the agency headquarters and regional offices, in the form of discretionary and NILECJ grants.

Annually every state is given $200,000 to support the development of a comprehensive state criminal justice plan, which details how

the state will be spending its LEAA funds. This plan must be approved by LEAA. The requirement for the submission of an annual criminal justice plan is part of LEAA's goal for the rationalization and nationwide coordination of the criminal justice system. The comprehensive criminal justice plan is designed to force the states to systematically organize and more efficiently deal with competing needs and the ordering of priorities for the various agencies within the system. Because of the lack of professional expertise in this field, state comprehensive criminal justice plans have been a mass of unorganized information, a nonspecific collection of facts on various aspects of the system, and even less specific descriptions of the problems and needs for action within an area. In spite of this, LEAA has never rejected a comprehensive plan; states may be required to make changes within the plan, and to follow agency guidelines more specifically. It is important to stress that even without the guidelines and the requirements, states would not act any differently in terms of awarding their funds; however, the LEAA requirements are important because they provide a systematized and professional model for the states to follow.

Each state is given a block of money, awarded as action grants, to support the projects and programs outlined in the criminal justice plan. The amount awarded is based on the state's population. This money goes to the individual state (criminal justice) planning agency. (Each state has a different name for that agency; in general, they are referred to as SPAs.)

State planning agencies (SPAs), staffed by criminal justice professionals, are under the control of a Supervisory Board, which is appointed by the Chief Executive of the state. The Supervisory Board is responsible for giving final approval for the allocation of block grant action money. The members of the Board represent vested interests in the criminal justice system. A 1973 nationwide survey of Supervisory Board members found that 46 percent of the members were representatives of criminal justice agencies (Judiciary, Prosecution, Corrections, Law Enforcement, and the FBI); 33 percent were elected and public agency officials; 3 percent were described as people connected with the defense of criminal suspects; and 18 percent were categorized as private citizens, the majority of whom were professional criminal justice social scientists and researchers. Needless to say there is little representation of Third World and poor people, who are disproportionately the most frequent victims of crime, as well as the most widely arrested and imprisoned group of people in this country. The Board members ensure continual support and increased funding for the repressive operations of the various criminal justice and professional interests they represent.

The protection of existing criminal justice operations is also maintained at the regional board level. In order to ensure that LEAA money would reach local units of government, the LEAA legislation requires that 40 percent of the planning money must be allocated to regional planning boards. This is to help these boards finance the development of a local criminal justice plan, which will be submitted to the state and incorporated into the state plan. The regional boards are also responsible for the initial approval of funding projects and programs for their area. The membership of the regional planning boards is very similar to that of the SPA Supervisory Board. In most states the members are originally selected by the state's Chief Executive; vacancies are then filled by the remaining board members. The majority of regional board members are with criminal justice agencies, and elected officials. Progressive and politically active community groups are not represented. There are no effective popular controls on what regional or supervisory boards do and how money is allocated. The respective boards respond to the interests and concerns of strengthening and protecting the operations of the criminal justice system.

HOW LEAA SPENDS ITS MONEY

As the primary agency responsible for Federal financing of law enforcement and criminal justice efforts, LEAA distributed more than one billion dollars between 1969 and 1975. Thirty-nine percent of this money has gone to support police and police-related activities; 13 percent of the funds has been spent on

courts' projects and programs; 28 percent of the money has been spent in the area of corrections; combined efforts, including any combination of courts, policing and corrections, account for 11 percent of the funds; non-criminal justice agencies received 7 percent of the funds. Between 1969 and August 1975, the police received 61 percent of all action grants.[3] In 1973, out of $483 million in LEAA funds, $158.92 million was used for "detection, deterrence, and apprehension of criminals," and $66.04 million went solely for crime prevention. Forty-six percent of total LEAA action funds went to law enforcement and police-related activities.[4]

During the past 5 years LEAA has supplied money to police departments for purchasing new guns, automobiles, riot control equipment, helicopters, computers, and sophisticated intelligence gathering systems. LEAA is generously assisting in the development of a police-industrial complex, by providing initial grants for law enforcement agencies to purchase hardware and reinforcing the police argument that this type of hardware is mandatory if crime is to be controlled.

LEAA also supports the soft approach to policing, encouraging police-community relations and sensitivity training for police, as well as greater community involvement in policing. The recently published *Standards and Goals Report* (funded by LEAA) stressed the importance of supporting greater community involvement. The Report stated:

> *Cooperation between the police and the community is the first step in effective crime control. . . . The police must obtain information from the community as to its needs, and the public also must be informed of the police agency's roles so that it can better support the police in their efforts to reduce crime.*[5]

LEAA has been a major influence in developing and implementing communications, information, and intelligence systems. It is estimated that since 1969, approximately $320 million has been used for this purpose.[6] A nationwide network for gathering, storing, and disseminating information on criminals, and suspected or suspicious persons, has been financed by LEAA (see chapter 8).

In the past year LEAA's concentration on supporting law enforcement activities has decreased. Currently, considerable emphasis is on developing standards and goals for criminal justice agencies. In addition, there is increasingly greater emphasis on the field of corrections, which corresponds to the increased militant activity within the prisons. LEAA is meeting the need to supply research and programs which will control and stabilize inmate populations.

STANDARDS AND GOALS

The LEAA effort to develop nationwide standards and goals for the criminal justice system was initiated in 1971. A National Advisory Commission on Criminal Justice Standards and Goals selected by the Administrator of LEAA, was directed to formulate standards and goals for "crime reduction and prevention at the State and local levels."[7] The Commission was created as a response to one of the major criticisms of the agency—that it was too scattered and not focused enough in its operations.[8] The establishment of a selected body of experts to formally outline standards and goals for all aspects of the criminal justice system would establish a specific direction for LEAA. The standards and goals would potentially act as a major force influencing the design and types of programs that would receive LEAA support.

After two years the Commission produced six volumes[9] outlining almost four hundred specific standards and recommendations for the police, courts, corrections, the justice system as a whole, and an area defined as "community crime prevention." The Commission concentrated its efforts on defining goals and standards that would reduce crime by increasing the efficiency and professional operations of criminal justice agencies. The first goal proposed by the Commission is a 50 percent reduction in high-fear crimes (burglary, robbery, assault, rape, homicide) by 1983. The emphasis is on restoring and rebuilding confidence in the mechanisms and agencies of the existing system.

Legally, states are not required to use the standards and goals selected by the Commission. The Commission was authorized to act only in an advisory capacity. However, while LEAA cannot mandate the use of standards and goals, through their funding process they can strongly "suggest" that states begin to use those standards and goals in the writing of their comprehensive plans (which must be approved by LEAA).

While in the past LEAA has been able to pursue criminal justice planning, standardization, uniformity, and coordination, their leverage has now increased enormously. Every state will be undergoing a process of examining what standards and goals will be established for their criminal justice system, using LEAA funded and directed Reports as guidelines—which are backed by authority and money.

The standards and goals presented in the Commission Reports are diverse, ranging from the recommendation to abolish plea bargaining, to the usual requirement of psychological examination of police applicants. All of the

Grants to Police Departments
As a Percentage of All Action Grants
1969–1975

Year	Number of Police Grants	Percentage of Action Grants	$ Amount (millions)	Percentage of Action Funds
1969	2,491	80	15.4	66
1970	8,928	73	86.3	49
1971	10,118	64	140.1	40
1972	10,255	60	169.5	42
1973	8,047	55	181.0	43
1974	5,843	52	130.6	36
1975*	1,198	50	36.0	43
TOTAL	46,875	62	758.9	46

*Partial figures

Source: LEAA computer printout, cited in *Law Enforcement: The Federal Role*, Report of the Twentieth Century Fund Task Force on the Law Enforcement Assistance Administration, New York: McGraw-Hill, 1976, p. 139.

recommendations have a common theme. They are aimed at improving the functional operations of the criminal justice system, managing conflict and changing some of the more devastating and dehumanizing practices of the police, the courts, and the correctional system. Such changes only minimally alter existing practices and policies, and seem to be made less because of concern for the practice itself than out of concern with public reaction.

The Reports stress that private citizens must begin to play a more active role in the criminal justice system. It is suggested that this can be accomplished through such things as community relations programs and volunteer activities. The theme of the entire *Community Crime Prevention Report* is that citizens can prevent crime by making their cars, homes, and businesses more secure against crime ("target hardening"), and by cooperating with the system. The Reports make it clear that the professionals who control and run the criminal justice system will continue to do so. The operation of the agencies of criminal justice may be marginally improved, but whom they protect and serve, and who is policed, punished, and jailed will remain the same.

Standardization and coordination for law enforcement agencies means that police departments will specify their needs, define goals and objectives, and develop long range plans. Policing, which has long been characterized as chaotic, is now beginning to be rationalized. Individual cities and towns must now coordinate and consolidate their policing efforts. For example, in 1973, LEAA funded the National Sheriffs' Association to develop a manual to "Assist in the Development of Law Enforcement Mutual Aid Systems."[10] The manual details the type of legislation needed to legalize mutual aid and an operational plan for implementing the proposed system.

THE NATIONAL INSTITUTE FOR LAW ENFORCEMENT AND CRIMINAL JUSTICE

Through the distribution of discretionary grants and research awards of LEAA's research arm, the National Institute for Law Enforcement and Criminal Justice (NILECJ), LEAA has been able to directly influence what types of new projects will be sponsored and what kinds of research will be supported. Discretionary grants are "the means by which LEAA can advance national priorities, draw attention to programs not emphasized in state plans and provide special impetus for reform and experimentation."[11] Between 1969 and 1975, over $486.7 million has been distributed in this form. Discretionary grants, like other LEAA awards, have gone primarily to building up law enforcement agencies. According to the most recently available statistics, between January 1969 and January 1972, 36 percent of all discretionary awards went directly to law enforcement activities. This figure does not include money that went for police involved in organized crime activities, narcotics enforcement, or juvenile delinquency prevention.[12]

NILECJ is responsible for encouraging training, education, research and development for the purpose of improving law enforcement and criminal justice and of developing new methods for the prevention and reduction of crime, and the detection and apprehension of criminals. The Institute was not included in the original LEAA legislation; it was introduced as the

liberal answer to crime. The emphasis on research and education for examining the causes and effects of crime was considered the appropriate liberal response to the demands for law and order. It was believed that with universities conducting objective and professional research, the crime problem could be solved rationally. Similar to the way think tanks and universities service the Pentagon, NILECJ was designed as the research and development arm of law enforcement and the Department of Justice. NILECJ would provide counter-insurgency research for the police.

NILECJ, like the discretionary grants and action funds of LEAA, has focused primarily on law enforcement activities. Between 1973-1975, 44.6 percent ($33.5 million) of all NILECJ awards were for police-related projects. The largest single amount ($21.4 million) was used for one specific purpose—the development and evaluation of equipment, techniques, and standards. Projects in this category included: a citizen alarm system, a reliable low-cost burglar alarm for residential and small business use, and

protective garments for the police.[13]

NILECJ operates two major projects designed to disseminate information and increase standardization and uniformity within the criminal justice system. The first of these is the "Exemplary Project Program." For this program, LEAA selects projects considered to represent outstanding criminal justice programs which are suitable for adoption by other communities. Manuals containing comprehensive guidelines for establishing and operating the selected program are then made available to agencies throughout the country.

"Prescriptive packages" are similar to the exemplary project program. For prescriptive packages, a *type* of program (not a specific existing project as in the exemplary program),

such as methadone maintenance or police-community relations, is carefully detailed in a manual. The manual describes how such a program would be started and operated. These manuals are then freely dispersed to criminal justice agencies interested in establishing the type of program outlined in the manual. NILECJ will also provide technical experts to assist in the development of these programs.

A variety of criticisms have been leveled at LEAA, ranging from the extreme of totally replacing it to specific recommendations for altering the operations and functions of the agency. Basically, the conflict is over which tactics and strategies will best meet the need for preserving capitalism in the United States. There is not a uniformly accepted formula to

THE FAILURE OF LEAA

*The evidence is overwhelming; the federal government has greatly increased its expenditures to combat crime, but these expenditures have had no effect in reducing crime . . .

*LEAA's tendency to "modernize" and to rely on overly technological solutions for police work is, in some cases, equipping law enforcement agencies to deal with crises that have never occurred and, in all likelihood, never will occur. The mere development of equipment and accompanying tactics, however, raises the possibility . . . of the new technology being applied to situations for which is is inappropriate and can only be harmful . . .

*The SPA structure, because of its lack of accountability to city councils and state legislatures or to traditional cabinet offices, is subject to political manipulation . . . and can be used to foster repressive police measures and a build-up of state military-type departments. Such risks are greater where the state has placed heavy emphasis on the development of centralized information and intelligence systems . . .

Rising crime rates have stimulated a public cry for more funds for police in order to reduce and prevent crime; this is occurring despite the fact that the police are stating that they lack the capacity to control crime and that prevention is the responsibility of other agencies that deal with people before they become involved in crime. This myopia is replicated at the federal level, where the Congress and LEAA have refused to look at the interrelationship of anti-crime efforts to other federal domestic policies . . .

*What can be said about our crime reduction capacity? Not much that is encouraging. We have learned little about reducing the incidence of crime, and have no reason to believe that significant reductions will be secured in the near future.—NILECJ Director Gerald Caplan

Excerpts from: Center for National Security Studies, Law and Disorder IV, Washington, D.C., The Center for National Security Studies, 1976, pp. 4, 6.

---

follow and there are differences as to how this goal can be met. Cities and towns criticize LEAA for providing only minimal financial support for local criminal justice problems, while state and Federal officials, and criminal justice personnel and professionals argue that LEAA is inefficiently managed, overrun with too many diverse, nonspecific programs and projects, and is not stopping the rapidly rising rate of crime.

Several private organizations have also criticized LEAA. A 1972 report by the Committee for Economic Development (CED), an advisory group to the Federal government made up of prestigious multinational corporate leaders, described the legislation that created LEAA as defective and the program a failure. The report, *Reducing Crime and Assuring Justice,*[14] proposed totally abolishing LEAA and establishing a Federal Authority to Ensure Justice.

The Twentieth Century Fund, also a private organization with prestigious members, including the former police chief of New Haven, Connecticut, the former executive director of the International Association of Chiefs of Police, and a number of lawyers, recently proposed a major reorganization of the agency, with the direct distribution of Federal funds to states, counties, and cities.[15] Another report on LEAA, titled *Law and Disorder IV,* released in May 1976, is the most recent in a series of critical reports.[16] This report has a more liberal perspective than the others, and criticized LEAA for ignoring the rights of criminal suspects, prisoners, and minorities, and for not providing adequate support for nontraditional approaches to the various criticisms leveled at the agency. Reports such as the *Law and Disor-*

"Officer Bill"

The most important program in
your community relations effort

"Officer Bill" . . . the Tested
and Proven Police Program for
lower elementary grades!

A complete program. Presented by
your own officers in about 30 min.
Pays off in respect and friendship!

der series have been attacked by LEAA as being
politically biased and written by people with no
expertise in criminal justice.

The response to the CED report was considered more significant because of the political
importance and influence of the Committee.
Testifying in March 1973 to a subcommittee of
the House Committee on the Judiciary, Attorney General Richard Kleindienst un-
equivocally described the recommendations of
the report as totally wrong and incorrect,[17]
while Richard Velde, Administrator of LEAA,
described various parts of the Twentieth Century Fund Report as superficial, false, and
confusing.[18]

In general, the conflict over how to change
LEAA is divided between the need to concentrate on reducing crime and the view that
LEAA should be primarily responsible for
providing the technology and ideology for
systematically improving criminal justice operations throughout the country. LEAA has attempted to meet these criticisms by supplying
both services; the agency is criticized for
accomplishing neither. The criticisms of LEAA
are made within a corporate rationale framework. This framework requires that LEAA be
operated in a well-defined, systematic manner,
which demands managerial and fiscal accountability, as well as responsibility and efficiency in
diffusing actively growing political opposition
and struggles against the repressive functions of
the criminal justice system.

LEAA, out of the political need to develop a
strategy to answer criticisms of the agency
responded in a variety of ways. Additional
audit officers were added to the staff, more
data on the disbursement of money was collected, and financial support was provided to a
variety of software programs and projects
including assisting rape crisis and intervention
centers, academic conferences, and innocuous
programs such as "Justice for Jurors." (Jurors
are given badges in order to give their temporary position some prestige.) LEAA is governed by the need to create the mechanisms
and organizations which will support the existing system. Therefore, LEAA will fund community groups, but this support is condition-

and is quickly terminated when an organization becomes politically progressive. In addition, this funding process permits increasing covert community surveillance and penetration. LEAA is not concerned with the repressive function and operations of the criminal justice system. The agency's goal is to offer an overall program which is generally acceptable to all factions of the ruling class. The purpose is to provide support which will both please and appease critics, without sacrificing or compromising its basic purpose of strengthening the internal security network. LEAA supplies the financial and theoretical support and guidance for developing both the ideological and the force components for the criminal justice system.

Through its various programs, Exemplary Projects and Prescriptive Packages, NILECJ

research projects and discretionary grants, and the requirement of LEAA approval of comprehensive state criminal justice plans, LEAA has become the major force influencing the "war on crime." LEAA is supplying the authority, the methods, and the money needed to rationalize the system of internal security in the U.S. As such, LEAA has enormous significance, because it represents the first serious attempt to develop a *national* apparatus of repression and control. Although LEAA is an expanding and very powerful agency, a really effective apparatus is still a long way off. One reason for this is the serious divisions *within* the police system which undermine efforts to develop a monolithic apparatus of repression. In the next chapter we will examine in depth one aspect of this issue.

1. For a legislative history of the Omnibus Crime Control and Safe Streets Act of 1968 see "Index to the Legislative History of the Omnibus Crime Control and Safe Streets Act of 1968," Office of General Counsel, LEAA, January 23, 1973; see also Richard Harris, *The Fear of Crime*, New York, Praeger, Inc., 1969.
2. For Fiscal Year 1974, the percentage distribution of total direct expenditures for the criminal justice system was: Federal 13.1%; State 26.1%; Local 60.8%. U.S. Department of Justice, *Trends in Expenditure and Employment Data for the Criminal Justice System 1971-1974*, Washington, D.C., Government Printing Office, 1976, p. 2.
3. LEAA computer printout, cited in *Law Enforcement: The Federal Role*, Report of the Twentieth Century Fund Task Force on the Law Enforcement Assistance Administration, New York, McGraw-Hill, 1969, pp. 109-110, 139.
4. U.S. Department of Justice, *Fifth Annual Report of the LEAA, Fiscal Year 1973*, Washington, D.C., Government Printing Office, 1973, p. 18.
5. National Advisory Commission on Criminal Justice Standards and Goals, *A National Strategy to Reduce Crime*, Washington, D.C., Government Printing Office, 1973, p. 72.
6. LEAA Responses to Issues Raised by the Subcommittee on Constitutional Rights, Committee on the Judiciary, U.S. Senate, March 11, 1974, p. 52.
7. National Advisory Commission, loc. cit., p. v.
8. The Reports submitted by the National Advisory Commission on Criminal Justice Standards and Goals are: *A National Strategy to Reduce Crime; Police; Courts; Corrections; Criminal Justice System; Community Crime Prevention.*
9. National Sheriffs' Association, *Mutual Aid Planning: A Manual Designed to Assist in the Development of Law Enforcement Mutual Aid Systems*, Washington, D.C., National Sheriffs' Association, 1973.
10. "Discretionary Grant Guidelines," LEAA, p. 1.
11. Center for National Security Studies, *Law and Disorder IV*, Washington, D.C., The Center for National Security Studies, 1976, p. 19. See also, Lawyer's Committee for Civil Rights Under Law, *Law and Disorder III*, Washington, D.C., Urban Institute, 1972, p. 22.
12. Public Law 93-83, "Crime Control Act of 1973," August 6, 1973, Part D, Section 401.
13. U.S. Department of Justice, *Fifth Annual Report of the LEAA, Fiscal Year 1973*, Washington, D.C., Government Printing Office, 1973, p. 100. See also *Law and Disorder IV*, p. 13.
14. Committee for Economic Development, *Reducing Crime and Assuring Justice*, New York, Committee for Economic Development, 1972.
15. See "Response to a Report by the Twentieth Century Fund Task Force," in the *Congressional Record—Senate*, May 25, 1976, S 7906 and Report of the Twentieth Century Fund Task Force on the Law Enforcement Assistance Administration, *Law Enforcement: The Federal Role*, New York, McGraw-Hill Book Co., 1976.
16. *Law and Disorder IV*, loc. cit.
17. U.S. House of Representatives, Committee on the Judiciary, *Law Enforcement Assistance Administration*, 93rd Congress, 1st Session, 1973, p. 277.
18. See "Response to Newspaper Reports Concerning A Report by the Center for National Security Studies, Richard Velde," in the *Congressional Record—Senate*, May 25, 1976, S 7905.

6. POLICE MILITANCY

"If you're going to buy a policeman as a mercenary, then you ought to pay him top dollar. We ought to get combat pay."
Patrolman Demurjian, N.Y.P.D.[1]

"Cops on strike? I thought they went on strike a long time ago. Like about ten years."
Woman, Bedford-Stuyvesant[2]

INTRODUCTION

The recent upsurge of police strikes, lobbying campaigns and lawsuits marks a new high of organized militancy within the ranks of the police. This militancy underscores the fact that the police institution is not monolithic, that it is full of divisions and conflicts, reproducing the social contradictions of advanced capitalism. Today's police, over 650,000 strong, are themselves a politically active sector of the state apparatus pushing its own interests and demands, sometimes against the capitalist state and, more frequently, in alliance with the ruling class against the working class. The fidelity of the police to their repressive function is not a given, but must be continually reproduced through the way in which the job is structured and the rewards available for loyal service. The current economic crisis threatens both the legitimacy and the fiscal base of the police, and they have responded with an unprecedented degree of occupational solidarity and a marked increase of reactionary political activity. In demanding higher wages, more weapons and increased police powers, the police, as never before, are both questioning the demands made upon them and insisting upon increased compensation for doing the dirty work of the ruling class.

Organizations of the police are not new. The New York Police Benevolent Association (NYPBA) was founded in 1894, and the police, along with the firemen, have been traditionally the best organized and most politically effective sector of municipal employees. By and large, the police have organized as a privileged special

interest group, pushing their demands with the threat that without their professional knowledge and daring courage, the people would be left to the agonies of crime and public disorder. Much of this agitation, especially in recent years, has been a racist appeal to Whites. While jealously guarding their economic privilege, especially job security and liberal pensions, the police have simultaneously lent their support to racist and reactionary politicians.

In the last 15 years, the police have become more tightly organized than ever before. The NYPBA, for example, was in 1958 a small fraternal society with an effective lobby in Albany and $900 in its treasury. By 1969, however, it had become a militant organization with an annual budget of almost $2 million and a Health and Welfare Fund that had paid more than $15 million since its inception in 1963.[3] Almost all police belong to citywide associations and a rapidly increasing percentage also belong to national groups such as the Fraternal Order of Police (FOP) or the International

Fred Wright, Union Cartoons

"You and I should stick together against those Blacks!"

Conference of Police Associations (ICPA). Command-level police frequently belong to the International Association of Chiefs of Police (IACP).

The main economic and political incentives to police organizations have not changed. What is new, however, is the increased willingness of rank and file police to embrace trade union tactics to advance their economic goals and the emergence of a vocal challenge, mostly from Black police, to intradepartmental racism and police brutality. City officials and police administrators have responded to this upsurge in militancy by White and Black police with enough sophistication to shape its impact in important respects. Police militancy poses a serious threat to the orderly functioning of class rule, but, when properly channeled, it has served as an important impetus to increasing both the repressive power and centralization of the state.

In this chapter, we survey the contemporary state of police organizations and attempt to assess the direction of their development. We start with a brief analysis of the history of police organizations and then sketch out the impact of the changing economic and political conditions of policing in the 1960's and 1970's on police militancy. We also look at the sudden blossoming of union-affiliation and the policy initiatives of the command-level police organizations. Finally, we discuss Black police societies, which sometimes act in concert with the predominantly White groups, but which have often acted in opposition to both the police administration and the police organizations.

HISTORY OF POLICE ORGANIZATIONS

Historically, the police have organized apart from and in opposition to the working class. Their claim to the mantle of professionalism has developed out of the nature of their work, the active encouragement of police administrators and policy-makers, and the initiative of the police themselves. As discussed in Section II, the nature of the police function under capitalism sets the police against the working class. Most police have been recruited from the

working class, but the vast majority of them have in the course of their work switched their class loyalty to the local bourgeoisie. These politicians and businessmen have, in turn, looked out for the police and rewarded their loyalty with relatively high wages. In Northern industrial cities, for example, police wages in the nineteenth century ran about double those of laborers, and everywhere police had little trouble keeping their scale well above those of other city employees such as teachers or sanitation workers. In addition, the police received at times ten times their regular salary in graft, payoffs for political support, and special bonuses for strike-breaking. The introduction of the three platoon system in the 1880's meant a reduced work week with no reduction in wages, and other improvements in working conditions followed through the 1890's. The semi-military organization of the police and the active promotion of a professional and racist ideology have also intensified the gap of consciousness and life style between the police and the working class.[4]

Police organizations developed initially as fraternal and benevolent societies. Providing a form of self-help, the societies also pushed for higher wages, improved working conditions, and retirement benefits. Typically composed of all of the police rank except the top command posts, these societies were frequently dominated by supervisory personnel such as lieutenants and captains. These officials reminded the ruling class of their responsibilities to the police with the aid of payoffs to city councilmen and state legislators. The police fraternal societies were an accepted part of the electoral machinery in many cities, and they worked to reinforce the formal hierarchy within police departments.[5]

Despite the political lobbying of police societies, city officials and police administrators have not, by and large, attempted to prevent such organizations. Until recently, however, the police command has strenuously resisted any move toward union-affiliation of the police. The officials have argued that unionization would complicate the loyalties of the police, erode departmental discipline, and raise the spectre of a city immobilized by a police strike.[6] Simply put, unionization was seen as a serious threat to the maintenance of class domination.

Like professionals and unlike almost all other workers, the police have historically been able to improve their standard of living and social status without recourse to unionization. Particularly in big city departments, they have had their economic battles fought for them by the civilian commissioners, police chiefs and top administrative personnel who couched demands for increased police budgets in the language of professionalization. The rank and file police, for their part, had made only two short drives for unionization before the current campaign.

POLICE UNIONIZATION, 1917-1919

In the first period of police unionization, 1917-1919, the police in several cities tried to ally themselves with the conservative trade union movement. Hurt by the severe inflation which accompanied World War I and spurred by the renewed militancy of the working class, local police organizations turned to the American Federation of Labor (AFL) for charters in the fall and winter of 1917. The AFL rejected these applications on the basis of an 1897 ruling refusing the admission of a group of private police in Cleveland which had declared that it was "not within the province of the trade union movement" to organize policemen as they were "too often controlled by forces inimical to the labor movement." The persistent clamor of police associations, however, led to a reconsideration of this ruling, and the next year the AFL changed its policy and began chartering police locals.

When spurned by their allies at city hall, the police were eager to embrace the trade union movement to win their demands, and within nine weeks after the adjournment of the AFL convention, 65 police organizations, mostly in small cities, applied for union charters. Within months, 37 charters had been granted, and the growth of these locals after admission to the Federation brought their membership to about 4,000. The AFL did not push police unionization. The initiative came from the police

themselves, and even in cities like New York and Chicago where the police did not apply for charters, pro-labor sentiment was rising and the issue of formal affiliation was widely discussed. In most cities, the officials grudgingly accepted police unionization. In a few cities, pro-labor officials encouraged it, while in Oklahoma City the policeman's union, 100 percent strong, had the support of the mayor. This sudden marriage of convenience between the police and organized labor was, however, ended almost as soon as it had begun.[7]

THE BOSTON STRIKE

The first wave of police unionization came to an abrupt halt with the defeat of the Boston police strike in 1919. Most accounts of the strike credit the violence and disorder which accompanied it as the reason for the sudden end of police unionism. In fact, however, the strike resulted in violence because of the calculated union-busting efforts of the Boston Police Commissioner and his corporate lawyer advisor. They were determined to break the police union, not because of opposition to the police officers' economic demands, but because of their fears that in a big city department unionization would undermine departmental authority and complicate the class loyalties of the police. In addition, they felt that breaking the back of the police union was an important precedent in the struggle against the other non-police municipal employee unions. The police were the best organized of these city workers and, if their unionization could be stalled, it lowered the resistance of the weaker organizations.[8]

The Boston police strike was defeated, all 1,200 of the striking policemen were fired, and the successful union-busting in Boston put an end at that time to both the police and municipal employees' unionizing drives. In New York, the police had wanted to join the AFL but were stopped by the vigorous opposition of the entrenched PBA officials and the example of Boston. Similarly, the Washington, D.C., police won a pay bonus but lost their AFL affiliation through President Woodrow Wilson's intervention in the courts.

In responding to the first wave of police unionization, city officials followed the lead of the intense 1919 open shop campaign in private industry. There was, however, an important difference. In private industry, the defeat of unionization meant that the workers continued to receive very low wages and oppressive working conditions. The police, on the other hand, were rewarded for their abandonment of the AFL with higher wages, shorter hours and improved working conditions. In Boston, the entirely new police force hired during and after the strike received almost all of the wage increases demanded by the union. On the whole, police wages rose faster than those in private industry until 1929 and the police continued to be among the best paid of municipal workers.[9]

Officials and city administrators in many cities used laws barring municipal unionization and the lesson of the Boston police strike to forestall police affiliation with the labor movement, but gave in nevertheless to police pressure for an independent association or FOP lodge. The Fraternal Order of Police, which was founded in 1915 to promote civil service reform and pension provisions for police, benefited from the defeat of unionization. Some police administrators continued to formally oppose police organizations but in fact tacitly encouraged them as a useful ally in pressing for increased police budgets. Frequently dominated by the police officials themselves, police groups, both independent and FOP-affiliated, promoted departmental loyalty, reinforced racist and anti-working-class law enforcement practices and bolstered police morale.

POLICE UNIONIZATION, 1937-1942

The second wave of police unionization, 1937-42, also developed in the context of working class militancy, increased class conflict, and the resurgence of the trade union movement in the public sector as a whole. The American Federation of State, County and Municipal Employees (AFSCME) had chartered a police local in 1937 and then launched a police organizing drive which resulted in about 49 locals, both North and South, by the end of

World War II. As was the case in 1919, however, even the city officials and police administrators who supported the police wage demands opposed their affiliation with the labor movement. In cities such as Chicago, Los Angeles and St. Louis, the AFL locals quickly succumbed to managerial insistence on autonomous or FOP-affiliated police organization.

The FOP capitalized on its anti-trade union image and, in most cities, police who desired the prestige, resources and support of an outside group turned to the FOP. During World War II, however, even the FOP was strongly resisted by city officials, especially in Detroit and Lansing, Michigan, and it adopted a restrictive organizing policy of only chartering local lodges if they had prior administrative acceptance and no other organization claimed majority status.[10]

While channeling police dissatisfaction into narrow interest groups, such as the police benevolent associations and the FOP lodges, police officials also developed their own national organization, the International Association of Chiefs of Police (IACP), founded in 1893. A professional organization, the IACP promoted strong management and improved technology, and in 1915 it pioneered the fingerprint file later taken over by the FBI. It has always stressed the value of high salaries to attract skilled administrators and police wages adequate to ensure loyalty. Until 1969, however, the IACP consistently opposed union-affiliation of the police.[11]

RENEWED POLICE MILITANCY

With the fiscal crisis of the 1970's, the police are once again turning to trade union tactics to advance and protect their interests. The recent

series of police strikes and slowdowns — San Francisco (1976), Baltimore (1974), Albuquerque (1975), New York (1971), Youngstown (1976)—as well as numerous job actions and protests in other cities, have drawn attention to the police demand for wage increases and collective bargaining, and again raised the issue of the legality of police strikes.[12] Most of the tremendous increase in organizations has taken place within the old city-wide police associations, such as the NYPBA or the Detroit Police Officers Association, and the FOP affiliated lodges. While not affiliated with the trade union movement, many of these organizations enjoy collective bargaining and formal grievance procedures.

The causes of the sudden upsurge of police militancy in the last two decades lie in the changing conditions of policing. In large measure, today's police are moved to collective action by the realization that the declining legitimacy of the state subjects them to the explicit hostility of large segments of the population. Police work has become harder. As the degree of race and class conflict intensifies, the police assume a more demanding role both in repressing strikes and demonstrations and in attempting to contain the escalating level of crime. They are attacked, on the one hand, by progressive groups demanding the curtailment of their coercive power and, on the other hand, by reactionary elements calling for law and order and increased police efficiency. In this struggle, the vast majority of the politically active police have taken sides with the most reactionary elements. Blacks, women and other minority police have, however, formed an important counter-tendency to the dominant thrust of police organization. Still only a small fraction of police forces, they have been organizing much more actively in the last decade to agitate against both departmental discrimination and police brutality. Contemporary police dissatisfaction also stems from the erosion of their traditionally secure and privileged economic status.

Although police are still among the best paid of city workers, their wages have been subject to the same periodic fiscal and economic pressures which have beset the state sector—and city government in particular—since the 1930's. The wages of all municipal workers have lagged behind those in unionized industry, and the police are no exception. Between 1939 and 1964, police wages rose an average of 18.4 percent annually while the average wages of unionized factory workers increased almost twice as much. Police wages increased dramatically during the 1960's, in part because of the tight labor market and also because the heightened level of class and race conflict increased the cities' willingness to pay. Between 1966 and 1971, the annual rate of increase of police wages exceeded both the rate of private industry and the consumer price index. The deteriorating fiscal base of large cities and the current economic crisis, however, set limits on the resources available to the police, and in cities of more than 100,000 people, the average annual rate of increase in patrolman's wages has declined from 10.5 percent in 1968/69 to 5.5 percent in 1970/71. Even with their gains from the 1960's, the increases in police wages have lagged behind both those of Federal employees and local transit workers, and the police still earn less than many public and private sector skilled workers.[13] Despite this levelling off, the relative privilege and security of police work has attracted thousands of applicants at a time when many cities are considering or implementing police personnel cutbacks.[14] Like other wage earners, the police have suffered from the sharp increase in the cost of living since 1967, and they want more money.

CONTEMPORARY POLICE ORGANIZATIONS

The causes of police militancy are both political and economic, and the police have pursued a variety of strategies in attempting to secure their position. There are five main types of police organizations: (1) local associations; (2) FOP lodges; (3) national professional organizations; (4) union-affiliated locals; (5) Black police associations.

The first three forms of organization are similar in that they have, for the most part, based their demand for economic advantage on a claim of professional expertise. They have in turn attempted to use their claim of special knowledge about crime prevention to support reactionary political demands. The Black police associations, which now exist in virtually all departments with more than 25 Black police, and the union-affiliated locals represent, to a certain extent, a new direction in police organizing. We will discuss each of these forms of police organization in turn.

The vast majority of today's police belong to police-only local organizations. The New York Police Benevolent Association (NYPBA) is the largest of these with some 18,000 members. Safely insulated from the trade union movement and in only weak alliance with the fire fighters, local police associations have virtually never made economic demands which went beyond their own narrowly perceived self-interest. Nowhere have they been active in defending other city workers from cutbacks, and in several cities police are agitating, usually without success, to end parity between the police and fire fighters wages. In 1973, the NYPBA quit the State Police Conference of New York because it had joined in a coalition to oppose any reductions in pensions for municipal workers, and, instead, the PBA joined with the fire fighters to lobby for increased pensions themselves. The next year the NYPBA tried unsuccessfully to break parity with the fire fighters.[15]

On the political front, local police organizations have been active in mobilizing rank and file police in support of racist and reactionary law enforcement policies. The NYPBA defeated civilian review in a two-year legal and electoral battle against Black and Puerto Rican organizations and White liberals, supported by Mayor Lindsay, who had created a Civilian Review Board to appease the Third World electoral constituency and to provide a mechanism to curb police brutality. The PBA, already experienced in staging rallies and running petition campaigns, spent half a million dollars and mobilized its membership for an aggressive campaign to win the 1966 referendum outlawing the Board. Their publicity appealed to the effective combination of White racism and the fear of crime; many Whites justified their racist position by accepting the police claim that civilians should not interfere with policing because it requires expert knowledge.[16]

The racist and reactionary politics of the NYPBA are similar to those of other local police organizations. The Los Angeles Police Protective Association League helped elect Mayor Sam Yorty and the Detroit PBA tried unsuccessfully to oust the progressive judge, Justin Ravitz. Elsewhere, police organizations and police wives have done court watching to monitor the bail and sentencing policies of liberal judges. Police organizations have also lobbied for increased weaponry and most of the California police—along with the district attorney, police chiefs, sheriffs, deputies, Highway Patrol and correctional personnel—helped finance and worked for the successful 1972 initiative campaign to restore the state death penalty.

FRATERNAL ORDER OF POLICE

Although most police organizations are primarily local, an increasing percentage are affiliated with state or national groups of police which cooperate in lobbying for improved police benefits and changes in the penal code and law enforcement policy. The Fraternal Order of Police (FOP) is the oldest and second largest national police organization with about 900,000 members in 800 departmental lodges across 50 states. It has expanded its activities to include all financial and job grievances, as well as a considerable degree of explicitly political agitation.

Like the independent police organization, the FOP has enjoyed its fastest period of growth in the last two decades. FOP has become more active and, rather than repudiating trade union strategy, now pushes collective bargaining for local lodges. Although it still formally prohibits police strikes, lodges in cities such as Cincinnati, Columbus, Oklahoma City and Asheville, N.C., have staged work slowdowns to win contract demands within the last two years. On the political front, the FOP lobby in Washington retains a public relations firm and works with Congress to demand economic benefits for the police and tougher law enforcement. In recent years, it has supported bills to exempt police pensions from Federal income tax and to grant a $25,000 indemnity to police killed while engaged on Federal cases. State associations of FOP lodges lobby for similar demands.

Despite regulations barring police membership in national political organizations, many police officials have chosen to accept the FOP's claim that its lodges are autonomous and do not subject the police to political pressure contrary to their law enforcement commitment. The FOP, however, actively promotes ties between the police and reactionary businessmen and politicians through its lobbying work and associate membership for civilians. The national FOP also helps finance local political campaigns, such as the Philadelphia FOP's successful 1969 campaign against one of the nation's first civilian review boards. It has consistently demanded greater severity in law enforcement and criticized judicial and constitutional restraints on police activity. The Chicago FOP, for example, praised Mayor Daley's illegal order to "shoot to kill" arsonists and "shoot to maim or cripple" looters in the Black riots which followed the assassination of Reverend Martin Luther King, Jr., in April 1968. FOP lodges engage in court surveillance to oust liberal judges and in 1970 the Atlanta

FOP staged a work slowdown to support their demand for shotguns and mace as regular equipment. In addition to demands for economic privilege and a greater voice in law enforcement policy, the FOP has also worked for the election of right wing politicians.[17]

The majority of the nation's police belong to organizations which press for both increased wages and reactionary law enforcement policies. Most groups devote their primary attention to immediate economic gain and, although they use trade union tactics, they frame their demands as professionals rather than as workers. This self-identification as "crime fighters" is encouraged by police administrators and city officials who, although resistant to spiraling wage costs, basically support the concept of police professionalism.

In many instances, local police associations have opposed particular LEAA-encouraged managerial or technical innovations such as the fourth platoon, one-man cars and centralized communication systems because such changes threaten police jobs. The police have won important local victories on these issues but the overall tendency of police work is toward the increased use of technology and of civilians paid less than uniformed police. Police officials are being encouraged by their own professional associations to cooperate with police associations in changing work rules and they anticipate that in the long run police resistance will be overcome.

IACP, ICPA, AND PORAC

The main impetus for expanding the police institution comes from the corporate ruling class but, within the police, two organizations have taken the lead in promoting professionalization: the IACP, and the International Conference of Police Associations (ICPA). The IACP represents approximately 8,000 command level police and private industrial security officers. Like the rank and file police associations, the IACP has increased in size and importance in the last 15 years. Its membership tripled between 1961 and 1969, and its annual budget now exceeds $2.5 million.

The IACP is funded by corporations in-

volved in law enforcement, the Ford Foundation and membership dues. It has also received grants from LEAA, which are currently suspended pending investigations for fraud, and consulting contracts from police departments to draw up reorganization plans. The IACP cooperates with the Defense and Labor Departments in developing police training programs.[18] Tied in tightly to national criminal justice policy-makers, the IACP publishes *The Police Chief* to promote the idea that police can be improved through better management, recruiting and training. This magazine, in which advertisements for police technology and weaponry figure prominently, and numerous IACP monographs stress the importance of increased Federal spending on law enforcement. To push for such appropriations and influence criminal justice policy, the IACP maintains a lobby in Washington.

For the rank and file police, the International Conference of Police Associations is the most important political pressure group. Started in 1953, the ICPA is made up of more than 100 police associations whose combined membership is about twice the size of the FOP. It is strongest in California, New York, Illinois and New Jersey, and many of the largest city associations are affiliated (New York, Detroit, San Francisco, Washington, D.C., Chicago, St. Louis, Milwaukee, Buffalo, and Seattle). Organ-

FORMER POLICE OFFICERS ASSN.
CARAVAN TO WASHINGTON

ized to promote professionalization and to "stimulate cooperation among law enforcement agencies," the ICPA demands greater privileges for local police and, like the IACP, demands increased Federal spending on law enforcement.

At the state level, many local police organizations have also joined forces to finance lobbying groups, the largest of which is the Peace Officers' Research Association of California (PORAC). Set up in 1951, PORAC is a professional organization which supports police demands for higher wages and improved working conditions as essential to upgrading the quality of law enforcement. Financed by dues, PORAC maintains a full-time lobbyist in Sacramento and retains a powerful San Francisco law firm to defend police in departmental investigations. In addition to lobbying for increased state law enforcement expenditure, PORAC also finances reactionary political campaigns, such as the 1970 fight against the community control of police initiative in Berkeley. Among its other victories, it counts the creation of the Commission on Peace Officer Standards and Training, the state teletype system, and the revival of the death penalty.

POLICE AND THE LABOR MOVEMENT

Alongside the increase in the size and militancy of the professional associations of both command level and rank and file police ha been a renewal of police interest in the organized labor movement. Fueled by the sam grievances which have given rise to the loca associations and FOP lodges, unionization i becoming an increasingly accessible alternativ because of the success of other municipa workers in winning collective bargaining rights New York City took the lead in legalizin unionization for all but police in 1956 an Wisconsin followed in 1959. Connecticut Massachusetts, Michigan, and New York Stat followed in the mid 1960's, and state secto unionization spread after President Kennedy' 1962 Executive Order legalizing collective bar gaining for Federal employees.[19] In 1955, ther were fewer than 1 million public employee unionized but by 1976 there are almost million unionized and more than 2 millio additional public employees in unaffiliated co lective bargaining units such as police bene volent associations or the National Educatio Association. Today, unions are growing faste in the state sector than in private industry an over half of local government personnel ar unionized. Police unions are legal in 27 state and they exist, regardless of legal status, i virtually all states where public employees ar organized.

Most of the police collective bargaining unit are organized as local police associations o FOP-affiliated lodges without organizationa ties to other municipal workers' unions. Onl about 15 percent of the unionized polic belong to locals affiliated with national union of which the two largest are the Internationa Brotherhood of Teamsters and AFSCME (AFL CIO).[20] Increasingly, however, police, especiall in small and medium-sized cities, are consider ing affiliation with the labor movement as means of gaining expertise at the bargainin table and improved regional police cooperatio on economic demands.

The Teamsters represent more police tha any other trade union, and they also hav contracts with sheriff's deputies, state troopers, prison guards and police command officers. Michigan is the most heavily organized state, with about two-thirds of the state police officers in 50 cities and towns belonging to Teamster Local 214, and Minnesota is second. The two largest police departments in South Dakota, Sioux Falls and Rapid City, are Teamsters. In addition to locals, the Teamsters also have representation contracts with San Diego's 1,100 police force and 2,300 other California police. Scattered police departments in thirteen other states give the Teamsters a total of perhaps 15,000 police represented either through membership or contract, a huge increase from the 2,500 police represented as recently as 1970. The Teamsters are conducting an aggressive police organizing campaign, but AFSCME still represents about 10,000 police, mostly in Connecticut and Illinois. Unlike the Teamsters, however, police membership in AFSCME does not appear to be increasing and it may be decreasing.[21]

In many respects, the union-affiliated police locals are very similar to their police association or lodge counterparts, and much of the contemporary literature on police organizations refers to both affiliated and unaffiliated organizations as police unions. This terminology reflects the fact that today many police organizations, whatever their professional aspirations, are raising the trade union demand for collective bargaining rather than relying on political pressure alone and are willing to engage in work stoppages, public demonstrations and strikes. Even the IACP dropped its formal opposition to police unionization in 1969 when it was forced to admit that almost a fourth of the nation's police forces belonged to *de facto* unions and that the police have a legal right to collective bargaining. The upper echelons of the police administration have been quick to recognize the potential of a union contract to discipline a frequently disaffected and unruly workforce. The IACP aggressively promotes sophisticated personnel practices and publishes two monthly journals to keep administrators on top of the most recent court decisions, statutes, administrative agency decisions, and arbitration awards in police labor relations.

Police administrators no longer oppose unionism of the police as strenuously as they once did. The legality of that position has been eroded and police unions have not had the disruptive effect that their early opponents had feared. There has been no indication of labor influence on law enforcement and Teamster contracts explicitly pledge that "law enforcement comes before union membership." In the 1950's, members of AFSCME-affiliated police locals raided a labor council bingo game in New Haven and broke up a picket line in Bridgeport. Recently, Teamster cops arrested Teamster organizers during a strike of dairy workers in Madison.[22] Police unions have not increased labor influence on police administration and in fact most police unions espouse an anti-working-class ideology of police professionalization. When the police have gone beyond their professional mystique to ally themselves with other city workers, however, they have been subjected to the sanctions familiar to trade unionists. After defeat of the 1974 municipal strike in Baltimore, for example, the AFSCME police local, which had struck in support of blue collar workers, lost its exclusive bargaining contract and was heavily fined. Although there is still important opposition to police unionism, some of the most sophisticated police administrators look to them as a means of facilitating regional centralization of the police.[23]

Police unions have not increased the frequency of police strikes and there is some indication that, in the long run, unionized police forces will prove more "responsible" in labor negotiations than independent associations. After an initial period of militancy, unions in private industry have for the most part come to cooperate with management in formulating contracts and in pacifying or eliminating more progressive and demanding elements within the unions.[24] Frequently, municipal workers' unions have also agreed to tie wage increases to layoffs or new productivity schedules, and the police can be expected to accept similar conditions on their unionization.

Most of the police strikes in the last ten

years have in fact been conducted by independent associations or FOP lodges. Until May, 1970, AFSCME police locals had charter provisions prohibiting strikes and the charter of the Joliet, Illinois, police force was revoked after a one-day strike in 1967. The Teamsters no longer oppose strikes of public employees and both AFSCME and the Teamsters are committed to the right of police unions to collective bargaining and striking when necessary. The unions are also, however, committed to winning acceptable contracts during negotiations and would greatly prefer to seek compulsory arbitration and preserve the myth of the essentiality of police services by not calling a strike.

Unlike production workers or city employees, who perform a visible service, the police have had difficulty in making their withdrawal of services felt. One obstacle to the success of a police strike is the overall ineffectiveness of police patrols in preventing crime. Short-term replacement of police by scabs is readily available and, even when the NYPBA walked out in a 10-day wildcat strike in 1971, the police commanders of the top-heavy bureaucracy proved sufficient to maintain normal police functions. While the small businessmen bought more locks and hired a few security guards, the largest banks and the stock exchanges relied on their own private security forces.[25] Police strikes have intensified the dissatisfaction of many people with police services and they have also tended to increase the resentment against public employee unions in general.

Within the police institution, unionization has yet to mark a change of rank and file political commitment, and unionization has evolved alongside of, and in basic agreement with, a professional ideology. This amalgam of unionism and professionalism may, however, prove to be a volatile mixture. The police have coveted the mantle of professionalism because it has meant higher wages, better working conditions and more privileges. When these prerequisites are challenged, as they have been repeatedly in recent years, the police have found that, like teachers, their "professionalism" precludes their right to strike and forces them to accept wage cuts or longer hours for
70

the public good. Most professionals, of course, rarely make such sacrifices. In striking, however, the police confront the reality that they are but one arm of a large and overlapping apparatus of repression and that they are not, in fact, a thin blue line between order and chaos. When they have acted alone and exclusively in pursuit of their own self-advancement, as was the case in San Francisco and New York in 1976, they cannot expect to receive support from other workers who also face cutbacks and whose strikes the police themselves have helped to break.

BLACK POLICE ORGANIZE

Unlike the predominantly White police associations and lobbies, Black police organizations are a relatively recent development. The racist hiring practices of the police have excluded Blacks and other Third World people from the force and even today Blacks make up, for example, less than 4 percent of the department in Boston where they have almost 20 percent of the population. The Civil Rights movement and the Black uprisings of the 1960's opened the police ranks to minorities, but racist discrimination is still the norm in police recruitment, job assignments, promotion, and disciplinary policies. Even in the relatively progressive department in Berkeley, California, at least 90 percent of all officers who were discharged or received severe discipline in 1974-75 were minorities.[26] In addition to departmental discrimination, minority officers also face overt racist hostility and not infrequently physical threats from White officers.

Black police have organized to combat racism within their departments and in police practices in minority communities. In 1969, the Connecticut Guardians called a mass sick call of Black police to end departmental discrimination. The next year, the Guardians defended a Black police officer charged with assaulting a White policeman who abused a Puerto Rican girl, and they warned that Black police would physically restrain White officers exercising brutality toward citizens. The New York Guardians, with about 2,000 members in 1970, publicized police beatings of Black prisoners and demanded safeguards to prevent further beatings. They have also been very active in trying to increase the number of Black police, as have the Black police associations in Cincinnati and many other cities.

Most of the Black police organizations are small and emphasize internal over community concerns. Some groups, however, such as the Chicago Afro-American Patrolman's Association (AAPA) and the Pittsburgh Guardians, focus their work on combating police racism and improving police-community relations. The AAPA defines itself as a primarily community service organization, and its members refused to act as strikebreakers against Black workers protesting racism in the building trades. It has also won a court ruling blocking federal funds to the Chicago Police Department because of its violation of affirmative action guidelines in employment practices. The Oakland Black Police Officers Association is currently fighting a $20 million class action suit against officials of LEAA and the U.S. Attorney General's office for discrimination against minority and women police officers. It is supported in this action by a broad progressive coalition, which also includes other Black police groups.[27]

In 1971, many of the Black police associations on the East Coast joined together to form the National Council of Police Societies (NCOPS). In contrast to the predominantly "law and order" ideology of the police establishment, NCOPS opposes indiscriminate stop-and-frisk policies and preventive detention, and it supports civilian review. The Midwest and Regional Council of Police is another multi-city

organization of Black police. Both groups are now zones of the National Black Police Association which was formed in 1972.[28]

At the command level, more than 60 senior Black police officers from 24 states formed the National Organization of Black Law Enforcement Executives in 1976. At a meeting sponsored by the Police Foundation and LEAA, the officials demanded a role for the expertise of Black police administrators in fighting crime. Their goals include many of the policies favored by the liberal criminal justice planners, such as increased minority recruitment, civilian complaint procedures, and police-community relations programs.[29]

On the whole, Black and minority police associations represent the most progressive tendency within the police institution. The role of the Black police administrators' organization remains to be seen, but even the smallest rank and file groups have protested departmental discrimination, and the larger and more militant organizations have taken on the task of exposing police brutality and systematic racism. In this progressive struggle, many of the Black officers groups have come into conflict with the racist and reactionary police organizations. None of the Black organizations represent police in wage negotiations, so most Black police belong to the White dominated police organizations as well. In 1967, however, the New York Guardians opposed the NYPBA by campaigning in favor of civilian review. Elsewhere, the right-wing political activity of police organizations has been criticized by Black police and, in 1970, the Atlanta Afro-American

BLACK POLICE IN KEY CITIES

CITIES	% BLACK	% BLACK POLICE
Washington	71.1	35.9
Baltimore	46.4	13.0
New Orleans	45.0	6.1
Wilmington, Del.	43.6	11.5
Birmingham, Ala.	42.0	1.9
St. Louis, Mo.	40.9	14.0
Cleveland	38.3	7.7
Pittsburgh, Pa.	20.2	6.4
Dallas, Tex.	24.9	1.9
Los Angeles	17.9	5.2
Boston	16.3	2.1

IN NEW YORK CITY

While more than 31% of N.Y.C.'s population is Black or Puerto Rican, only 8% of the 30,000 policemen are from these two groups. "As one progresses up through the ranks ... the incidence of racial discrimination becomes more blatant. Thus, while 9.4% of patrolmen and detectives are from minority groups, only 4.66% of the sergeants, 2.61% of the lieutenants and 1.4% of the captains and above are from minority groups."

—N.Y. Times, February 12, 1973

Patrolman's League denounced the FOP's ten-week job action.[30] Officers for Justice (OFJ) supports the Berkeley Police Review Commission, which is actively opposed by both the Berkeley Police Officers Association and PORAC. Although OFJ members belong to the SFPOA, they opposed the 1976 San Francisco police strike on the grounds that the police did not deserve pay raises while some of the communities they patrol suffer 40 percent unemployment.

By taking positions in opposition to the dominant police establishment and expressing a determination to challenge brutal police practices, many Black police associations have exposed the racist functions of criminal justice. Today, this struggle is an integral part of their own effort to end racial discrimination in law enforcement employment. The most advanced sector of the criminal justice policymakers, however, also formally oppose job discrimination and have attempted at every level to incorporate Black police into a fundamentally racist system. Only by continuing to expand their alliances with the communities they police can the Black police expect to maintain the progressive character of their struggle and avoid cooptation. The rapid expansion of police unions points to the increased contradictions of the repressive apparatus, but, unlike many Black groups, the unions have raised no objections to the reactionary and anti-working-class political initiatives of the police. By simply demanding more money for themselves, without supporting other city workers facing similar cutbacks, the police unions are objectively aiding the corporate bourgeoisie's efforts to slash social services while bolstering the repressive apparatus.

In this chapter, we have attempted to describe and analyze the roots of contemporary police militancy. While the present situation is by no means clear or settled, it is possible to identify the direction and political thrust of police organizations and unions. Compared to other workers in industry and in the public sector, the police have been overall the recipients of economic rewards and privileged working conditions. This is due to the aggressive organizing of the police, especially in recent years, and to the support of the local and national bourgeoisies who find it necessary to maintain the police as an anti-working-class and racist force. With the fiscal crisis of the last decade, the police have turned to more militant organizing and unionism in order to protect their eroding privileges.

The development of trade unionism among the police, however, has not meant a deeper class consciousness nor greater unity with the working class. By organizing around their own narrow self-interest—often against the interests of other public employees and service workers—and in defense of their status as "professionals," the relationship between the police and workers has become even more antagonistic. Some Black police associations, feeling the special pressure of on-the-job discrimination and often outright racism from White officers, have attempted to steer a different course and have organized around affirmative action and reordering the priorities of policing. While these Black organizations offer a progressive alternative to the sole demand for higher wages and reactionary politics of the conventional police organizations, they should not be regarded as analogous to the militant rank-and-file caucuses that have emerged in recent years to challenge the union bureaucracy; while relatively progressive, they too organize primarily around their own special interests and do not fundamentally challenge the functions of the police in capitalist society.

In organizing against the police it is important to take into account their new organized militancy. We should not make the error of interpreting it as a sign that the police are about to join the working class. On the other hand, it is just as incorrect to regard it as indication of a growing "police state." Rather it should be seen generally as an aspect of how the contradictions in the larger society are reproduced within the state apparatus and, more specifically, as a reflection of the problems faced by the ruling class in maintaining the loyalty and reliability of the police. These internal conflicts and struggles within the police apparatus indicate that repression is by no means automatic nor monolithic.

1. *New York Times,* January 20, 1971.
2. *New York Times,* January 16, 1971.
3. Margaret Anne Levi, *Conflict and Collusion: Police Collective Bargaining,* Technical Report No. 07-74, Cambridge, Mass., Operations Research Center, MIT, 1974, p. 9.
4. Sidney Harring, "The Development of the Police Institution in the United States," *Crime and Social Justice,* Vol. 5, Spring-Summer 1976.
5. Emma Schweppe, *The Firemen's and Patrolmen's Unions of the City of New York: A Case Study in Public Employee Unions,* New York, King's Crown Press, Columbia University, 1948.
6. Raymond Fosdick, *American Police Systems,* Montclair, N.J., Patterson Smith, 1972 (reprint of 1920 edition), pp. 318-321.
7. Sterling D. Spero, *Government as Employer,* New York, Remsen Press, 1948, pp. 245-294.
8. "The Boston Police Strike Tragedy," *The Searchlight on Congress,* Vol. 10, No. 2, September-October 1924, pp. 9-17.
9. Bruce Smith, *Police Systems in the United States,* New York, Harper and Brothers, 1940, pp. 134-135.
10. Levi, op. cit.; John H. Burpo, *The Police Labor Movement: Problems and Perspectives,* Springfield, Charles Thomas, 1971.
11. I.A.C.P., *Police Unions,* Washington, D.C., 1944; "Public Employee Organizations," *The Police Chief,* Vol. 36, December 1969.
12. Between 1966 and 1969, there were 127 work stoppages in police and fire departments compared to only 16 in the preceding seven years. There were 13 police work stoppages between May 1970 and January 1971. Harvey A. Juris and Peter Feuille, *Police Unionism,* Lexington, Mass., Lexington Books, 1973, p. 19.
13. Levi, op. cit., pp. 201-218; Juris and Feuille, op. cit., pp. 20, 45-55; David L. Stanley, *Managing Local Government under Union Pressure,* Washington, D.C., The Brookings Institution, 1972, pp. 68-75.
14. *New York Times,* July 22, November 6, 1971. As of January 1973, the top patrolman's pay in New York City, Oakland, San Francisco, and Los Angeles exceeded $14,000, exclusive of overtime, longevity, night shift differential and other monetary fringe benefits. Juris and Feuille, op. cit., p. 54.
15. *New York Times,* August 11, 1973; June 2, 1974.
16. Edward Rogowsky, et al., "Police: The Civilian Review Board Controversy," in Jewel Bellush and Stephen David, eds., *Race and Politics in New York City,* New York, Praeger Publishers, 1971.
17. Leonard Ruchelman, *Police Politics,* Cambridge, Mass., Ballinger Publishers, 1974, p. 55.
18. William Turner, *The Police Establishment,* New York, G.P. Putnam's, 1968, p. 287.
19. Levi, op. cit., pp. 3-6; Juris and Feuille, op. cit., pp. 6-12.
20. *Wall Street Journal,* May 5, 1976.
21. *New York Times,* October 28, 1975; *Los Angeles Times,* January 21, 1971; Juris and Feuille, op. cit., p. 29.
22. Burpo, op. cit., pp. 69-70; *Wall Street Journal,* May 5, 1976.
23. *New York Times,* July 19, 1974; Juris and Feuille, op. cit., p. 3.
24. Levi, op. cit.; Harvey A. Juris and Peter Feuille, *The Impact of Police Unions,* Summary Report, U.S. Department of Justice, LEAA, NILECJ, December 1973.
25. *New York Times,* January 14-19, 1971; *U.S. News and World Report,* February 1, 1971.
26. Berkeley Personnel Board, quoted in *Daily Californian,* June 7, 1976.
27. *New York Times,* January 6, 1976; *The Black Panther,* September, 1975.
28. Juris and Feuille, op. cit., pp. 165-172; *New York Times,* June 13-14, 1971.
29. *New York Times,* September 10, 1976.
30. Levi, op. cit., pp. 187-194.

IV. THE IRON FIST

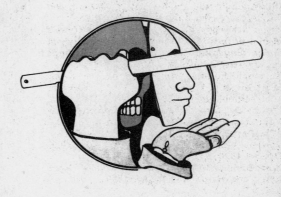

7. THE MILITARY-CORPORATE MODEL

Initially, police strategists responding to the crises of the 1960's relied mainly on adapting already tried and tested managerial and military principles to problems of domestic "order." Confronted with the inefficiency and lack of coordination of local police units, many government and corporate reformers found it natural to look to the corporations and the armed forces for more effective models of organization and planning. The result was a concentration of money and research on the development of improved technology (especially in weapons and in communication and information systems), and on devising sophisticated planning strategies, often based on "systems analysis" and usually borrowed from the military. Although from the beginning some lip service was paid to the need for more subtle approaches involving improved "community relations," the primary focus was on technical and administrative problems, and the overall thrust was toward reorganizing the police as an effective combat organization.

Behind this emphasis on technical and managerial improvement is a specific ideology about the sources of crime and disorder which supports the use of technical solutions to problems that are actually social and political. Although virtually all of the major commission reports and other official and semi-official discussions of crime produced in the sixties give at least some attention to the social and economic sources of crime, they all ultimately regard crime as a basically inevitable feature of modern life in the cities. In this perspective, the problems police are called on to deal with are usually explained as the result of processes that are inherent in urbanization and population growth, or of diversities of values and beliefs that are held to be an inherent part of American culture. The report on police of the 1967 Crime Commission, for example, is full of references to the idea that crime is caused by the "complexities" of modern society, with its heterogeneous and mobile population, its general prosperity, and the congestion and ano-

nymity that go along with a high degree of urbanization.[1] It isn't made clear why any of these things should be a cause of crime, or how exactly they do cause it, but the idea that they do is an essential part of modern police ideology. The police section of the Report of the National Advisory Commission on Criminal Justice Standards and Goals, similarly, has this to say about the basic sources of crime in America:

> Widely varying beliefs and changing life styles mark the structure of this complex and competitive society. Extremes in ideals, emotions, and conduct are trademarks of life in the United States.[2]

Again, it isn't ever made clear why or how these things actually contribute to the high rates of crime in the U.S., but the implications of this view are very important. Instead of being seen as the product of a specific set of oppressive social and economic relationships that can be changed by conscious political action, crime is regarded as primarily the result of certain *inescapable* natural, cultural and technological processes. According to this argument, dealing with the social sources of crime is at best a long-range problem, which has to take a back seat to the practical and technical priority of devising means of controlling and containing crime. As the Crime Commission put it in 1967, the police "must accept society as it is."[3]

From this point of view, the failure of the police in the crises of the sixties was mainly technical, a failure of technology and organization, rather than of basic direction or purpose. The solution to police problems, therefore, is regarded as essentially the same as that for any other technical problem. As the keynote speech to a 1970 symposium on science and technology in law enforcement put it,

> the problems of crime demand the same kind of research techniques that have been so dramatically effective in other national programs; in the space program, in the fight against disease, and in the defense effort.[4]

76

Since the problem of crime is seen as similar to the problem of ending disease or going to the moon, it follows that the best means of fighting crime is to mobilize scientific and technological skills and resources toward improving the technical capacity of the criminal justice system. In 1967, the Task Force on Science and Technology of the Crime Commission bemoaned the fact that while "more than 200,000" scientists and engineers were working on military problems, and hundreds of thousands of others were at work in other areas of modern life, only a handful were working to "control the crimes that injure or frighten millions of Americans each year."[5]

The emphasis on police technology comes out of this perspective, and it has built on the fact that many of the basic principles have already been developed for the military, especially in the course of the war in Southeast Asia. Early discussions of police technology requirements, in the mid-1960's, very often drew explicit parallels between the situation in Vietnam and the situation in U.S. cities. As a systems engineer for North American Aviation put it in 1967,

The technological and tactical problems of military and law enforcement agencies are

similar in many aspects. . . . The legal, socio-logical, and political implications and constraints may be different in dealing with the Viet Cong terrorist hiding in the outskirts of Saigon as contrasted to the agitator instigating a riot in the streets of Chicago, but some of the technical and tactical problems associated with detection, identification, and apprehension are the same. The law enforcement official is required to detect and identify his enemy—the criminal; the military man must detect and identify his enemy on the battleground.[6]

A key concept here is the idea of "technology transfers"[7]; the application to law enforcement of techniques and innovations originally developed in other fields—in this case, specifically the aerospace and defense industries. Consequently, a major development in the last few years has been the entry of important corporations in these industries (such as IBM, Sylvania, Rockwell, Motorola, and Hughes Aircraft) into the business of law enforcement technology, as well as the growing attention on the part of private research institutes (Stanford Research Institute, IIT Research Institute, etc.) and government agencies not initially concerned with criminal justice (such as NASA) in research related to police problems. One of many examples of the growing corporate interest in law enforcement was the "exploratory program" developed jointly by the General Electric Company and the city of Syracuse, New York. The program was designed to discover what services the technical resources of GE could provide for the local police. The police toured GE laboratories, and GE personnel rode with the Syracuse police on patrol. The suggestions made by the GE staff included TV recording systems for patrol cars, automated police communication systems, and improved burglar alarms.[8] (For more detailed analysis of recent police technology, see the chapter on Technology, below.)

But the emphasis on technology is not the only side of the military-corporate perspective. Nearly as important is the stress on developing more sophisticated techniques of management and operational strategies within police departments. Police theorists generally agree that no

amount of technical hardware will be very useful unless it is combined with more effective internal organization than most police departments have had in the past. In the words of one police management specialist,

we have produced systems and hardware "tools" which, in their sophistication, cannot merely be used. They must be managed with all the skill and expertise a system-oriented, change-dominated environment demands. The applications of science and technology to the law enforcement function will increasingly depend on the development of more advanced management technology within the police organization. In our zeal to take advantage of technical "hardware" and systems, we must remain mindful that success in the final analysis will depend more on our ability to develop our most crucial asset, our human resource.[9]

But all police commentators and theorists writing during the sixties agreed that the level of managerial skills developed in American police departments was uniformly low. The model here for comparison was the big corporation. The Crime Commission pointed out that many departments were "not organized in accordance with well-established principles of modern business management,"[10] and the prestigious corporate policy-making group, the Committee for Economic Development, similarly calls for new managerial policies that will

reduce the "organizational and administrative chaos that characterizes the nation's uncoordinated system of criminal justice."[11]

An example of the concrete programs that have emerged out of this concern for organizing the police along corporate lines is the management development program of the Los Angeles police. In looking for models to pattern their program after, the LAPD made visits to a number of corporations to study *their* management training programs, including Ford, North American Rockwell, Union Oil, Pacific Telephone, and IBM. This resulted in the creation of a "Management Development Center," funded by LEAA, whose main function is to provide intensive seminars for high and middle-level police officials to enhance their managerial skills. The series of seminars for lieutenants and sergeants, for example, which is designed to increase their "personal, managerial, and conceptual skills," includes such subjects as "Creative Thinking," "Effective Memory Techniques," "Speed Reading," "Managerial Communications," "Implementing Organization Change," and **Motivation** in Theory and Practice." The emphasis in the program is on developing "practical approaches" to "universal executive problems"; the problems faced by police officials are presumed to be the same as those faced by any other management, and the concepts used in the program are those that "have proven successful in corporate industry and in the academic community for some time."[12]

If the organizational forms and techniques

are modeled after the corporations, the actual operational strategies derived from this perspective are borrowed from the military. Military terms and concepts like "command and control" or "operations research" have become a common feature in many police departments since the late sixties. In the police context, "command and control" means devising the organizational and technical means of helping the police commander "facilitate his command of policemen and police vehicles through control of communications networks and equipment at his disposal."[13] The importance of effective "command and control" is stressed in a brochure issued by the Motorola corporation:

> *The land must be safe.*
> *The problems are here. Now. And the solutions always begin the same way: identify the problem, accurately. Stay on top of it. Move fast. Don't waste anything. Not time. Not manpower. Make the right decision. Make another decision. Get more facts. No mistakes. No stumbling. No wavering. And through it all—complete control. Complete command efficiency.*
> *Nothing less will do.*[14]

To this end, companies like Motorola and North American Rockwell have devised entire "command and control" packages (or, in Rockwell's terms, "modular command and control concepts") for urban police departments. These include everything from designs for the physical layout of "command control centers" to specific designs for new communications equipment for patrol cars, to organizational charts detailing the various functions for different personnel. The Emergency Command Control Communications System (ECCCS) designed by Hughes Aircraft for the Los Angeles PD, for example, includes such things as an automated dispatch center, a two-way digital radio communications system for all patrol units, complete with "anti-jamming" equipment (to stymie attempts by militants to jam police transmissions during civil disturbances) and special mobile command centers to be used in emergencies.[15] Again, the model for these systems is the military; when the New York PD began planning its Command and Control Center in 1969, it sent its planners to visit the existing command centers at the Strategic Air Command Headquarters in Omaha, the Pentagon, and the Manned Spacecraft Center in Houston; and the Center was candidly described by then-mayor John Lindsay as a "war room."[16]

Another concept borrowed from the military is "operations research," a complicated phrase for the process of trying to figure out how best to allocate police resources in a given area by using advanced mathematical and statistical techniques. The stilted language and nearly incomprehensible technical jargon this often involves would be somewhat comical if it were not deadly serious. The Operations Research Task Force of the Chicago PD, for instance, which began in 1968 under a grant from LEAA, comes up with conclusions like this:

> Demands for service are predictable with considerable accuracy. The preferred method is to use an exponential smoothing technique. For demonstration purposes, a simple linear prediction based on the experience of 1969, and the observed increasing trend have been used and found to be accurate to 5%. The queuing model assumes poisson arrival of calls for service and negative exponential distribution of service times. Statistical test of the negative exponential hypothesis indicated that the assumption is weak. Unit requirements can be more accurately specified using an Erlanq type distribution or through use of the detailed computer simulation of the response force that has been carried out by the OR Task Force.[17]

Once again, the military origins are very explicit. According to the Chicago Police OR Task Force, "There is an analogy between the problem of estimating search effectiveness in anti-submarine warfare and in estimating the effectiveness of preventive patrol."[18]

If all of this seems a little like caricature or science fiction, it should be remembered that the application of this kind of systems analysis and technology to the police is still in its early stages. At the moment, a lot of it promises more than it delivers in terms of effective repressive force. And there are some signs that the early uncritical enthusiasm for new law

enforcement technology has been somewhat dampened, at least for some police agencies and some major corporations. A report prepared in 1972 by Sylvania's "Sociosystems Product Operation," for example, proposes that Sylvania should de-emphasize its concern with the "public safety market," citing problems of funding and "political constraints" on the size of the market for police technology. (The report seemed more optimistic about sales to overseas clients—including the Buenos Aires police and the Guatemalan government—where some of these constraints are less pressing.)[19]

But despite these limitations, the potential is still there. The special danger of the military-corporate approach to policing is that it is based on the conception of an inner warfare in the United States between the police and the people, and it is committed to using whatever scientific and technical resources are available, or could be made available, to enhance the possibility that the police will win that war. And although more sophisticated and subtle strategies of police work are now emerging, this still the one that provides the underlying muscle that makes the others possible.

In the following three chapters, we look closely at the various forms of new police technology, and at one dramatic illustration of the military model of policing—the development of special paramilitary tactical units, of which Los Angeles' Special Weapons and Tactics (SWAT) team is the most prominent example. Finally, we will examine recent developments in the intelligence network in which the counter-insurgency functions of the police are most clearly revealed.

1. President's Crime Commission, *Task Force on Police*, Washington, D.C., Government Printing Office, 1967, p. 2.
2. National Advisory Commission on Criminal Justice Standards and Goals, Volume on *Police*, Washington, D.C., Government Printing Office, 1973, p. 2.
3. Crime Commission, *Police*, op. cit., p. 2.
4. (Honorable) Clark MacGregor, "Criminal Justice: Priorities and Programs for the Seventies," in S. I. Cohn and W. B. McMahon, eds., *Law Enforcement, Science and Technology II, Proceedings of the Third National Symposium on Law Enforcement Science and Technology*, Chicago, IIT Research Institute, 1970, p. 8.
5. Crime Commission, *Task Force on Science and Technology*, Washington, D.C., Government Printing Office, 1967, p. 1.
6. Keith L. Warn, "System Engineering Approach to Law Enforcement," in S. A. Yefsky, ed., *Law Enforcement Science and Technology: Proceedings of the 1st National Symposium on Law Enforcement Science and Technology*, Chicago, Thompson Book Company, 1967, p. 651.
7. Cf. G. Bay et al., "The Application of Aerospace Technology to Law Enforcement and Criminalistics Problems," in Cohn and McMahon, op. cit., pp. 571-75. This article describes a "technology utilization center" under NASA devoted specifically to transferring aerospace innovations to other fields, including law enforcement.
8. W. H. T. Smith, et al., "An Exploratory Program of the Syracuse Police Department and the General Electric Company on Law Enforcement Problems," in Yefsky, op. cit., pp. 773-78.
9. Allen T. Osborne, "The Management Development Program of the Los Angeles Police Department," in Cohn and McMahon, op. cit., p. 291.
10. Crime Commission, *Police*, op. cit., p. 44.
11. Committee for Economic Development, *Reducing Crime and Assuring Justice*, New York, CED, 1972, p. 7.
12. Osborne, op. cit., pp. 293, 296.
13. Robert J. Reider, "Police Information-Communications Network: a Systems-Analysis View," in Cohn and McMahon, op. cit., p. 210.
14. Motorola Communications and Electronics, Inc., "Motorola Total Police Communications Systems," N.D., p. 1.
15. Hughes Corporation, Ground Systems Division, "Space-age Systems Engineering Can Be Used to Improve Law Enforcement," Sept. 1971. See also *Los Angeles Times*, May 4, 1971.
16. *New York Times*, Oct. 14, 1969.
17. Albert M. Bottoms, et al., "Operations Research in Law Enforcement: A Report on the Chicago Police Department Operations Research Task Force," in Cohn and McMahon, op. cit., p. 354.
18. Ibid., p. 355.
19. Sylvania Corporation, "Sociosystems Products Operation, 1973-1977, Business Plan," July 1972, Sections 1 and 4.

8. TECHNOLOGY

*"Let's not forget that there is always some-
one behind each technological device."*[1]
—Ernesto Che Guevara

INTRODUCTION

Until the late 1960's, the police had not
relied very extensively on technology to carry
out their work. In 1967, a task force report
from the President's Commission on Law Enforcement and the Administration of Justice,
headed by then-Attorney General Nicholas Kat-
zenbach, emphasized the need to employ more
science and technology throughout the criminal
justice system, especially within the police
apparatus. This Science and Technology report
was prepared by the Institute for Defense
Analyses (IDA), a consortium of universities
specializing in military research for the Department of Defense. IDA pointed out that over
200,000 scientists and engineers have helped
solve military problems but "only a handful are
working to control the crimes that injure or
frighten millions of Americans each year."[2]
Today, the handful has grown to thousands and
the emphasis now is to apply the research in
every way possible. In 1973, the National
Advisory Commission on Criminal Justice Standards and Goals urged that:

> In addition to allocating human resources in
> the most efficient manner possible, police
> agencies need to concentrate on obtaining
> and applying sophisticated technological and
> support resources. Communications systems,
> information systems, and criminal laborato-
> ries are tools that multiply the effectiveness
> of police officers.[3]

Besides the argument of increased efficiency,
technology is being pushed because it can be
extremely profitable for the large corporations
that produce and sell complex police equipment. Thus corporations producing technological systems are using agencies in the federal,
state, and local governments in an attempt to
increase the sale of their products to the police.
An editorial in *Police Chief* magazine talked

about this process: "LEAA [Law Enforcement
Assistance Administration], both through state
grants and Institute funding, is fostering the
recognition of police by industry as a specific
market."[4]

LEAA, through the Advanced Technology
Division of its National Institute of Law Enforcement and Criminal Justice, is coordinating
and funding major research to develop a comprehensive police technology. According to its
new administrator, Richard Velde, "LEAA
must be a leader in helping state and local
governments apply the most modern technology to all criminal justice system functions."[5] In
fiscal 1974, the Institute budgeted $8.6 million
for three phases of technology research:

(1) The Analysis Group identifies and analyzes
criminal justice problems to determine
whether, and how, new or improved equipment can solve them. The prime contractor
is the MITRE Corporation, a spinoff from
MIT's Lincoln Laboratory located in Bed-
ford, Mass. Previously, MITRE had con-
tracted exclusively with the Department of
Defense to design highly classified strategic
command systems, space surveillance systems and military communications networks.[6]

(2) The Development Group translates equipment needs into practical hardware systems.
The prime contractor is the Aerospace Corporation located in El Segundo, Calif., with
laboratories in nearby San Bernardino. Aerospace was founded in 1960 with the support
of the U.S. Air Force to develop ballistic
missile systems.[7]

(3) The Law Enforcement Standards Laboratory
works with the National Bureau of Standards and evaluates currently available
equipment to provide local agencies information on performance.

Some of the defense contractors which
relied on the Vietnam War to provide the
market for their products are now selling
similar items to domestic police departments:
examples include helicopters from the Bell and

Hughes companies; communications equipment from General Electric, Honeywell and Motorola; computers from IBM, RCA and UNIVAC; and gases from Federal Laboratories. Even the electronic battlefield developed by Sylvania Electronics to monitor troop movement along the Vietnamese DMZ and Ho Chi Minh trail has been brought home and erected along the U.S.-Mexico border in an attempt to control drug traffic and illegal entry of Mexican nationals.[8] Other projects, such as the government's space program, are also generating technological systems which are being transferred to law enforcement agencies.[9]

Some of the new technological systems will certainly increase the efficiency of the police. Computer information systems will allow the police to increase their surveillance of the population. New communications systems involving digital computers, electronic maps and radios with coded channels will allow the police to respond faster to certain situations. With the aid of technology the number of arrests will probably grow. However, these and other forms of technology are subject to failure. Los Angeles County is suing the Ampex Corporation because the county-wide computer system is not functioning properly,[10] police helicopters are extremely noisy and have unexpectedly

crashed, and many non-lethal weapons either cannot be controlled (e.g., tear gas on a windy day) or are ineffective as riot control techniques. The corporate policy of planned obsolescence and mass production has affected the quality of many products. Moreover, since Watergate, the general public is more sensitive to the massive use of technology by government agencies, especially the police apparatus which has the power to control and coerce the population.

Clearly, police technology does not solve the social and economic problems which cause crime; it only attempts to control them more efficiently. We do not mean to suggest that there is necessarily anything *inherently* wrong with technological development. The important question is *who controls* that development, and what purpose they have in using it. Technology should be supported if its purpose is to meet people's needs (in education, work, health, etc.); but if technology is used to protect and maintain an economic and political system which disregards or is unable to fulfill those needs, then its development should be opposed.

What follows is a brief discussion of five areas of police technology: information systems, command and control, area surveillance, weaponry, and identification techniques.

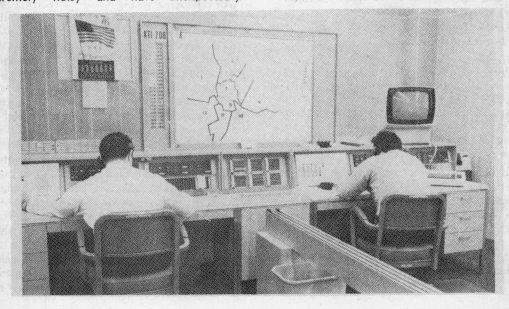

COMPUTERIZED INTELLIGENCE SYSTEMS

The computerization of police information is rapidly on its way to completion. In 1968, only 10 states had automated state-level criminal justice information systems. By 1972, computerization existed in 47 states with the main centralized intelligence files being held by the FBI's National Crime Information Center (NCIC) in Washington, D.C.[11] The Federal Government's Law Enforcement Assistance Administration has made this development possible by providing nearly $90 million to over 100 computerized information systems.[12] (See chapter 21 for a chart of various computerized information systems.)

The computer is used for rationalizing various aspects of the criminal justice system, but its primary function will be to develop a fast and efficient intelligence-retrieval network on people (criminal histories) and events (crimes, identification of stolen autos, weapons, etc.).

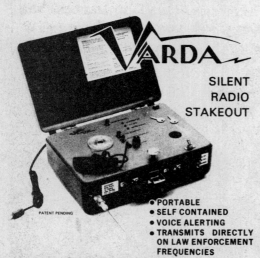

SILENT RADIO STAKEOUT

- PORTABLE
- SELF CONTAINED
- VOICE ALERTING
- TRANSMITS DIRECTLY ON LAW ENFORCEMENT FREQUENCIES

PATENT PENDING

FOR LAW ENFORCEMENT USE ONLY

Installed quickly by a police officer in a stakeout area this machine, when tripped by an intruder or victim, will broadcast a prerecorded VOICE MESSAGE directly to police vehicles, beatmen and station. Its effect is to move the police department to the scene of the crime, while the crime is occuring.

P.O. BOX 6343 • 2901 FERNVALE ROAD • BAKERSFIELD, CA. 93306

The computerized intelligence systems will allow the police and other agencies quicker access to more information. Previous examples of political fugitives eluding detection and identification because of delays in receiving FBI reports will occur less frequently with the new systems. Also, police intelligence agents will use the network in their attempt to penetrate and disrupt progressive work (see chapter 10 for examples). A significant result of the computer technology will be a lessening of inter-agency and regional rivalry within law enforcement, which previously has caused much inefficiency. With the computerized systems, requests for information will be directed to machines instead of personnel.

The use of computerized information systems has generated intense debate concerning invasion of privacy. In February, 1974, the Justice Department and Senator Sam Ervin, Jr. [D-N.C.], both presented privacy bills to Congress which would regulate the kinds of information that police can collect and disseminate.[13] While these bills will control some of the more blatant police tactics, they will not prevent the police from routinely using the computerized systems to enforce the status quo.

NATIONAL CRIME INFORMATION CENTER (NCIC)

The largest computerized intelligence system is the FBI's National Crime Information Center (NCIC). NCIC was established in 1967 as a national index of wanted persons, stolen autos, and stolen property, consisting of less than 500,000 entries that could be retrieved by only 15 computer terminals throughout the country. By 1974 there were links to 94 law enforcement agencies plus all 55 FBI field offices. The system contains 400,000 computerized criminal histories, 4.9 million total entries, and handles about 130,000 transactions daily.[14] In many cases, NCIC is linked to state and regional terminals which are entire systems in themselves. For example, in Michigan, NCIC links with the Law Enforcement Intelligence Network (LEIN) which holds 150,000 entries and links to 225 terminals, including the ichigan Secretary of State's files.

Federal agencies which contribute and re-
:eive information with NCIC include the Secret
:ervice, the Internal Revenue Service, Alcohol
nd Tax Division of the Treasury Department,
ustoms Service, Immigration and Naturaliza-
on Service, U.S. Courts, Attorneys and Mar-
als, and the Bureau of Prisons.[15]

The NCIC takes its present form from an
EAA computer information project—SEARCH
System for Electronic Analysis and Retrieval of
riminal Histories), which was initiated in
969 out of Sacramento, California. Starting
ith the same concept of state-held files and a
entral index, SEARCH brought together infor-
ation from Arizona, Connecticut, Florida,
lichigan, Minnesota, New York, Texas, the
istrict of Columbia, and the FBI onto its
omputer network, and began to expand the
dex to contain the histories of individuals on
e system. From July 1969 to December
970, a test run of the system was carried out
which Michigan acted as the central index
ith 2.5 million records. The states participat-
g plus five "observer" states accounted for 75
ercent of the crime in the United States. Prior
this test, SEARCH was considering some of
e following points: standardizing data input,
pdating records in the central file, accessibility
y persons whose records were in the system,
ccessibility, by commercial and other non-law
nforcement agencies, and further computer
evelopment to enable the transmission of
ngerprints. Evaluation of the 18-month test
aised additional questions: 1) location of the
entral file, 2) type of controls and responsibili-
es to be imposed on the system, and 3)
rocedures for maintaining short retrieval time
hen the file becomes extremely large.

However, by the end of 1970 the primary
ssue became who would control the system. In
November, the security and privacy committee
f SEARCH recommended that individuals
hould be allowed to review their files. The
BI disagreed and in December, only ten days
fter money had been budgeted by LEAA to
ontinue SEARCH, Attorney General John
Mitchell transferred authority to develop the
ystem to the FBI, with the NCIC acting as
he centralized file.[16]

Since the take-over, the FBI and LEAA
money have encouraged more states and their
local law enforcement agencies to join the
system by feeding their files into the NCIC
computer. At present, Massachusetts is the only
state to openly refuse to enter the system,
claiming that the NCIC's massive invasion of
privacy results in misleading and incorrect
information on individuals being indiscriminately circulated by the federal government. NCIC's
potential role in large-scale repressive control is
clear when a Presidential Commission on Law
Enforcement estimates that at the present rate
50 million Americans will have criminal arrest
records by the end of the decade.[17]

COMMAND AND CONTROL

Another area of police work in which
sophisticated technology is being increasingly
utilized is in command and control—the structures and equipment police agencies use to
coordinate their activities and maintain commu-

nications (See discussion above, in chapter 7). This includes radio communications, telephone switchboards, patrol car allocation schemes, portable two-way radios, electronic maps, and patrol cars with digital computers.

Much of day-to-day command and control involves receiving telephone complaints and dispatching police units to service them. However, during the urban disorders and mass demonstrations since the 1960's, weaknesses in the command and control system became apparent. According to the National Advisory Commission on Criminal Justice Standards and Goals,

> Many police communications systems are actually chaotic assemblies of independent radio networks that somehow manage to move a monumental volume of radio traffic despite considerable inefficiency. They operate on the threshold of collapse, with radio traffic overloads the rule rather than the exception. In a major civil disorder, disaster, or other emergency, most policy communications systems will break down.[18]

One example of the problem occurred in Berkeley, California, during a militant anti-war demonstration. At the height of the action someone telephoned a bomb threat to the police headquarters at which point communication from the main radio room to the streets was stopped for ten minutes, causing tremendous confusion for the anti-riot police.

The addition of more sophisticated electronic systems is an attempt to more rapidly respond to increasing requests. As metropolitan areas require more police personnel, radio channels become more crowded, the location and management of large numbers of patrol cars becomes more complicated, and the retrieval of requests for police-related information is more time-consuming. In order to better keep track of patrol cars, electronic systems have been developed which include direction finders, patrol car emitters, and patrol box sensors. At police stations the signals are monitored in a computer and are either displayed on video screens or directly onto an electronic map. This information then allows a computer to dispatch the most readily available cars on request. The switchboard operator

86

types the activity and location of the complaint. Immediately the computer assigns a car and begins to develop records of the specific complaint. The radio dispatcher is shown the assignment and broadcasts it. Some patrol cars are now equipped with digital computers consisting of a video screen and teletype keyboard which are attached to radio equipment for transmitting and receiving all messages.

WEAPONRY

Weaponry, the ultimate instrument of police force, is constantly used—specifically to subdue "criminals" by killing or injuring them, and in general to intimidate the entire population. The racism of the police (and the society) can also be gauged by the police use of weapons, since Blacks and other Third World people are fired upon and killed by police much more than those in White communities.[19] Weapons are generally classified into lethal and non-lethal.
Lethal weapons: The standard lethal police weapon is the .38-caliber revolver, although recently some police departments are starting to use the more powerful .357 magnum. Perhaps more significant is the widespread use of dumdum bullets, which are flat- or hollow-tipped and expand as they enter the body. They rip wider wounds, resulting in more bleeding and death in many cases. Although the 1907 Hague convention outlawed the expanding dumdum bullets on the grounds that they were "calculated to cause unnecessary suffering" (and they are not used by the U.S. armed forces), close to 900 police departments were using dumdums in 1972.[20]

Recently, community organizations in Seattle, Washington have protested the police department's decision to use hollow-tipped bullets. The Third World community has led this struggle, since police figures show that 60 percent of the suspects fired upon by police officers in the last three years have been Blacks, Asians, and Chicanos. The opposition forced suspension of the bullet's use until further research could be done, and the final decision was left to the city council. The council voted eight to one in favor of the hollow-tipped bullet after the American Civil Liberties Union, one of the original opponents, withdrew its objections.[21]

Also, now standard equipment in many patrol cars is the riot gun—a 12-gauge shotgun which can fire dumdum slugs as well as double-0 buckshot (each shell contains nine lead pellets the size of a .32-caliber slug). Police shotguns firing double-0 buckshot were responsible for killing three Black students at Orangesburg, South Carolina, in 1968, two Black students at Jackson State College (Mississippi) in 1970, and two Black students at Southern University (Louisiana) in 1972.[22] Most police arsenals also contain machine guns, sniper rifles, etc. The National Guard in 1970 issued to its troops the M-16 automatic rifle for riot control.[23]

Less than lethal weapons: Most of the recent research and development in police weaponry has been done on the so-called less than lethal weapons. The National Science Foundation defines them as coercive devices and agents intended in normal law enforcement application not to create a substantial risk of permanent injury or death. Less than lethal weapons range from various nightsticks, stun guns, the rubber bullets used by the British in Northern Ireland, and water cannons, to the various chemical gases (CN, CS, DM) and electrified baton to the sound curdler, paint gun, and instant banana peel.[24] (See chapter 21 for a detailed chart of these weapons.)

Again, it was the political protests and demonstrations against racism and the Vietnam War which forced the escalated development of less than lethal and anti-riot weapons. Some of these weapons were used in Vietnam and other overseas wars, but many were developed specifically for the "war at home." Presently, many of the weapons are not being used, or are in the early stages of development, but research, funded primarily by LEAA, continues.

AERIAL SURVEILLANCE

Police agencies began using aerial patrols little more than a decade after the first flight of the Wright brothers. The Los Angeles County

STRIKE™

the *safer*

CS grenade controls violence *fast!*

Sheriff formed a reserve aero-squadron as early as 1925, and by 1933 it became a full-time police unit. The New York City police had an aviation section by 1929, and in 1947 the New York Port Authority began using helicopters for surveillance.

In 1964, Los Angeles County developed their helicopter program into what they called a rescue unit, which was used extensively for the first time during the Watts riot in 1965, during which the helicopters were a major part of the police and military surveillance command network.

This experience resulted in the heavy funding of aerial patrol programs through funds from the National Highway Safety Act of 1966 and the Crime Control and Safe Streets Act of 1968 (LEAA).[25] The first major LEAA helicopter project was the creation of "Project Sky Knight" in the city of Lakewood, California (in Los Angeles County). In 1966 Lakewood received an initial grant of $159,000 to set up a helicopter patrol system of intensive day and night patrols using three helicopters. Project Sky Knight had six goals: 1) to improve police response time, 2) demonstrate successful daytime surveillance methods, 3) initiate effective nighttime surveillance, 4) increase patrol observation, 5) increase officer security, and 6) reduce crime in the project area.[26] These helicopters were equipped with communications equipment to fully integrate them into existing police communications systems, high intensity directional lights called night suns, which are capable of lighting the area of a baseball field from a height of 300-600 feet and are equipped with infra-red filters for covert observation in total darkness, and with a powerful public address system. One report outlines the helicopters' use in riot control:

> Civil disturbances often result in a vast amount of confusion, particularly at night, with ground patrol units unable to identify the key points of difficulty, and participants often claiming they did not hear an order to disperse. The helicopter's overall view of the scene, together with loud speaker and riot suppression equipment, will do much, both tangibly and psychologically, to bring the situation to a rapid and acceptable conclusion.[27]

In New York City, police helicopters have been equipped with closed circuit T.V. cameras and also computerized reporting systems which are designed to determine the deployment of ground units. This system is called ACTIONS, an acronym for "Allocation and Control Through Identification of Ongoing Situations." The ACTIONS system is part of New York's "Electronic War Room" which utilizes a large CCTV network (including numerous cameras at fixed locations throughout the city).[28]

The helicopters most widely used by the police are from Bell Helicopter and Hughes Aircraft, and their cost ranges from $40,000 to $150,000 per operational helicopter. There were 150 police helicopters in 1972, which seems to be the year when such purchase reached its peak.[29]

Surveillance by police helicopters has brought about much adverse community reaction; complaints of intimidation and harassment are numerous, and in some communities, been mobilized to block the purchase of helicopters by city police. Most complaints have

resulted from the constant noise caused b[y] patrols, and the intensity of the "night suns" which are heavily used during night survei[l]lance.

Opposition to police helicopters has recentl[y] been expressed by citizens of Atlanta, Georgi[a.] Since the Atlanta Police Department's six hel[i]copters began 24-hour surveillance in fall, 197[3] community groups have complained about th[e] helicopters flying over houses at all hours of th[e] night, shining searchlights into windows, lan[d]ing in parks and following innocent people.[30]

Such complaints have led police to conside[r] the STOL (short take-off and landing) aircraf[t] which was originally developed for use by th[e] U.S. military and was used extensively i[n] Indochina. These fixed-wing aircraft are muc[h] quieter than helicopters and operate at min[i]mum altitudes of 1000 feet. They can b[e] equipped with similar equipment as helicopter[s] can remain airborne for 10-12 hours (helico[p]ters are limited to 2½ hours flight time), ca[n] operate from small landing strips (600 feet[)] and can fly at very low airspeeds (30 mph[)]

Helio Guardian... right arm of the law.

The Helio Guardian is recognized as one of the world's premier C/STOL (Controlled Short Take-off and Landing) aircraft. This ability, along with its toughness and versatility, make the Helio a proven asset to law enforcement agencies. Search and rescue...traffic control...surveillance...utility transportation — the Helio Guardian is ideally suited to do the job. It's your right arm in the air.

Introducing the Rockwell Printrak 250.

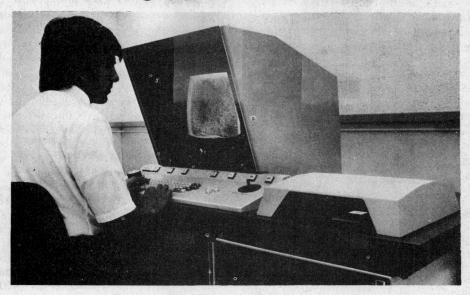

TOL aircraft cost from $39-140,000 to purchase and are much cheaper to operate than helicopters (1/3 to 1/2 as costly).

DENTIFICATION TECHNIQUES

Advanced technology is being used extensively by law enforcement agencies in their ttempt to identify suspects. Research from the military, aerospace, and the physical sciences in general is being applied daily in many crime aboratories with instruments like the gas chromatograph, X-ray fluoroscope, emission spectograph, and infra-red spectrophotometer. Identication research is receiving large government rants to perfect known techniques and develop ew methods.

—A microbiologist at the University of Maine claims that criminals can be identified by he germs they leave at the scene of the crime.[31]

—Dental X-rays were used by the FBI in heir attempt to identify victims of a New York townhouse explosion.[32]

—A scientist at the Internal Revenue Service claims that a radioactivation analysis is in use to determine the validity of supporting tax documents by determining the age of the paper and ink.[33]

—NASA applied its aerospace research for the Chicago Police Department by developing a fiber optics profilometer which deciphers impressions left on a writing pad after the page bearing the writing has been removed.[34]

—The Stanford Research Institute received a $150,000 grant from the National Science Foundation to study the costs and benefits derived from the application of scientific resources in the criminalistics field.[35] Two examples of highly developed identification techniques are the standard fingerprint system and the recently-developed voiceprint method.

Fingerprints: Due to their uniqueness, fingerprints have become the most widely used method of identification, with voluminous files stored at local, state, and federal agencies. However, the extensive use of fingerprint identification has led to problems in maintaining and searching these files. The largest fingerprint collection is held by the FBI in Washington, D.C. It contains about 16 million sets of different criminal prints plus about 62 million different prints from civil service applicants and

VOICEPRINTS

members of the armed forces. With duplication, the total number of fingerprint cards in the FBI files is around 200 million. Each day 30,000 sets (10,000 from arrests) of prints are received and processed by over 1,000 FBI personnel.[36]

A main weakness of the fingerprint classification system is that it requires ten ordered prints in order to file a card and also to retrieve a match from the file. Therefore, when a manual retrieval method is used, latent fingerprints (those few, usually poor quality prints left by a suspect) are almost impossible to match with a person's ten-finger card in the file. To alleviate this problem, some law enforcement agencies maintain a small "latent file" to allow a finger-by-finger search of those individuals considered to be involved in certain types of crimes. All these identification procedures assume the person in question has already been fingerprinted. Consequently, latent prints are primarily used to confirm identification or eliminate suspects.

Until recently, if an agency wanted the FBI to check their print records on a suspect to determine if the person was a fugitive or had a record they would mail a set of the suspect's prints to Washington and FBI personnel would examine many print cards to determine if the suspect's prints were on file. By the time the agency received an answer a week to ten days had elapsed and the suspect might be out of custody.

Technology is now being employed to reduce both the transmission and file-search time. The transfer of prints from agency to agency is now almost instantaneous through facsimile reproduction techniques, with the most recent means of transmission being satellites. The California Crime Technological Research Foundation under an LEAA grant has directed a project to test the feasibility of using a space satellite to transmit fingerprint card facsimiles from coast to coast in seconds. The agencies which participated were the Los Angeles County Sheriff's office, the California Department of Justice, the Florida Department of Law Enforcement, and NASA.[37]

For searching the files, the FBI is attempting to develop a semi-automatic storage/retrieval system using electronic scanners to locate and classify prints through a process of comparing fingerprint details (pattern recognition). Technicians would help in the classification process and would examine print cards when more than one was chosen by the computer. The prototype system was designed by Cornell Aeronautical Laboratories (now Calspan Corporation) of Buffalo, New York, and delivered to the FBI in August, 1972. After experimentation the FBI has requested five additional production models.[38]

For law enforcement agencies with smaller fingerprint files, Eastman Kodak has developed an automated microfilm information retrieval system called Miracode, which can scan up to 900 fingerprints in a minute. The fingerprint file, which is kept on microfilm, is scanned electronically with the suspects's fingerprints. If they are on the microfilm, the system will find them. Also, this method is being used now to match latent fingerprints.[39]

Voiceprints: Voiceprints are based on the principle that speech is uttered differently by each individual due to physical differences in the larynx, mouth, tongue, teeth, and lips. Voice identifications were first developed at the Bell

Suppress crime at night

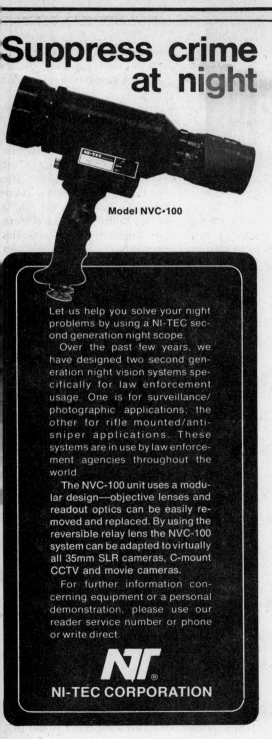

Model NVC-100

Telephone laboratories through a method called voice spectrography. The technique's early law enforcement proponent was Lawrence Kersta, who formed the Voiceprint Laboratory in Somerville, New Jersey. Others who have specialized in voiceprint research have included Michigan State University's School of Criminal Justice and Audiology and Speech Sciences Department. The law enforcement application of voiceprint has been carried out most extensively by the Michigan State Police, but many other law enforcement agencies are now acquiring equipment to record and analyze voiceprints.[40]

Two methods have been developed for voice recognition. The first method involved the visual comparison of graphs which are records, over time, of frequency and amplitude patterns of the voice. However, the courts are reluctant to admit these voiceprints as evidence since identification involves a subjective interpretation by an examiner in order to match two prints. In summer, 1974, the U.S. Court of Appeals ruled that voiceprint identification cannot be used as evidence in criminal trials. While the ruling is only binding in Federal courts in Washington, D.C., it is expected to influence other federal and state courts.[41]

These court decisions have prompted LEAA to fund Rockwell International and the Aerospace Corporation to develop a purely scientific method of voice identification, using a digital computer. Currently, LEAA claims highly accurate results in identifying voices by matching phonemes (the smallest recognizable unit of sound made by combining a vowel and a consonant).[42] LEAA is also funding the development of a voiceprint filing system comparable to the fingerprint system. Their goal is a voiceprint identification system that will be admissible in the courtroom.

The increased use of technology by the police signals an escalation of conflict within U.S. society. It means that the repressive apparatus is preparing for a prolonged conflict, since establishing technological systems for crime control requires a large investment in capital and training. These systems have a permanency which will affect all police opera-

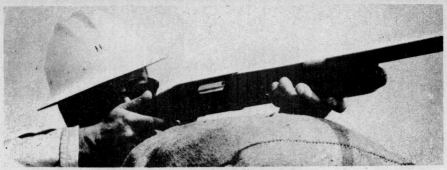

Standard riot shotgun

tions in the future. In addition, certain war-related technology will increase the combat role of the police and serve to intensify the conflict between the state and the communities; and the worsening economic conditions will accelerate this process.

1. *Granma,* Havana, Cuba, January 5, 1975.
2. President's Commission on Law Enforcement and Administration of Justice, *Task Force Report: Science and Technology,* Washington, D.C., U.S. Government Printing Office, 1967, p. 1.
3. National Advisory Commission on Criminal Justice Standards and Goals, *The Police,* Washington, D.C., U.S. Government Printing Office, 1973, p. 86.
4. *Police Chief,* November, 1969, editorial.
5. National Institute of Law Enforcement and Criminal Justice, "Advanced Technology: An Overview," *LEAA Newsletter,* December, 1974, p. 6.
6. North American Congress on Latin America, *The University-Military-Police Complex,* 1972, p. 27.
7. Ibid., p. 25.
8. Robert Barkan, "War's Technology is a Peacetime Spy," *San Francisco Chronicle,* January 19, 1972.
9. The National Aeronautics and Space Administration publishes annually *Technology Applications Progress Report,* which describes inventions that can be applied in other fields.
10. *San Francisco Chronicle,* January 23, 1975.
11. National Advisory Commission on Criminal Justice Standards and Goals, *Criminal Justice System,* Washington, D.C., U.S. Government Printing Office, 1973, p. 33.
12. J. Taylor DeWeese, "Giving the Computer a Conscience," *Harpers,* November, 1973.
13. *Washington Post,* February 3, 1974.
14. *F.B.I. Bulletin,* January, 1974.
15. *New York Times,* November 30, 1971.
16. *Washington Post,* February 27, 1972.
17. DeWeese, op. cit.
18. National Advisory Commission on Criminal Justice Standards and Goals, *A National Strategy to Reduce Crime,* Washington, D.C., U.S. Government Printing Office, 1973, p. 88.
19. Paul Takagi, "A Garrison State in a Democratic Society," *Crime and Social Justice,* 1, Spring-Summer 1974, p. 29.
20. *Washington Post,* October 8, 1972.
21. *Seattle Post-Intelligence,* January 10, 1975.
22. *New York Times,* February 7, 1973.
23. *Los Angeles Times,* August 22, 1970.
24. Security Planning Corporation, *Non-lethal Weapons for Law Enforcement,* Washington, D.C., 1972.
25. *New York Times,* February 9, 1969.
26. Robert Dyment, "Los Angeles County Sheriff's Department Helicopter Patrol," *American County Government,* November, 1968, p. 25.
27. Ibid., p. 27.
28. *New York Times,* June 1, 1969.
29. Lawyers' Committee for Civil Rights Under Law, *Law and Disorder III,* Washington, D.C., 1972, p. 37.
30. *Great Speckled Bird,* Atlanta, April 1, 1974.
31. *Los Angeles Times,* June 30, 1972.
32. *New York Times,* April 3, 1972.
33. *New York Times,* March 1, 1970.
34. *Attorney General's First Annual Report,* Washington, D.C., U.S. Government Printing Office, 1972.
35. Ibid., p. 516.
36. Thomas C. Bartee, "Fingerprint Classification," *Task Force Report: Science and Technology,* President's Commission on Law Enforcement and Administration of Justice, Washington, D.C., U.S. Government Printing Office, 1967, p. 107.
37. *LEAA Newsletter,* November, 1971, p. 11.
38. *Los Angeles Times,* June 6, 1974.
39. *Los Angeles Times,* November 12, 1972.
40. Department of Michigan State Police, *Voice Identification Research,* Washington, D.C., LEAA, February, 1972.
41. *LEAA Newsletter,* July 1974, p. 22.
42. *LEAA Newsletter,* December 1974, p. 14.

9. SWAT

The domestic unrest in the sixties gave rise to a paramilitary conception of police work in certain police and government organizations. Special training programs in handling civil disorders run by the army for domestic police, the International Chiefs of Police Bomb Detecting School, new weaponry and technological systems were all designed to counter the "threat from within." The establishment of the Los Angeles Police Department's Special Weapons and Tactics (SWAT) unit is a good example of this trend.

According to a report issued by the LAPD in July 1974,[1] SWAT was initiated in late 1967 in response to the increased incidence of urban violence, and in particular the emergence of the sniper as a threat to police operations, the appearance of the political assassin, and the threat of urban guerrilla warfare. Many police officers were being killed due to carelessness and poor training. As one SWAT instructor put it, "Those people out there—the radicals, the revolutionaries, and the cop haters—are damned good at using shotguns, bombs or setting up ambushes, so we've got to be better at what we do."[2] Conceived by an ex-marine as part of a total counterinsurgency plan, the iron fist in the velvet glove, SWAT was set up as a unit within the LAPD tactical operations group, which also includes helicopter operations, unusual occurrences control planning, and the 200-man Metropolitan division (which handles high frequency crime areas, labor disputes, and riots, and is on call 24 hours a day). There are six squads, each of which has two five-man teams.

SWAT's RESPONSIBILITIES

The same report lays out the following tasks that SWAT teams are trained to carry out: protecting police officers engaged in crowd control from sniper attack, providing high ground and perimeter security for visiting dignitaries, rescuing hostages, providing for the nonviolent apprehension of desperate barricaded suspects, providing control assault firepower in certain non-riot situations, rescuing officers or citizens endangered by gunfire, and neutralizing guerrilla or terrorist operations directed against government personnel, property, or the general populace. The language describing SWAT's duties reveals the extent to which the police see themselves as a military unit fighting a domestic war. Many SWAT members have had military experience, and all are volunteers who have gone through an extensive and rigorous screening process. Regular members of the department, they carry their uniforms and equipment in their car trunks as they may be called to action at any moment.

Each SWAT member receives instruction in the history of guerrilla warfare, scouting and patrolling, camouflage and concealment, combat in built-up areas, chemical agents, first aid, and ambushes. Originally trained by Marines at Camp Pendleton, SWAT officers now train their own men although they still enjoy close cooperation and rapport with the Marine Corps. And while they still do some training at Pendleton, they also use the Universal Studios movie set where they can create the real life situations encountered by SWAT—a riot, bank robbery, ambush, and so on. Ambush training is considered to be extremely important, given the number of police officers who have been killed in recent years. For example, SWAT members are trained to get out of a car under fire without exposing themselves to snipers, use their car for cover, and fire from a prone position. Autopsy pictures of slain policemen are used to reinforce the lesson.

Each team trains as a self-sufficient unit and each member can handle any assignment within

the unit. After the initial instruction, the team trains once a month. The teams include a leader, scout, marksman, observer, and rearguard. SWAT teams are equipped with automatic rifles, semi-automatic shotguns, gas masks, gas canisters, smoke devices, ropes, pry bars, manhole hooks, and walkie talkies. They are accompanied by a mobile command post that carries communications systems, armored vests, steel helmets, extra ammunition, tear gas projectiles, battering rams, first aid supplies and "c" rations. Most large city police departments and the FBI now have SWAT-type units or are in the process of developing them. There are an estimated one thousand SWAT teams throughout the country. The LAPD receives four to five requests a week for officer and material to train men in other cities. Just after the SWAT assault on the house occupied by suspected members of the Symbionese Liberation Army (described below), the LAPD received over one hundred letters from other departments asking for information on SWAT.

In April 1975, San Francisco newspapers revealed that most Bay Area county sheriff departments and many cities had SWAT-like units. The FBI has trained officers from at least 40 Northern California police and sheriff agencies. While most Bay Area police departments have received training from the FBI, some conduct their own training. Smaller departments form units with police officers from neighboring towns.

It is not a town's population size but rather its wealth that determines the "need" for a SWAT unit. For example, the town of Belvedere has a heavily armed SWAT team. Belvedere, with four officers on the police force, organized a SWAT team made up of citizen volunteers. The SWAT team has at its disposal a two and a half ton Army surplus tank, with a fifty caliber machine gun mount. Belvedere has less than 3000 people in two square miles, but it is the wealthiest city in Marin County in terms of median family income and its property was assessed at nearly $24 million.[4]

WHAT SWAT HAS DONE

Since its inception in 1967, SWAT has been activated close to 200 times. Teams have acted as security for the president and vice president, visiting diplomats and heads of state, and have protected officers engaged in crowd control during campus disorders, rock festivals, and other civil disturbances. They have helped officers investigate "armed strongholds" and rescued wounded officers and hostages. Since 1971 when they were assigned to handle situations involving barricaded suspects, they have been involved in 96 such incidents, and according to their own report have only fired on four occasions, have wounded one suspect and killed seven. Six of those seven were suspected members of the Symbionese Liberation Army (SLA).

The language of the LAPD report is deceptive, and does not indicate which individuals or groups are subjected to SWAT operations. For example, one of the "armed strongholds" investigated by SWAT was the Black Panther Party headquarters in Los Angeles. The *Los Angeles Times* reported that at 4 a.m. on December 8, 1969, a 40 man police team clad in black coveralls and black baseball caps, armed with automatic rifles and sniper rifles, opened fire on the headquarters. During the siege that followed, police planted dynamite charges on the roof to blast their way in from the top, a police helicopter circled over the building, and an armored personnel carrier stood by for possible use in the final assault. It wasn't until after the Panthers had surrendered that the press was allowed to come to the scene.[5] Thirteen Panthers were arrested for conspiracy to commit murder, conspiracy to commit assault on a police officer, and conspiracy to possess illegal weapons. When they finally came to trial in July 1971, the jury acquitted them of all but the last and least serious charge. The jury's decision showed that the LAPD's attempts to portray the Panthers as a threat to the community failed, and that it was clear to the citizens of Los Angeles that the Panthers had been set up and attacked by an overzealous and over-armed police assault team, for reasons that had nothing to do with public safety.

The 1975 shoot-out in Los Angeles involving members of SWAT, the FBI, and the SLA was similar to the attack on the Panthers in that both times massive amounts of firepower were expended in the middle of the Black community and no attempt was made to insure the safety of those inside the house under attack or in the community. In both cases, SWAT itself terrorized the community in its efforts to "neutralize terrorist operations." The police report states that during the SLA shootout 29

SWAT members and 7 FBI men used weapons, including four automatic weapons, that expended 5371 rounds and launched 83 tear gas canisters into an area equivalent to a 25 x 30 foot room. At one point the SWAT commander in charge was reported to have requested fragmentation grenades, but his request was denied. (In any case, fragmentation grenades were unnecessary. The types of tear gas used, the Flite Rite and Spedhete projectiles, can ignite a firestorm when used indoors in a flammable atmosphere, and did in fact totally destroy the house. See photo below.)

As the American Civil Liberties Union (ACLU) has pointed out, the police made no attempt to evacuate the community or to communicate with SLA members inside the house before opening fire.[6] Although they had been previously informed that a Black woman re-mained hostage in the house after the shootout began, when the woman ran out of the house, SWAT members dragged her to the ground and kicked her. The house was levelled, and houses on both sides were severely damaged by fire. Homes, cars and apartments were riddled with bullets and angry residents demanded compensation from the city. While the mayor and the governor commended the LAPD, parents of the dead, witnesses to the event, and many others were horrified. Independent investigations were conducted by the ACLU, Citizens Research and Investigating Committee (CRIC), and Lake Headley, a private investigator hired by the father of one of the slain SLA members. All their reports raise serious questions about the intentions of the police and indicate that lives could have been saved.

While there has been no organized response

to the actions of SWAT in Los Angeles, SWAT and units like it in other cities will probably be increasingly subject to public scrutiny as their existence becomes known to community groups already engaged in struggles around the police.

The FBI SWAT teams are euphemistically called Apprehension Units. Approximately 10 percent of the Bureau's 8,500 special agents receive SWAT training. In September, 1975, several Units consisting of over one hundred agents raided the Oglala Sioux Nation at Crow Dog's Paradise on the Rosebud Reservation in South Dakota, searching for native Americans charged with murdering two FBI agents. The suspects were never found.[7]

The SWAT program of military strategy, efficiency and tactics is expanding. In 1976, San Quentin Prison authorized the establishment of a Correctional Emergency Response Team (CERT), modeled after SWAT. The CERT team is made up of prison guards who have successfully completed a 40 hour course in specialized FBI training. The CERT squad consists of three five-man teams, plus a commander and an assistant commander. CERT has not yet been called into action, but it is certain that incidents similar to the murder of George Jackson will now be handled more "professionally."

The actual behavior of SWAT seems to contradict its avowed purpose of employing restraint in curbing incidents of urban violence. Quite to the contrary, the net effect of SWAT's police-state tactics is to induce fear and outrage on the part of the community it purports to protect. The actions taken against the SLA and the Panthers seem designed less to minimize violence than to serve as a warning to anyone or any group that seriously challenges the forces of repression. The SWAT concept is an indication of the extent to which the police are willing and able to use the most brutally effective military tactics to ensure "order" at any cost in a time of social upheaval and mass discontent. It's important to keep this in mind when looking at the new, softer police strategies of community pacification, described in the next section. No matter how much money and effort is poured into sophisticated pro-

grams aimed at improving police relations with the community, ultimately the basis of police power is the capacity to use force—and the emergence of SWAT shows how serious the police are about refining that capacity.

1. Los Angeles Police Department, "Special Weapons and Tactics," July 1974, p. 101.
2. Bill Hazlett, "Police Specialists—Grim Training Aimed at Saving Lives," *Los Angeles Times*, October 29, 1972, Section C, p. 2.
3. *Christian Science Monitor*, June 19, 1974.
4. *San Francisco Chronicle*, April 2, 1975.
5. *Los Angeles Times*, December 9, 1969.
6. ACLU, "Report on the SLA Shoot-Out May 14, 1974," July 1974, pp. 1-5.
7. "Garden Plot and SWAT: U.S. Police as New Action Army," *Counterspy*, Winter 1976, Vol. 2, Issue 4, p. 17.

S.W.A.T. Equipment

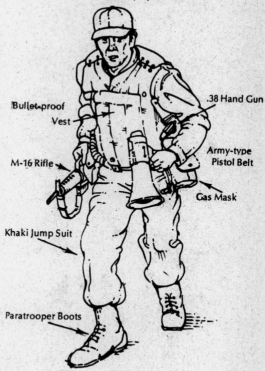

Bullet-proof Vest

.38 Hand Gun

M-16 Rifle

Army-type Pistol Belt

Gas Mask

Khaki Jump Suit

Paratrooper Boots

Other Equipment: .12 Gauge Tear Gas Launcher
Remington 308 Rifle with Long-range Scope

10. POLITICAL SURVEILLANCE

Political surveillance in the United States developed in response to the rising resistance to capitalism by the working class. Since World War I, there has been a steadily expanding and increasingly sophisticated effort by Federal, state and local police agencies to "detect, disrupt, or otherwise neutralize" individuals and organizations considered a threat to the capitalist system. While this development has been characterized by the anarchy of organization and interrelationships of the various agencies, it has nevertheless resulted in the creation of a powerful intelligence gathering apparatus.

The recent disclosures in the wake of Watergate have revealed massive amounts of information about the political surveillance activities of the CIA, FBI, IRS, local police and other agencies. It is necessary to remember, however, that this is but the tip of the iceberg of domestic repression, and that the suggested "reforms" of these agencies are largely cosmetic or designed to rationalize and assist the operations of these agencies. Congressional committee reports do not challenge the legitimacy and in fact uphold the necessity of domestic intelligence for maintaining capitalist rule. Their criticisms are of individuals who overreacted (J. Edgar Hoover) or of the failure of agencies to stick to legal arrangements for doing this work (the CIA should not be doing domestic intelligence, that's the FBI's job).

We can also be sure that none of these agencies have disclosed their most sensitive operations, but have instead moved them under deeper cover. Recent disclosures of past operations and purges of officials are only sacrifices on the altar of democracy designed to cover their more important work.

ORIGINS

The first major federally organized surveillance operation was directed against the socialist and communist movements and the anti-war movement at the time of World War I. This surveillance resulted in the round-up and deportation of about 10,000 immigrant anarchist and revolutionary workers by the Justice Department in the 1919-20, Palmer Raids, and mass raids against draft resisters involving some 50,000 persons in 1918.[1]

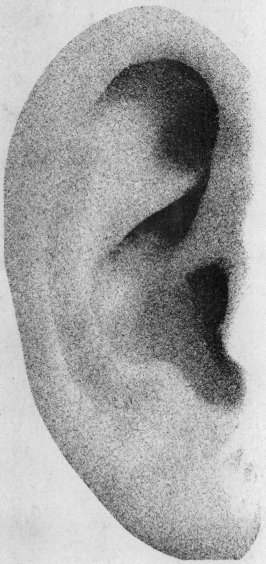

Recognition of the need for a continuous surveillance program resulted in the creation of the Federal Bureau of Investigation in 1924. The FBI became the main agency for the domestic surveillance of revolutionaries, and from time to time it worked with the U.S. Army in this effort. It was not until the mass uprisings of the Black and anti-war movements in the 1960's that the CIA, local police and other agencies came to play a significant role in domestic spying.

The rise of the Communist Party (CPUSA) in the 1930's and its leadership in labor and social reform movements provided the focus of nearly all of the FBI's work until the 1960's. It was President Roosevelt who directed the FBI in 1936 to collect information on "subversive activities."[2] This category was not limited in practice to investigating suspected criminal acts, but provided a blanket authorization for the FBI's attempts to subvert the communist movement. This was not the work of a paranoid J. Edgar Hoover, as liberal critics would have us believe, but rather reflected the view of the ruling class and its government on the necessity of suppressing communism.

The FBI's work thus entered the realm of pure intelligence, that is, information-gathering for the purpose of formulating policies of repression. According to a Hoover memo to Roosevelt, by 1938 the FBI was investigating subversion in the maritime, steel, garment and fur, coal and auto unions (all CPUSA strongholds) as well as in newspapers, educational institutions, youth groups, Black groups, the government and the armed forces. This intelligence, gathered through burglary, bugging, mail opening and infiltration, was transmitted directly to the White House.[3]

THE 1960's

Following World War II, the FBI continued under its COMINFIL program to seek out and destroy what was left of the CPUSA. This program was directed, in the FBI's own words, at "the entire spectrum of the social and labor movements in the country."[4] This was followed by COINTELPRO-CPUSA (1956) and other COINTELPRO programs described below.

The Black nationalist and anti-war movements provoked an enormous growth in the domestic intelligence apparatus. Now the U.S. Army, Central Intelligence Agency, National Security Agency, Internal Revenue Service, Alcohol, Tobacco and Firearms division of the Treasury Department, Bureau of Narcotics and Dangerous Drugs (later the Drug Enforcement Administration) and local police departments

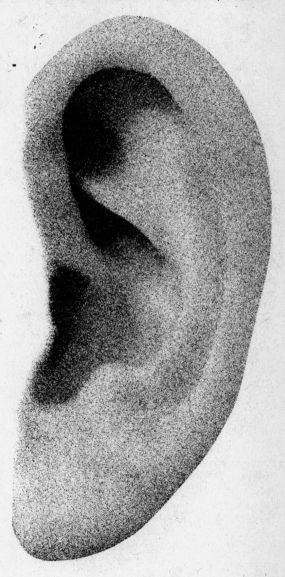

99

joined the FBI in its attempts to infiltrate, disrupt and destroy progressive organizations and their leaders. The mass uprisings in the Black ghettos of Watts (1964), Detroit and Newark (1967) caught the government by surprise and revealed its ignorance of the size, strength and leadership of the Black movement. Likewise, the growth of the anti-war movement frightened and puzzled the ruling class, and they began to infiltrate and seek the "foreign source" of this movement.

The Justice Department attempted to strengthen the intelligence gathering capability by coordinating the work of the various agencies through the Interdepartment Information Unit (later the Interdivisional Information Unit—IDIU).[5] In addition to the agencies listed above, its members included: Community Relations Service (Justice Dept.), Neighborhood Legal Services, Office of Economic Opportunity, Housing and Urban Development Model Cities and survey programs, and the U.S. Post Office. Federal social welfare programs were used as listening posts in the ghettos and barrios for identifying leaders and collecting information. The IDIU compiled and computerized files on individuals and organizations (receiving 42,000 entries per year by 1970) which were later turned over to the CIA, IRS and FBI. In 1974, the IDIU's computer operations were transferred to the Civil Disturbance Unit of the Justice Department where

they continued in full operation.

Evidently the IDIU did not fulfill its role because of the lack of cooperation from member agencies. Indeed, the history of the U.S. intelligence agencies reflects a resistance to joint work based on a fear of disclosing operations to others. In response to this situation, President Nixon made another attempt to bring the intelligence "community" together.

THE "HUSTON PLAN":
Nixon's White House
Secret Police Force

In July 1970 an ad hoc Inter-Agency Committee on Intelligence was set up to make recommendations for increased and improved intelligence gathering techniques and operations to President Nixon. The Committee was comprised of J. Edgar Hoover, FBI (chairman); Richard Helms, Director, CIA; Lieutenant General Donald Bennet, Director, Defense Intelligence Agency (DIA); and Admiral Noel Gaylor, Director, National Security Agency (NSA). The Committee, after several work sessions, submitted to the President for approval the "Huston Plan" (named after the coordinator of the committee and liaison to the President—Tom Charles Huston). Despite warnings that in some respects the plan was illegal and contained serious risks, President Nixon gave his approval of the operation. The "official" written approval, however, came from H. R. Haldeman after Huston told him, "We don't want the President linked to this thing with his signature on paper . . . all hell would break loose if this thing leaks out."[6]

Briefly, the Huston Plan proposed the use of electronic surveillance, burglary, wiretaps, and mail coverage against "violence-prone" campus and student related groups, and any "individuals and groups in the United States who pose a threat to the internal security."[7]

The intelligence information thus gathered was to be analyzed by a body created by Huston and Nixon, called the Inter-Agency Group on Domestic Intelligence and Internal Security (IAG), which was made up of the same members as the original ad hoc committee. The IAG was not only to analyze intelligence, but to initiate and coordinate field operations.[8]

According to his May 22, 1973 Watergate statement, Nixon rescinded his approval of the plan five days after he authorized it.[9] The reason for this was the unyielding opposition to the plan by J. Edgar Hoover, who did not want anyone else supervising his FBI.[10] The President's disapproval of the plan did not mean it was totally lost. The NSA communications surveillance and the CIA's mail opening program were continued. And the CIA and NSA continued to press for authorization to expand into and gain access to domestic intelligence.[11]

With the larger plan shattered, Nixon established the secret Intelligence Evaluation Committee (IEC) made up of members of the White House staff and representatives from the FBI, CIA, NSA, Secret Service, and Departments of State, Justice, and Defense. The IEC was housed in the Justice Department, first in the Internal Security Division and later in the Criminal Division.[12]

Nixon failed to unite the agencies in a program of *action*. Thus the IEC remained no more than a means of collating information. The secret White House intelligence police, the "plumbers," grew out of the desire to put such information to use. Their actions were later to become known as Watergate. James McCord, member of the plumbers and of the Committee for the Re-Election of the President (CREEP), received intelligence reports directly from the IEC, as did John Dean and Egil Krogh.[28]

Included in this section (see below) are excerpts from the texts of top secret documents concerning the Huston Plan: the President's "decision memorandum" and the plan for the organizational structure of the Inter-agency Group on Domestic Intelligence and Internal Security. These documents were taken by John Dean when he was fired from the White House, probably as bargaining tools for his salvation, and were leaked to the *New York Times* on June 6, 1973.

TOP SECRET
Decision Memorandum
The White House
Washington
July 15, 1970
TOP SECRET
Handle via Comint Channels
Only
Subject: Domestic Intelligence

The President has carefully studied the special report of the Interagency Committee on Intelligence (ad hoc) and made the following decisions:
1. Interpretive Restraint on Communications Intelligence

National Security Council Intelligence Directive Number 6 (NSCID-6) is to be interpreted to permit N.S.A. to program for coverage the communications of U.S. citizens using international facilities.
2. Electronic Surveillances and Penetrations

The intelligence community is directed to intensify coverage of individuals and groups in the United States who pose a major threat to the internal security. Also, coverage of foreign nationals and diplomatic establishments in the United States of interest to the intelligence community is to be intensified.
3. Mail Coverage

Restrictions on legal coverage are to be removed, restrictions on covert coverage are to be relaxed to permit use of this technique on selected targets of priority foreign intelligence and internal security interest.
4. Surreptitious Entry

Restraints on the use of surreptitious entry are to be removed. The technique is to be used to permit procurement of vitally needed foreign cryptographic material and against other urgent and high priority internal security targets.
5. Development of Campus Sources

Coverage of violence-prone campus and student-related groups is to be increased. All restraints which limit this coverage are to be removed. Also, C.I.A. coverage of American students (and others) traveling or living abroad is to be increased.

6. Use of Military Undercover Agents

Present restrictions are to be retained.

7. Budget and Manpower

Each agency is to submit a detailed estimate as to projected manpower needs and other costs required to implement the above decisions.

8. Domestic Intelligence Operations

A committee consisting of the directors or other appropriate representatives appointed by the directors of the F.B.I., C.I.A., N.S.A., D.I.A., and the military counterintelligence agencies is to be constituted effective August 1, 1970, to provide evaluations of domestic intelligence, prepared periodic domestic intelligence estimates, carry out the other objectives specified in the report, and perform such other duties as the President shall, from time to time, assign. The director of the F.B.I. shall serve as chairman of the committee. Further details on the organization and operations of this committee are set forth in an attached memorandum.

The President has directed that each addressee submit a detailed report, due on September 1, 1970, on the steps taken to implement these decisions. Further such periodic reports will be requested as circumstances merit.

The President is aware that procedural problems may arise in the course of implementing these decisions. However, he is anxious that such problems be resolved with maximum speed and minimum misunderstanding. Any difficulties which may arise should be brought to my immediate attention in order that an appropriate solution may be found and the President's directives implemented in a manner consistent with his objectives.

Tom Charles Huston.

TOP SECRET
Handle via Comint Channels
Only

Organization and Operations of the Interagency Group on Domestic Intelligence and Internal Security (IAG)

1. Membership

The membership shall consist of representatives of the F.B.I., C.I.A., D.I.A., N.S.A., and the counterintelligence agencies of the Departments of the Army, Navy, and Air Force. To insure the high level consideration of issues and problems which the President expects to be before the group, the directors of the respective agencies should serve personally. However, if necessary and appropriate, the director of a member agency may designate another individual to serve in his place.

2. Chairman

The director of the FBI shall serve as chairman. He may designate another individual from his agency to serve as the FBI representative on the group.

3. Observers

The purpose of the group is to effectuate community-wide coordination and secure the benefits of community-wide analysis and estimating. When problems arise which involve areas of interest to agencies or departments not members of the group, they shall be invited, at the discretion of the group, to join the group as observers and participants in those discussions of interest to them. Such agencies and departments include the Departments of State (I & R, Passport); Treasury (IRS, Customs); Justice (BNDD, Community Relations Service); and such other agencies which may have investigative or law enforcement responsibilities touching on domestic intelligence or internal security matters.

4. White House Liaison

The President has assigned to Tom Charles Huston staff responsibility for domestic intelligence and internal security affairs. He will participate in all activities of the group as the personal representative of the President.

5. Staffing

The group will establish such subcommittees or working groups as it deems appropriate. It will also determine and implement such staffing requirements as it may deem necessary to enable it to carry out its responsibilities, subject to the approval of the President.

6. Duties

The group will have the following duties:

(A) Define the specific requirements of member agencies of the intelligence community.

(B) Effect close, direct coordination between member agencies.

(C) Provide regular evaluations of domestic intelligence.

(D) Review policies governing operations in the field of domestic intelligence and develop recommendations.

(E) Prepare periodic domestic intelligence estimates which incorporate the results of the combined efforts of the intelligence community.

(F) Perform such other duties as the President may from time to time assign.

7. Meetings

The group shall meet at the call of the chairman, a member agency, or the White House representative.

8. Security

Knowledge of the existence and purposes of this group shall be limited on a strict "need to know" basis. Operations of, and papers originating with, the group shall be classified "top secret handle via Comint channels only."

9. Other Procedures

The group shall establish such other procedures as it believes appropriate to the implementation of the duties set forth above.

TOP SECRET
* From the *New York Times*, June 7, 1973.

"How many times do I have to explain, Henderson? There are good guys and there are bad guys and no matter how it looks, we're still the good guys!"

FBI's DOMESTIC INTELLIGENCE OPERATION *

The FBI has come under investigation recently for illegal activities carried out during its domestic intelligence operations. Through the use of hundreds of informers, electronic surveillance, mail openings, burglaries and other techniques, the FBI along with other government agencies has launched an unprecedented attack against individuals and organizations attempting to challenge the imperialism, racism and sexism endemic to U.S. capitalism. Many progressive forces fighting to establish socialism as the only solution to this country's problems are the special focus of the FBI's political surveillance. The congressional and Justice Department investigations may temporarily

* While other agencies such as the CIA and DIA are involved in domestic intelligence activities, our discussion focuses only on those like the FBI which see such activities as their primary purpose.

restrict some of the blatantly unconstitutional activities of the FBI, but as long as political struggle continues the state's repressive apparatus will attempt to prevent revolutionary change.

What follows is a summary of one of the better studies of the FBI's activities conducted by the U.S. General Accounting Office (GAO) at the request of the House Judiciary Committee Chairman, Peter Rodino, Jr. The study is entitled *FBI Domestic Intelligence Operations— Their Purpose and Scope: Issues that Need to be Resolved.* The GAO examined 898 cases (randomly selected) which were investigated in 1974 at 10 of the 59 FBI field offices. A case, or investigation, represents the total effort by the FBI on a specific subject (individual or group). During 1974, the 10 field offices alone were responsible for 19,659 domestic intelligence cases. It should be noted that the GAO investigation did not receive the full cooperation of the FBI.

(1) Structure of the Intelligence Division

Among the 13 organizational divisions of the FBI, the Intelligence Division is responsible for all investigations of foreign and domestic intelligence. The domestic branch is structured according to the chart shown below.

The *Extremist section* investigates individuals and organizations categorized as "black, white or American Indian extremists." It is concerned with the extent of communist influence among extremists and it attempts to develop informants who can supply information. This section in the Washington Headquarters has a Civil Disorders Reporting Unit and four other units responsible for investigations in other regions. The Extremist section, with 8 agents, formulates policy and gives guidance to field offices. It also develops special programs for handling "racial intelligence" relating to riots and lesser forms of protest, and passes this information to other government officials and agencies. Some of the organizations the FBI categorizes as extremist are: Black Panther Party, Black Liberation Army, Symbionese Liberation Army, Nation of Islam, American Indian Movement, Ku Klux Klan and National Socialist White Peoples' Party.

The *Subversive section* investigates the activities of revolutionary communist organizations, groups and individuals including fugitives. It also develops informants who infiltrate or are close to these organizations. This section, with 19 agents, has 2 units investigating communist groups, 2 units for revolutionary, urban guerrilla-type groups and 1 unit for informant control. In addition to formulating policy, guiding the field office investigations, disseminating intelligence to other agencies, the Subversive section maintains the FBI's Administrative Index (ADEX) of individuals it considers extremely dangerous. Some of the organizations the FBI categorizes as subversives are: Communist Party-USA, Socialist Workers Party, Progressive Labor Party, Students for a Democratic Society, Venceremos Brigade, Revolutionary Communist Party, October League, Weatherman, and Vietnam Veterans Against the War.

The *Research section* acts as a service agency for the entire Intelligence Division by preparing research and analysis on requested topics. It is also involved in electronic surveillance through requesting authorization, maintaining FBI policy and the monitoring of surveillance records. The Research section instructs agents and also advises the Bureau about the effect of new legislation on the Intelligence Division. This section has 20 agents in 4 units—

ORGANIZATIONAL STRUCTURE OF DOMESTIC INTELLIGENCE OPERATIONS

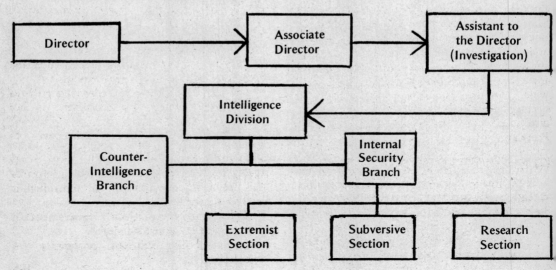

EXTENT OF FBI DOMESTIC INTELLIGENCE CASES AND AGENTS (1974)

Field Offices	Domestic Intelligence Cases	Domestic Intelligence Agents (full-time)	Total Agents in office	Percent of Total
San Francisco	4,881	86	350	24
Los Angeles	4,026	59	497	12
New York	3,988	82	973	9
Chicago	1,795	36	361	10
Dist. of Columbia	962	3	70	4
Buffalo	883	8	81	10
Sacramento	842	11	93	12
San Diego	790	11	91	12
Springfield	772	3	80	4
Atlanta	720	14	132	11

Source: Report to the House Committee on the Judiciary by the Comptroller General of the United States, *FBI Domestic Intelligence Operations—Their Purpose and Scope: Issues That Need to be Resolved.*

Training, Central Research, Special Records & Related Research, and Analytical Research.

The actual domestic intelligence investigations are carried out by agents within the 59 various FBI field offices. At the Washington Headquarters, a unit chief and his supervisors are responsible for monitoring and supervising the field investigations. For example, within the Subversive section of the Intelligence Division, one unit supervises investigations in the East, and another unit supervises the West. Within the eastern unit, one supervisor is responsible for investigating a Maoist organization nationwide. Another supervisor, in addition to overseeing the investigation of an organization, also supervises the FBI's False Identities Program.

(2) What the FBI Looks For

When the FBI investigates an organization it categorizes as a threat to national security, its agents look for the following information:
—stated aims and purposes
—identities of leaders, especially those with extremist and subversive backgrounds
—membership
—publications
—foreign influence
—connections with other extremist or subversive organizations
—summary of activities, especially those involving violence or threatened violence and the success or failure of the organization in achieving its goals

The FBI investigates individuals who are:
—current, active members of extremist and subversive organizations or movements
—actively supporting the subversive goals of a movement when the movement is not formally organized
—in contact with known subversives, to determine the purpose of the contacts

Agents allegedly collect the following information to determine whether an individual is involved in criminal violations:
—details of the subject's involvement in subversive or extremist activity
—assessing the subject's propensity for violence

105

—background data for identification purposes, including: date and place of birth, past and present residences, occupations and employments, citizenship status, family background, military records, education, arrest record, physical description and photograph, automobiles, license plates, social security number and close associates

Sources for this information include public material, government agencies, private firms, neighbors, fellow employees, informants, and physical and photographic surveillance when needed. Finally, the FBI Manual of Instructions states that unless there is good reason not to, subjects under investigation should be interviewed. The main purpose is to develop intelligence information, but additional reasons are 1) assessing whether an individual would be a good informant, which can only be done through personal contact, and (2) to confront the individual with the FBI's investigation, which could intimidate the subject from continuing his or her political activity.

The Manual of Instruction indicates that subversive organizations are investigated differently than extremist organizations, since subversive groups tend to have "rigid organizational structures with centralized control exercised by the national leadership." Chapters and members are under discipline and the organiza-

INVESTIGATIVE SOURCES OF INFORMATION
(used at least once during 797 cases)

Source	Number of Cases	Percent of 797 cases
Informants	659	83
State & local police	611	77
Confidential source[1]	430	54
State motor vehicle division[2]	411	52
Other FBI offices	394	49
Other state & local agencies[3]	332	42
FBI headquarter indexes	314	39
Credit bureaus	313	39
Other Federal agencies	312	39
Other private sources[4]	266	33
Educational institutions	169	21
Bureau of Vital Statistics	161	20
State computers	144	18
Utility companies	143	18
Military records	52	7
Banks & other financial firms	31	4

1. An individual who, on a confidential basis, furnishes information available to him or her through his or her present position (e.g., employees of utility companies, educational institutions, state employment services, banks or a landlord).

2. Frequently used for identifying information (e.g., date of birth, residence and the subject's picture).

3. Primarily, voter registration units and departments of correction.

4. Includes newspapers, telephone directories, rental agencies, airlines, insurance companies, bonding companies and realtors.

Source: Report to the House Committee on the Judiciary by the Comptroller General of the United States, FBI Domestic Intelligence Operations—Their Purpose and Scope: Issues That Need to be Resolved.

Sara Krulwich

tion makes heavy demands on members' time, talent and finances. These demands may include participating in front groups or moving to another area of the country. Since these organizations hold closed meetings and may have secret members involved in clandestine work, the FBI subjects individuals in these types of organizations to fuller investigations. The FBI assumes that these members recognize that the use of violence as a political tool is inevitable. The FBI tries to identify all members of subversive organizations for the following reasons:

—to develop a complete picture of the organizations' activities

—to assess the ability of a group to act to achieve its stated goals

—to identify all members, including secret members

—to conduct an effective Security of Government Employees Program, since the FBI is concerned that members will gain responsible positions in government, industry and education

—to assess potential informers

The FBI does not consider extremist organizations to be as well structured or their members as well disciplined as those of subversive organizations.

(3) Indexes of Individuals

J. Edgar Hoover, as a Department of Justice attorney investigating sabotage during World War I, started to keep index cards on thousands of individuals. Hoover was placed in charge of the Justice Department's General Intelligence in August 3, 1919, and his wide-ranging investigation of radical activity resulted in 150,000 index cards by October 1920. The names of individuals arrested during the Palmer Raids came from Hoover's list.

Custodial Detention List: The FBI, under a 1939 Presidential directive, took charge of investigative matters relating to espionage, sabotage and violations of neutrality regulations. It compiled a "suspect list" of individuals considered to exhibit Nazi or Communist tendencies. FBI offices were instructed to submit names of individuals to be considered for custodial detention in the event of a

"It *does* frighten one. It is the special file on dissenters."

national emergency.

Security Index: In July 1943, the Attorney General advised the FBI that no legal justification existed for maintaining the Custodial Detention List. However, the FBI did not destroy the list, but instead renamed it the Security Index. In 1946, the FBI advised the Justice Department of its intention to compile a list of Communist Party members and others who it considered dangerous if diplomatic relations with the Soviet Union were broken. The Justice Department responded by developing a new detention plan to be used during a national emergency. In 1950, Congress enacted the Internal Security Act. Title II of the Act, called the Emergency Detention Act, permitted the government to detain persons considered dangerous to internal security during a national crisis. By 1951, the Security Index contained 13,901 names and the criteria was later broadened to include members or affiliates of other left groups. With the rapid expansion of the list, the FBI and the Justice Department established three categories of importance. Priority I was names of national and state leadership of revolutionary organizations, and persons preparing for underground activity. Priority II was names of second-level leadership, and Priority III was all other names on the index. By 1954, the index had grown to approximately 26,000 names. The Index was allegedly discontinued in 1971 when the Emergency Detention Act was repealed.

Communist or Reserve Index: In addition to the Security Index, from 1948 to 1960 the FBI maintained a Communist Index which included persons known to be affiliated or sympathetic with the Communist Party. In 1956, this listing was called the Reserve Index and it included members from other left organizations. This Index was also abolished in 1971.

Administrative Index (ADEX): In 1971, when Congress withdrew the legal basis for maintaining the previous lists, the FBI received approval from Attorney General Mitchell to keep a list for "administrative purposes only." Thus, the FBI established ADEX "... solely to list individuals who constitute a potential or actual threat to the internal security of the United States and/or whose activities and statements indicate that they would resort to violent, illegal, or subversive means." ADEX was computerized at FBI headquarters in 1972, and in January 1976 the Index was allegedly terminated.

Rabble-Rouser or Agitator Index: In response to the Black urban rebellions and the anti-war movement, the FBI created the Rabble-Rouser Index in August 1967 "to follow the activities of extremists who had demonstrated by their actions and speeches a propensity for fomenting disorders of a racial and/or security nature." This index provided personal data and a short summary of activities of the indexed individuals. In 1968, it was renamed the Agitator Index. In October 1970, five months before it was discontinued, the Index contained 1,131 names.

(4) Investigate and Disrupt the Leadership

In 1968 and 1970, the FBI initiated respectively the key activist and the key extremist programs to gain intelligence on the day-to-day activities and future plans of various leaders. An FBI internal memorandum stated that, "we should cover every facet of their current activities, future plans, weaknesses, strengths, and personal lives to neutralize the effectiveness . . . [of Key Black Extremists]."

FBI officials found the principal way to neutralize leadership was to tie them up in the courts and perhaps prison. In justifying their Key Activist program, the FBI announced that

more than one-half of those being investigated were under prosecution. In order to develop evidence (often fabricated) for a prosecution, the FBI used high-level infiltrators and electronic and physical surveillance. Also, in the early 1970's, the FBI's intelligence investigations became more efficient through the use of computers. The existence of this program was supposedly unknown outside the FBI.

Stop Index: The computer was used to develop a file of key individuals and to follow their travel and activities. The Stop Index included information supplied by local and state police agencies to the computerized National Crime Information Center (NCIC). Criteria for inclusion in the Stop Index were considerable travel, active participation in subversive or extremist activities and a strong propensity for violence. Of specific interest were Venceremos Brigade members, Weatherman suspects and individuals from the high priority ADEX file. When the Stop Index was allegedly discontinued in 1974, the computer contained 4,300 names.

Foreign Travel of Extremists and Other Subversives: The FBI was so concerned about the foreign travel of new left and Black activists that it maintained a computerized file, especially of travel to communist countries. An official from the FBI's Intelligence Division admitted that these investigations have found no evidence that left organizations are controlled or directed by foreign governments. This project was allegedly discontinued in 1973 "because the small number of submissions from field offices made the program financially inefficient."

Computerized Telephone Number File: Originally created in 1969 for criminal investigations, this file was expanded in 1971 to include domestic intelligence investigations. The main purpose of the computerized analysis was to map out the interrelationship of left individuals and organizations. Telephone numbers used by leftists were entered on the computer. The FBI would analyze what numbers were called and with what frequency. The telephone company would also supply the FBI with the toll records of all numbers listed on the computer. During a two year period (1971-73), 83,913 telephone numbers were processed through this computerized file.

Primary investigative techniques used by the FBI are 1) infiltration, 2) electronic surveillance (usually without a warrant), 3) mail covers (examining envelopes to determine the addressee and the addressor), 4) mail openings, 5) surreptitious entries, and 6) access to Federal income tax returns. The FBI also has established the False Identities program to investigate the trend toward clandestine activity. The FBI is concerned about the increasing use of false identity papers and realizes this trend will continue as clandestine work becomes an important aspect of revolutionary activity. In May 1974, the FBI called a conference on false identification which led to the creation of the Federal Advisory Committee on False Identification to study the extent of the problem and to propose remedies.

COINTELPRO: Another Counterintelligence Watchdog

On the night of March 8, 1971, a group calling themselves the Citizens' Committee to Investigate the FBI "liberated" hundreds of political documents from the FBI branch office in Media, Pennsylvania.[14] It was from the Media papers that FBI "COINTELPRO" activities first became public knowledge.

COINTELPRO is a general term to describe seven separate "counterintelligence" programs which the Bureau implemented at various times between 1956 and 1971. In 1973, under a U.S. District Court order, FBI Director Kelley was forced to release COINTELPRO—New Left, describing counterintelligence practices conducted against radical and anti-war groups. The release of COINTELPRO-New Left subsequently led to the release on November 18, 1974, of additional FBI documents that shed further light on domestic political surveillance, sabotage and infiltration.[15] These documents point out that COINTELPRO programs additionally functioned against the Communist Party—U.S.A. (CPUSA), Socialist Workers Party (SWP), White Hate Groups, and so-called Black Extremist groups as well as certain foreign-based intelligence services.

According to COINTELPRO documents, the earliest known COINTELPRO activities were against the CPUSA in 1956.

The activities carried out by COINTELPRO were considered "legitimate" and "proper" intelligence practices. What was *new* was the *targeting* of these activities against a specific group or category of organizations.

In October 1961, as a "direct outgrowth" of COINTELPRO-CPUSA, an order was given to establish a counterintelligence program based on disruption against the Socialist Workers Party (SWP). The order called for "carefully thought out operations with the widest possible effect."[16]

The next COINTELPRO undertaking was against White Hate Groups. This program, which began in 1964, grew out of national pressure on the F.B.I. to stop right-wing, racist attacks, lynchings, burnings and other terrorist activities perpetrated against Blacks. In his strategy for carrying out this program, both Hoover's racism and political bias are clearly demonstrated. In a memo he cautioned his agents that there are only a "relative few individuals in each organization who use strong arm tactics."[17] His distinction between the "right-wing" being a "relative few individuals" and the "left-wing" being the *whole* organization is quite evident.

Soon (1967) COINTELPRO-Black Extremist was instituted and became a counter-subversive priority. The Bureau claimed these "extremist group activities" included "police shootings, inciting riots, sniper attacks as well as the leadership being sympathetic to communism." A memo from Hoover dated August 25, 1967, indicated that the aim was to "expose, disrupt, misdirect, discredit and otherwise neutralize black national groups." The goals set out by Hoover included: 1) Prevent the *coalition* (his emphasis) of militant Black nationalist groups, 2) Prevent the rise of a Black "Messiah" (Dr. King was a primary target at this time), 3) Prevent violence on part of Black nationalists, 4) Discredit the leadership, and 5) Prevent long range goals of Black nationalist organizations (here he particularly stressed "preventing the conversion" of young people).[18] Another Hoover memo dated May 11, 1970, (see below) shows an order for a disruptive-disinformation operation targeted against the Black Panther Party (BPP). Recent articles published by the Black Panther Intercommunal News Service have suggested that COINTELPRO (among other counter-intelligence agencies) was involved in many attacks against the Panthers, including the assassination of Chicago Black Panther Party Chairman Fred Hampton. Hoover, himself, often publically attacked the Panthers as the number one threat in the nation—calling them "thugs," "criminals" and "hoodlums."

From the Fifth Estate *Intelligence Report:*

SAC, San Francisco   5/11/70
Director, FBI

COUNTERINTELLIGENCE AND SPECIAL OPERATIONS (RESEARCH SECTION)

The Bureau would like to offer for your consideration a proposal for a disruptive-disinformation operation targeted against the national office of the Black Panther Party (BPP). This proposal is not intended to be all inclusive or binding in any of its various phases, but only is a guide for the suggested action. You are encouraged to submit recommendations relating to revisions or innovations of the proposal.

1. The operation would be affected through close coordination on a high level with the Oakland or San Francisco Police Department.

2. Xerox copies of true documents, documents subtly incorporating false information, and entirely fabricated documents would be periodically anonymously mailed to the residence of a key Panther leader. These documents would be on the stationery and in the form used by the police department or by the FBI in disseminating information to the police. FBI documents, when used, would contain police routing or date received notations, clearly indicating they had been pilfered from police files.

3. An attempt would be made to give the Panther recipient the impression the documents were stolen from police files by a disgruntled police employee sympathetic to the Panthers. After initial mailings, brief notes by the alleged disgruntled employee would be included with the mailed documents. These notes would indicate the motive and sympathy of the police employee, his bitterness against his department, and possibly a request for money.

4. Depending on developments, at a propitious time, consideration would be given to establishing a post office box or other suitable "drop" address for the use of the alleged disgruntled employee to receive responses, funds, and/or specifications relating to the documents from the Panthers.

Fred Hampton

5. Although the operation may not require inclusion of a live source to represent the disgruntled employee, circumstances might warrant the use of such a source for face-to-face meetings with the Panthers. During early stages of the operation, an effort should be made to locate and brief a suitable police employee to play the role of the alleged disgruntled employee.

6. A wide variety of alleged authentic police or FBI material could be carefully selected or prepared for furnishing to the Panthers. Reports, blind memoranda, LHMs, and other alleged police or FBI documents could be prepared pinpointing Panthers as police or FBI informants; ridiculing or discrediting Panther leaders through their ineptness or personal escapades; espousing personal philosophies and promoting factionalism among BPP members; indicating electronic coverage where none exists; outlining fictitious plans for police raids or other counteractions; revealing misuse or misappropriation of Panther funds; pointing out instances of political disorientation; etc. The nature of the disruptive material and disinformation "leaked" would only be limited by the collection ability of your sources and the need to insure the protection of their security.

Effective implementation of this proposal logically could not help but disrupt and confuse Panther activities. Even if they were to suspect FBI or police involvement, they would be unable to ignore factual material brought to their attention through this channel. The operation would afford us a continuing means to furnish the Panther leadership true information which is to our interest that they know and disinformation which, in their interest, they may not ignore.

Although this proposal is a relatively simple technique, it has been applied with exceptional results in another area of intelligence interest where the target was of far greater sophistication. The Bureau believes with careful planning this technique has excellent long-range potential to disrupt and curtail Panther activity.

San Francisco is requested to submit comments and/or recommendations relating to the implementation of this proposal.

Copies of this letter have been designated for Los Angeles for background and information purposes. Any suggestion Los Angeles may have for strengthening or further implementing the technique will be appreciated.

(Last paragraph deleted by FBI)

The last domestic COINTELPRO was instituted in 1968 against the "New Left." In a December 7, 1973, press release, F.B.I. Director Kelley stated,

In the late 1960's, a hard core revolutionary movement which came to be known as the "New Left" set out, in its own words, to bring the Government to its knees through the use of force and violence.

... At this time of national crisis, the Government would have been derelict in its duty had it not taken measures to protect the fabric of our society ... Because of the violent actions of the leadership of the New Left, F.B.I. officials concluded that some additional effort must be made to neutralize and disrupt this revolutionary movement. This effort was called ... "COINTELPRO-New Left." [19]

As with other COINTELPRO programs, COINTELPRO-New Left called for a wide range of counter-insurgency actions. Much of the program centered on "neutralizing" the anti-war movement.

In all, some 2,370 disruptive actions were carried out under these programs. On April 20, 1971, six weeks after the "Media Papers" exposure, Hoover called for a termination of all COINTELPRO activities,[20] but left very open the question of further counterintelligence operations. In a directive, he informed his field agents that, "In exceptional instances where it is considered counter-intelligence action is warranted, recommendations should be submitted to the bureau under the code caption to which it pertains. These recommendations will be considered on an individual basis."[21]

112

While the COINTELPRO programs have been formally phased out, the use of the tactics they utilized has not. At a press conference on November 18, 1974, Attorney General William Saxbe and F.B.I. Director Clarence Kelley disagreed sharply over the question of the F.B.I.'s future policy on political surveillance and disruption. Saxbe, who legally is Kelley's boss, vowed to prevent a recurrence of anything like COINTELPRO. Kelley, on the other hand, defended the program, arguing that it had "helped bring about a favorable change"[22] and that failure to have carried out such disruptive actions would have been an abdication of duty by the F.B.I. In the future, Kelley went on, the F.B.I. might well engage in the same actions again "under emergency situations." Saxbe's attempt to regain public confidence was based on his formal power over Kelley, but even in the event that denouncing COINTELPRO was intended as more than a public relations stunt, it must be remembered that the previous attorneys general denied any knowledge of the existence of COINTELPRO. Kelley himself admitted that although the attorneys general were informed of some of the activities carried out against right wing groups, they were not informed of actions against Black groups or the New Left.[23]

Although COINTELPRO is "officially" dead, the theory and method behind it are very much alive.

One of the most important sections of a twenty-one page document released by the Justice Department on COINTELPRO is called "Analysis of Types of Activities Conducted Under COINTELPRO Domestic-Based Programs." This section lays out the tactics that the Bureau used against the Movement. Some of the tactics used in all the programs are:

1. Sending anonymous or fictitious materials to members or groups

The vast majority of these actions consisted of information designed to create dissension and cause disruption within the various groups. Of the total number of actions implemented under all five domestic based programs, approximately 40% fell under this category.

2. Dissemination of public record information

SAC, Baltimore
Director, FBI
COUNTERINTELLIGENCE PROGRAM
BLACK NATIONALIST - HATE GROUPS
RACIAL INTELLIGENCE (BLACK PANTHER PARTY)
(SUDED 12/2/68)

. . .

        In order to fully capitalize upon BPP and US differences as well as to exploit all avenues of creating further dissension in the ranks of the BPP, recipient offices are instructed to submit imaginative and hard-hitting counterintelligence measures aimed at crippling the BPP.

. . .

2 - Boston
2 - Chicago
2 - Cleveland
2 - Denver
2 - Indianapolis
2 - Los Angeles
2 - Newark
2 - New York
2 - Omaha
2 - Sacramento
2 - San Diego
2 - San Francisco
2 - Seattle

Cartoons distributed by the FBI in 1968-69 to provoke deadly conflicts between the US organization led by Ron Karenga and the Black Panther Party, whose members included Dave Hilliard, Bobby Seale, etc. Above, excerpts from an FBI memo leading to the use of such tactics.

113

to media sources

Actions implemented under this category consisted primarily of making public source material available to friendly media representatives for the purpose of using such material in a newspaper, magazine, or radio or television program in order to expose the aims and activities of the various groups. This type of activity represented approximately 20% of all actions implemented under domestic COINTELPRO efforts.

3. Leaking informant based or non-public information to media sources

Most of the actions implemented in this category related to the leaking of investigative material to friendly media sources for the purpose of exposing the nature, aims and membership of the various groups.

4. Advising local, State and Federal authorities of civil and criminal violations by group members

This activity—which is legal—represented approximately 8% of the total number of actions implemented under all five domestic based programs.

5. Use of informants to disrupt a group's activities

Most of the actions implemented under this category were for the purpose of using informants to disrupt the activities of various groups by sowing dissension and exploiting disputes. This type of activity represented less than 2% of the activities undertaken in connection with the four other (besides CPUSA) domestic based COINTELPRO programs.

6. Informing employers, credit bureaus and creditors of members' activities

The majority of actions implemented under this category consisted of notifying credit bureaus, creditors, employers and prospective employers of members' illegal, immoral, radical and Communist Party activities in order to affect adversely their credit standing or employment status.

7. Informing or contacting businesses and persons with whom members had economic dealings of members' activities.

The majority of actions implemented under this category consisted of notifying persons or businesses with whom members had economic

dealings of the members' association with the various groups involved for the purpose of adversely affecting their economic interests (mostly used against so-called Black Extremists).

8. Interviewing or contacting members

This type of activity—again, totally legal—was implemented in only a small number of instances for the purpose of letting members know that the F.B.I. was aware of their activity and also in an attempt to develop them as informants. It should be noted that many F.B.I. field offices carried on this activity routinely but did not attribute it to a counterintelligence function but rather to the routine investigation of individuals or organizations.

9. Attempting to use religious and civil leaders and organizations in disruptive activities

The majority of actions implemented under this category involved furnishing information to civic and religious leaders and organizations in order to gain their support and to persuade them to exert pressure on state and local governments, employers and landlords to the detriment of the various groups (used mostly in connection with Black Extremists).

10. Activity related to political or judicial processes

Although small in number (12), the actions in this category are among the most troubling of all the COINTELPRO efforts. Consequently, we will describe these tactics in detail, as follows: tipping off the press that a write-in candidate for Congress would be attending a group's meeting at a specific time and place; leaking information to the press that a group official was actively campaigning for a person running for public office; furnishing the arrest and conviction record of a member of a group who was a candidate for a local public office to a friendly newspaper which published the information; sending an anonymous letter to a political candidate alerting him that a group's members were active in his campaign and asking that he not be a tool of the group; sending an anonymous letter to a local school board official, purporting to be from a concerned parent, alerting him that candidates for the school board were members of a group; mailing an anonymous letter to a member of a group who was a mayoralty candidate in order to create distrust toward his comrades; furnishing information to news media on a group member running for public office, including data on arrests and marital status; furnishing public source data on a group to a local grand jury chairman who had requested it in connection with the grand jury's probe of the shooting of police by group members; furnishing information concerning arrests of an individual to a court that had earlier given this individual a suspended sentence and also furnishing this same information to his employer who later discharged the individual; making an anonymous telephone call to a defense attorney, after a Federal prosecution had resulted in a mistrial, advising him (apparently falsely) that one of the defendants and another well known group individual were F.B.I. informants.

11. *Establishing sham organizations for disruptive purposes*

This type of activity was utilized only in connection with the White Hate Groups program and was implemented in only five instances primarily for the purpose of using the organizations to send out material intended to disrupt various such groups.

12. *Informing family or others of radical or immoral activity by persons known to them.*

The majority of actions implemented under this category involved the sending of anonymous communications to family members or groups to which individuals belonged advising them of immoral or radical activities by persons known to them. For example, making telephone calls to parents of members of a group advising them of the connections of their children with the group; or advising the parents of a group leader that his or her actions will put the leader in danger.

In addition to these twelve categories of actions, there were about twenty miscellaneous actions which do not fit in any category. The most outrageous examples of these are:
—arranging for local police to stop two group members on a narcotics pretext, and having a police operator radio to the officer's car that a person who is also a member of the group wants the officer to call that member. The purpose of this is to have the two members who were stopped hear the radio message and suspect that the person mentioned is a police informer.
—use of citizen band radio, using the same frequency being used by demonstrators, to provide disinformation.
—reproducing a group leader's signature stamp.
—obtaining tax returns of group members, in hopes of finding errors or misstatements to use against them.
—reproducing a group's recruiting card.
—investigating the love life of a group leader, for dissemination to the press.

THE ROLE OF LOCAL POLICE

Local police departments began to expand their intelligence-gathering operations in response to the Black liberation and anti-war movements of the 1960's. The Watts uprising in 1964 revealed to the Justice Department that local police did not have "any useful intelligence or knowledge about ghettos, about black communities in the big cities."[24] The local nature of police departments was seen as offering the potential for developing this information. The police were to develop "procedures for the acquisition and channeling of intelligence" for "those who need it."[25] Following the rebellions in Detroit and Newark in 1967, this recommendation was repeated by the National Advisory Commission on Civil Disorders:[26]

> An intelligence unit staffed with full time personnel should be established to gather, evaluate, analyze, and disseminate information on potential as well as actual civil disorders . . . It should use undercover police personnel and informants . . .

As a result of this need, the FBI has become the national center and clearinghouse for intelligence gathered by local police departments. (See chapter 21, E, for a sample of intelligence projects created in California through Federal funding.) While there are no specific written agreements regulating the exchange of information between the FBI and state and local police, the FBI almost always

115

ALBUQUERQUE POLICE DEPARTMENT
CRIMINAL INTELLIGENCE UNIT
P. O. BOX 25806

Known Offenders
Extremists
Organized Crime

"Information is our thing"

DETECTIVE HENRY NUNEZ
766-7066   766-7613   766-7650   766-7652

receives what it asks for. [It must also be remembered that the Bureau not only passively receives information from the police, but actively directs their attention to specific individuals and organizations.]

The recent GAO study reveals, however, that the FBI receives a lot more information than it gives out to police. In a recent interview, Lt. J. O. Brannon, a police officer in the Houston Police Department's intelligence unit, put it this way:

> "The FBI is a good organization, but it's useless to us. It prides itself on its files, but do you know where the information in the FBI files comes from? Your local police department. They come over here and have access to everything they want, but when we try to get some information on a suspect from them, it's a different story. They pull the guy's file, then sit there holding it, and say, 'Okay, what do you want to know?' Well, I want to look through the whole file, but they won't allow that. They won't even let us hold it in our hands. They figure we're a bunch of dumb-dumbs, and we figure they're a bunch of bureaucrats, and it's hard to break down that barrier."[27]

Thus while the Bureau is centralizing the domestic intelligence gathering operations of the police, it is retaining control over these operations through its monopoly of information.

Almost every major city police department has its own intelligence unit for political surveillance. These units are always hidden within the police organizational structure, sometimes under the cover of Internal Security, Inspectional Services, or Organized Crime details. By 1968, the Detroit police had 75

officers in such a unit; Boston had 40; New York had 90 with 55 additional undercover; and by 1970 Los Angeles had 167 agents.[28] The trend is toward very rapid growth of these units.

The relations between these units have been characterized by competition rather than cooperation, by anarchy rather than by planned joint work. In the recent trial of the San Quentin Six, for example, it was revealed that the Los Angeles Police Department's Criminal Conspiracy Section and the state's Criminal Identification and Investigation agency had developed two separate plans to kill George Jackson.[29] This is due mainly to the nature of the work; given its illegal nature and its need for secrecy, most units have enough problems preserving their security within their own department much less worrying about the reliability of other police. But the main trend is toward coordination of this work through the FBI.

THE LAW ENFORCEMENT INTELLIGENCE UNIT

In addition to the FBI, there is another organization that coordinates police intelligence work—the Law Enforcement Intelligence Unit (LEIU). The LEIU is a private organization of about 230 police intelligence units in the major cities of the U.S. and Canada. As a private organization, the LEIU operates beyond the reach of city, state and Federal governments, exchanging files and conducting investigations, and is virtually unknown outside police circles.

The LEIU was founded in March 1956 at a secret meeting called by top California police officials and attended by representatives of twenty-six police and sheriff's departments from seven western states. A former member described its purpose:

> "He (Captain Hamilton, founder of LEIU and head of Los Angeles Police intelligence at the time) wanted to take police intelligence away from the FBI. Police departments do the street-level work to collect information and Hamilton didn't like the idea of turning it over to the FBI and making them the monitor; so he formed the

Former FBI agent Virginia Miller, also called "Blue Dove," as she is in real life and in her Indian disguise. In 1973-76, supported by local California police, she infiltrated the American Indian Movement (AIM) and framed Paul Skyhorse, Richard Mohawk, and others.

LEIU to circumvent the FBI's network. It was established to form an intelligence network independent of any Federal agency."[30]

This purpose is being carried out today; the LEIU files are the private property of its membership, and are not shared with other government agencies, civilians, or even other police officers in the department to which the intelligence unit is attached. In some cases, a single officer is designated as an affiliate member of the LEIU; he is then the only person in the department who has access to the files.

Membership in the LEIU is far from automatic. A police intelligence unit must be sponsored by a member agency and recommended by three more members. Upon application by a unit, all members are notified and a thorough investigation is made of the applicant agency and the individual officers who would be working with the LEIU. An executive board makes the final decision.

While it is a private organization, the LEIU enjoys extensive support of state and Federal government agencies. The files of the LEIU are coordinated and centralized by the Special Services Section of the Bureau of Criminal Identification and Investigation, a branch of California's Department of Justice Law Enforcement Division. Cards are made up and sent to member agencies to be kept in specially locked file cabinets. Some of the LEIU files are entered into a computerized file system operated by the LEIU under a 1.3 million dollar grant from the LEAA. The Interstate Organized Crime Index, as it is called, is an international network centered in the Michigan State Police computer in East Lansing, Michigan. In 1975, following the domestic spying scandals, the project was defunded, but the LEIU expects the project to be renewed soon.

Since its beginning, the LEIU has constantly defended itself against charges that it is engaged in domestic political surveillance, insisting that

117

THE MANY
FACES
OF
DOUG DURHAM

CEDAR RAPIDS, IA
18782   3·9·71

it is only concerned with organized crime. Recent disclosures by the Houston Police Department (a member agency) and Douglass Durham (a former member) show that the LEIU is in fact engaged in gathering information on political activists. Durham, a member of the Des Moines Police Department at the time, infiltrated the American Indian Movement and became its national security director. From this position he passed information on AIM's membership and legal defense efforts and attempted to frame two AIM members on a murder charge.[31] The Houston Police Department was the subject of a recent investigation that disclosed its 10 year spying program carried out with the help of Southwestern Bell Telephone, which provided information for more than one thousand files on Black activists,

civil libertarians and politicians. In fact, the general chairman of the LEIU in 1974, Donald Carroll, told a U.S. Senate committee investigating criminal justice data banks that LEIU targets were defined as "individuals and organizations involved in, *but not necessarily limited* to organized crime" (emphasis added). Another LEIU member recently admitted that the LEIU data base contains "a few of what I would call 'arrested or identified terrorists.' "[32]

It is safe to assume that the police intelligence network developed by LEIU is taking advantage of the organization's private status for the purpose of political surveillance. It provides the most secure information gathering and sharing system the police have developed, and is beyond the reach of public accountability.

CASE STUDY: CHICAGO

The operations of the Chicago Police Department's Security Section (SS) were recently exposed by a lengthy grand jury investigation which began after the Afro-American Patrolman's League requested a subpoena of the Chicago Police Department's files on the League. The investigation uncovered the operations of the SS in conjunction with the FBI, CIA, U.S. Army Intelligence and a right wing terrorist group which were aimed at destroying and disrupting anti-war and Black organizations and discrediting political opponents of Mayor Richard Daley.[33] Undoubtedly, the most important work of the SS escaped investigation; notably absent from the report of the grand jury are any references to the assassination of Fred Hampton, and surveillance of communist and Puerto Rican nationalist organizations active in Chicago. Nevertheless, this remains one of the most complete exposures of an intelligence unit and it is useful to study. Between 1967 and 1972, then Superintendent of Police James Conlisk met several times with the CIA for the purpose of strengthening the department's political intelligence work. During this time, he also attended, along with other Chicago police, weapons demonstrations and training sessions on the CIA's Virginia "farm." Chicago police received training, along with police from other departments, in clandestine operations, intelligence theory, explosive detection and disarmament, lock picking, and electronic surveillance and counter-surveillance.[34] At that time, then CIA director Richard Helms had offered the agency's help to five major city police departments for the purpose of developing their intelligence gathering and recording systems. According to Helms, only Chicago accepted, and the agency worked there in 1969-70.

The Chicago police then launched a massive intelligence gathering operation, infiltrating 57 Black, anti-repression, civil liberties and community organizations. These included the ACLU, Southern Christian Leadership Conference, People United to Save Humanity, Alliance to End Repression, and, on orders from the FBI, the Afro-American Patrolman's League. The agents attended the meetings of these organizations, recorded statements of members and sought to identify members and sources of finances of the organizations. In addition, several hundred informants, both paid and unpaid, volunteer and recruit, were established in these organizations.[35]

In some cases, agents and informants assumed leadership positions in these organizations up to and including the presidency. From these positions they had access to maximum information and influence over policy (in one case the agent succeeded in driving out the membership and bankrupting the organization). In classic fashion, agents in some organizations sought to incite members to violent confrontations with other organizations and/or the police (in one case the agent demonstrated the most effective downtown sniper posts and urged the assassination of police officers). The information gathered by these agents and informers was recorded in the files of the SS and passed on to the FBI and the U.S. Army 113th Military Intelligence Group headquartered in Evanston, Illinois.

The other part of the police department's domestic spying program was its work, in conjunction with the U.S. Army, with a right wing terrorist group, the Legion of Justice. The Legion first surfaced in 1969 under the leadership of an attorney, S. Thomas Sutton, a local right wing activist previously involved in the segregationist movement. Over the next three years, the Legion carried out a number of operations, including:

—raids on the offices of, theft of files from, arson, and beating and gassing of members of the Young Socialist Alliance and Socialist Workers Party
—theft of records of the Chicago Seven defense committee
—burglary of the office of Newsreel, a radical film distributor, to steal a Vietnamese film for the Pentagon
—tear gassing of a Soviet ballet performance and a performance of the Chinese acrobatic troupe

These operations were financed, directed and equipped by the SS and the 113th Military

119

Intelligence Group. Tear gas, mace, electronic surveillance devices, false identification, and expense money were all provided for Legion members. On a number of occasions the police also stood guard to make sure that other police did not arrest Legion burglars.

This picture of the operations of the Chicago police is far from complete. Clearly, the most important surveillance work remains known only to the Security Section itself; what was uncovered was mainly the least important and discontinued operations against liberal organizations. It would be a mistake to conclude from this that these operations represent a misguided, irrational "mistake" on the part of the police; in fact, they reveal, if only to a small degree, an essential part of the police role: suppressing popular movements which direct themselves against particular aspects of capitalist oppression (slum housing, repression, racism, etc.) or the capitalist system itself. While the police may misidentify the real strengths and purposes of some organizations, this should not obscure the fact that they are carrying out an essential police function, and that this function is recognized, directed and supported by the Federal state apparatus.

THE AGENT PROVOCATEUR
A Special Kind of Cop

All political police are basically *informer* (police prefer the term "informants"). Th informer may be a former group member wh defected ("stool pigeon") or a trained office who hides his/her true identity and joins group ("police infiltrator") or any private cit zen who for some reason—not always jus money—provides information to police ("pai informer"). And then there is that very impo tant type of informer, the *agent provocateur* who serves not merely to gather information i a passive way but becomes an actor, an activ participant in the group.

The provocateur's main function in th United States today is to provoke politica activists into illegal and/or violent action which then "justify" repression—which can b anything from criminal prosecution to on-the spot killing of activists. Provocateurs ar "super-militants" who incite others into foolis confrontation or violence with talk of "let's d something real—what's the matter, you chick en?" They play on the activist's frustration an

eams of guerrilla warfare, often forcing an
:tion that was never seriously intended, and
ius creating a set-up. Provocateurs sometimes
ke part themselves in the illegal action but
ore often they just provide the final inspira-
on or the weapon.

Provocateurs often begin as mere informers,
om either inside or outside the police force.
hey graduate to provocateurs for various
asons: police need for evidence, their own
eed to provide action which will justify their
ontinuation on the police payroll, or psycho-
gical drives in the individual provocateur such
; a desire for violence with no fear of being
osecuted. Whatever the reason, there is a
storic tendency for the informer to become
rovocateur, especially when the person is not a
gular police officer.

In a recent study of provocation, Paul
hevigny believes it was "originally a tool of
ternational espionage, brought over into
omestic politics." [36] Many nations provoked
r faked incidents to justify invasion and war
gainst other nations. The use of provocation
gainst people *within* a nation goes back at least
o France after the Revolution (the term, agent
rovocateur, is French). Later, in 1827, French
olice staged riots "to influence public opinion
n favor of the dominant order." [37] In Germany,
olice tried to frame Karl Marx and other Com-
nunists with faked documents about a sup-
osed conspiracy hatched in England, but the
vidence was exposed. These two incidents,

however, were not yet provocation in the
modern sense: they were pure fakery. [38] In Czar-
ist Russia, especially during the Bolshevik Revolution, the Okhrana (political police) used the
modern type of provocation. [39]

In the United States, provocateurs were
hired by private capitalists to destroy labor
struggles of the 1800's. They were used by officials in the Palmer Raids of 1919, to smoke out
radical labor organizers for arrest and/or deportation. J. Edgar Hoover used them to scare
Congress into giving the FBI more funds. In
1912, New York police instituted a "radical
bureau" (Bureau of Special Services, or BOSS)
against workers and radical groups. Today,
BOSS agents have been used to infiltrate and
provoke many radical organizations.

The use of provocation always increases
when the ruling class is trying to maintain its
control against a strong drive for social change.
It is a sign of political desperation, and may
indicate the coming of fascism. (However,
totally fascist societies do not use provocation,
simply because they have no use for legalistic
set-ups.) [40]

Traditionally, after an arrest is made the
charge is some type of conspiracy to overthrow
the government and the provocateur turns up as
chief witness for the state. Defense lawyers
often challenge the charge on the basis of "illegal entrapment." Entrapment is defined as
inducing an individual to commit *an act he or
she otherwise would not take part in*. Many

EXAMPLES OF AGENTS AS WITNESSES FOR THE STATE[43]

Agent	Agency	Organization Infiltrated
Ray Wood	N.Y. police (NYPD)	CORE, East Harlem Revolutionary Unit, Black Lib-eration Front, witness Statue of Liberty case.
Gene Roberts	NYPD	Malcolm X, Black Panther Party, witness Panther 21.
William Frapolly	Chicago PD	SDS, witness Chicago 8.
George Demmerle	FBI (informer)	Indictment of "Rat Bombers."
Larry Grathwohl	Cincinnati PD	Weatherpeople bombing conspiracy
Boyd Douglas	FBI (informer)	Berrigan conspiracy case.
Robert Hardy	FBI (informer)	Camden Draft Board bombing.
David Sannes	FBI (informer)	Seattle 7 Conspiracy Case
Tommy Tongyai	FBI (informer)	SDS, Hobart College bombing.
Douglas Durham	FBI (informer)	American Indian Movement.

Frank Martinez

judges, and much of the general public, disapprove of obvious entrapment. The case may backfire, especially if a mass defense campaign is mounted and there is wide exposure. Thus the state is tripped up by the same legal system that provocation is intended to utilize.

The state may answer by claiming it was not entrapment; it was "encouragement"—which is legal, and defined as "a set of techniques used by law enforcement agents to bring out the criminal intent in individuals *committed to* a particular type of illegal activity."[41] But whatever the terminology, the important point here is that the state sanctions and uses provocateurs. The extent of such use is indicated by a recent article that states:

> Of the 40 substantive witnesses for the prosecution of the Chicago Seven, 34 were undercover agents ... despite the growing use of electronic surveillance, several police authorities estimate that 90 percent of all intelligence gathered on the movement activity is the work of infiltrators and informers.[42]

The following account of the behavior o[f] one agent provocateur is presented in detail t[o] demonstrate the extent and nature of the use o[f] such agents to infiltrate and destroy progressiv[e] and radical organizations.

THE MARTINEZ CASE

"It does not pay to be an informer becaus[e] when they no longer need you, they'll fram[e] you."

Frank Martine[z]
Agent Provocateu[r]

Commenting to a local newspaper on ho[w] the police broke up the Chicano Moratoriu[m] Committee, Los Angeles Police Chief Dav[is] boasted:

> ... we had this orbiting satellite. That's t[he] way I'll put it, and when they'd (Brow[n] Berets) walk out with brass knuckles, w[e] made all those arrests, or an illegal gun o[r] something ... We were knocking them o[ff] right and left.[44]

That so-called "satellite" was one Eustac[io] Frank Martinez, informer/agent provocateur fo[r] the Alcohol, Tobacco and Firearms Enforc[e]ment Division (ATF) of the U.S. Treasur[y] Department. In October 1971 Martinez went t[o] La Casa de Carnalismo, a Chicano communit[y] anti-drug center, and told them he was an agen[t] and was willing to give evidence for the defens[e] in the case of "Los Tres del Barrio."[45] Subs[e]quently he was interviewed by members of L[a] Raza Unida, La Casa and Citizen's Research an[d] Investigation Committee. His story is a cas[e] study in the use of provocateurs.[46]

Following arrest for possession of an illeg[al] weapon in Houston, Texas, in 1969 he made [a] deal with ATF agent Tito Garcia to become a[n] informer/agent provocateur in return fo[r] dropped charges. His assignments included infi[l]tration of the Mexican American Youth Organ[i]zation (MAYO) and Brown Berets in Houston [and] to: 1) provide intelligence information on bot[h] groups and 2) to perpetrate acts of provocatio[n] and violence in his role as "militant Chican[o] leader." During this period he burned down [a] VISTA worker's house, provoked police vio[lence at a MAYO rally, and bought explosive[s] for the Brown Berets.

After his actions began to make him suspect in the Houston area, Martinez was sent to Los Angeles in 1970 to infiltrate the National Office of the Brown Berets and the National Chicano Moratorium Committee.[47] Under this assignment, he became the National Chairman of the Chicano Moratorium Committee and a high-ranking leader in the Brown Berets. During this time he "supplied intelligence information" for both organizations and "committed illegal acts" which led to police raids and arrest of organization members. He continually advocated violence and the use of illegal weapons, and stole documents and "perpetrated rumors" to discredit Chicano leader Rosalio Muñoz. In October of 1970 he organized a plan to disrupt with violence a campaign appearance of Senator John Tunney in East Los Angeles.

His next assignment was to infiltrate La Casa de Carnalismo. His job was to pick out leaders of the Chicano Liberation Front (CLF) that supposedly belonged to La Casa, and were responsible for recent bombings. He had full authority from his superiors to not only participate in any bombing attempts but to supply the explosives. Martinez later stated that the primary purpose of that organization as he saw it "was to eliminate drugs from the Chicano community."

In September, 1971 he appeared in court on charges arising out of a demonstration on August 29, 1971, the anniversary of the "Chicano Moratorium." His ATF superiors tried to frame him to plead guilty and be sent back to Texas. It was at this point that he defected.

CONCLUSION

During the recent period, there has been both a rapid expansion and diversification of the intelligence apparatus, and a growing popular dissatisfaction with its secrecy and contempt for civil liberties. While the modern system of political surveillance has its roots in the class and political struggles during the World War I era, beginning in the 1960's it developed much greater resources and sophistication in response to the Black and student movements. Recent exposures have documented a vast domestic intelligence apparatus— including the CIA, the military, and local police agencies in addition to the FBI—involved in assassinations, infiltration and disruption of legal political organizations, interference with constitutionally protected freedoms of assembly, speech and press, the collection of dossiers on progressive organizations and individuals, and more. This new information, resulting from Congressional and journalistic investigations, tells us a great deal about the functioning of the intelligence apparatus but the full story still remains to be told. Current proposals for legislative reform are for the most part designed to eliminate the gross abuses of political surveillance rather than attack its underlying functions. This ruling class concern for legitimating and reforming the institutions of repression is most clearly seen in the "velvet glove" police programs, which we address in the next section.

1. William Preston, *Aliens and Dissenters*, Cambridge: Harvard Univ. Press, 1963, chs. 7-8; Senate Select Committee to Study Governmental Operations with respect to Intelligence Activities (Church Committee), *Intelligence Activities and the Rights of Americans, Final Report, Book II*. Washington, D.C.: Government Printing Office, 1976, p. 21 fn.
2. Church Committee, p. 24 ff.
3. Ibid., p. 32.
4. Ibid., p. 48.
5. Ibid., pp. 78-81.
6. *New York Times*, June 7, 1973.
7. Huston Plan, in *New York Times*, June 7, 1973.
8. *New York Times*, November 11, 1974.
9. Ibid.
10. Ibid. Hoover never objected in principle to anything in the report. He just did not want *his* agents carrying out these objectives.
11. Church Committee, op. cit., p. 115.
12. Sanford Ungar, "Justice to Abolish Intelligence Panel," *The Washington Post*, May 13, 1973.
13. Seymour Hersh, "White House Unit Reportedly Spied on Radicals in '70s," *New York Times*, May 21, 1973.
14. The complete Media papers can be found in *Win* magazine, Vol. VIII, Nos. 4 and 5, March 1 and 15, 1972, and the majority of the "papers" along with analysis can be found in Paul Cowan, et al., *State Secrets*, New York, Holt, Rinehart and Winston, 1973, pp. 105-219.
15. Most of the information for the analysis of the

COINTELPRO documents came from the files in our library or directly from the materials released on November 18, 1974, by Attorney General Saxbe and FBI Director Clarence Kelly detailing certain aspects and activities of the Bureau's counterintelligence programs. The release is really only an outline of these programs. It deletes much of the information considered secret. It is therefore very difficult to understand the full extent of COINTELPRO operations.

16. Fifth Estate Intelligence Report, "COINTELPRO: An Analysis of the FBI Memos," reprinted from *Counter-Spy, The Journal of the Fifth Estate,* p. 1.

17. Ibid.

18. FBI memo from Director of FBI to SAC, Albany in Fifth Estate Intelligence Report.

19. Department of Justice release on COINTELPRO, p. 6.

20. The actual termination memo was from C. D. Brennan to W. C. Sullivan. Besides supervising COINTELPRO, Sullivan, now Assistant FBI Director, was part of the working group that established the Huston Plan.

21. Fifth Estate, op. cit., p. 4.

22. Quoted in Editorial, *The New York Times,* November 11, 1974.

23. *U.S. News and World Report,* December 2, 1974, p. 38.

24. Written testimony of Fred M. Vinson to the Church Committee, January 27, 1976, p. 32.

25. President's Commission on Law Enforcement and the Administration of Justice, *The Challenge of Crime in a Free Society,* Washington D.C.: Government Printing Office, 1967, p. 118-119.

26. *Report of the National Advisory Commission on Civil Disorders,* Washington D.C., Government Printing Office, 1968, p. 269.

27. George O'Toole, "America's Secret Police Network," *Penthouse,* December 1976, p. 204.

28. Frank Donner, "The Theory and Practice of American Political Intelligence," *The New York Review of Books,* April 22, 1971, p. 29.

29. See Karen Wald's articles in the *Guardian* newspaper on the San Quentin Six trial, especially "Quentin Defense Rests," *Guardian,* June 16, 1976, p. 9.

30. O'Toole, op. cit., p. 78.

31. *Guardian,* "FBI Pins Brutal Slaying on AIM," December 1, 1976.

32. O'Toole, op. cit., p. 194.

33. For a short summary see "Improper Police Intelligence Activities," A Report by the Extended March 1975 Cook County (Illinois) Grand Jury, November 10, 1975. The Repressio[n] Research Group has compiled a collection o[f] newspaper articles that detail the investigation[n.] Available for $3.00 from Repression Researc[h] Group, c/o Dr. Dan Stern, 5500 N. St. Louis Ave[.,] Chicago, Illinois 60625.

34. See Betty Washington, "Tell CIA, Conlisk Talk[ed] while He was Cop Chief," *Chicago Daily New[s,]* April 2, 1975; Commission on CIA Activiti[es] Within the United States (Rockefeller Commi[s]sion), *Report to the President,* Washington, D.C[.:] Government Printing Office, 1975, pp. 236-4[0,] 294-99; Richard Helms' testimony to the Sena[te] Foreign Relations Committee during his confirm[a]tion hearings for U.S. ambassadorship to Iran.

35. Larry Green and Rob Warden, "Police Spies aide[d] by Informer Army," *Chicago Daily News,* June [6,] 1975.

36. Paul Chevigny, *Cops and Rebels,* New Yor[k,] Pantheon Books, 1972, p. 223.

37. Ibid., p. 231.

38. Ibid., pp. 220-233.

39. Ibid., p. 238.

40. Ibid., p. 249.

41. Andrew Karmen, "Agents Provocateurs in th[e] Contemporary U.S. Leftist Movement," in Charl[es] Reasons, *The Criminologist: Crime and th[e] Criminal,* Pacific Palisades, California, Goodye[ar] Publishing Company, p. 210.

42. "Where are the Clark Kents of Yesteryear? The[y] are Infiltrating the Movement, and Here is How t[o] Get Rid of Them," *Ramparts,* December 1970.

43. These cases of agents provocateurs were take[n] from the following sources: Paul Cowan, et al[.,] *State Secrets,* pp. 17-19; CRIC, *The Glass Hous[e] Tapes,* pp. 133-180; and Anthony Platt and Lyn[n] Cooper, eds., *Policing America,* pp. 91-96.

44. CRIC and Louis Tackwood, *The Glass Hous[e] Tapes,* New York, Avon Books, 1973, p. 138.

45. Los Tres del Barrio were three Chican[o] community leaders (Juan Fernandez, Albert[o] Ortiz and Rodolfo Sanchez) charged wit[h] shooting a Federal Agent and sentenced to ove[r] 75 years in prison between them. Los Tres we[re] feared because they were beginning to organiz[e] the oppressed and expose the government[']s involvement in heroin trafficking. They were se[t] up, wounding the agent in pure self-defense.

46. Information in this discussion, including quot[a]tions, is from our file on Martinez. Especially use[e]ful was a joint press release by CRIC and La Cas[a] de Carnalismo dated January 31, 1972.

47. Martinez's superiors at ATF were Jim Riggs an[d] Fernando Ramos.

V. THE VELVET GLOVE

11. THE PACIFICATION MODEL

During the later 1960's, the technical and managerial approach to police work represented by the military-corporate model came under increasing criticism. More sophisticated analyses of crime and urban disorder suggested that massive spending on military hardware, by itself, would not only fail to stop rising crime rates and urban discontent, but would probably serve to further alienate large sectors of the population. This approach stressed the need for the police to develop closer ties to the communities most heavily patrolled by them. The emphasis began to be placed less on paramilitary efficiency and more on insuring popular consent and acquiescence. The idea that police departments should engage in some sort of "community relations" had, of course, been around for some time, but community relations programs, in practice, were few, and those that did exist were generally regarded as ineffective window-dressing. The new emphasis, on the other hand, represented a serious attempt to supplement the growing technological prowess of the police with programs that could make the police role more acceptable to the people most affected by it.

SOCIAL SCIENCE AND SOCIAL DISORDER

This focus on community pacification was strongly influenced by academic social science. The turmoils of the 1960's took most social scientists in the U.S. by surprise. Most of them operated on the assumptions of what was usually called the "consensus" model of U.S. society, which portrayed the country as a relatively conflict-free society in which most potentially disruptive political problems had been solved. The disorders of the sixties shattered this cheerful perspective and sent many social scientists scurrying to develop new theories that were more in line with the realities of Watts, Newark, and Detroit. Substantial amounts of money began to be poured into

126

research on the "urban crisis," and especially on the various parts of the criminal justice system. Although the specifics vary considerably, there are two common themes in much of this liberal social science of the sixties that have had an important (though sometimes indirect) influence on the new police-community pacification programs. The first was a theory of the causes of crime and urban violence that attempted to explain them as problems rooted in the culture or psychology of poor people rather than basic structural problems of U.S. society. The second was an emphasis on the decisive role played by the agencies of "social control" in influencing the level of violence and militancy in the cities.

VIOLENCE AND THE CULTURE OF THE POOR

American social scientists have traditionally downplayed or ignored the political and economic meaning of crime and mass social protest. Crime and rebellion have been defined as "irrational," purely "expressive" outbursts of mindless violence, without any genuine political content.[1] This perspective was developed further during the sixties. According to James Q. Wilson, for example—a Harvard political scientist whose work has had considerable influence on recent thinking about police strategy:

When people destroy their own communities, even at great risk to themselves . . . it is difficult to assert that the riot was an instrumental act—that is, an effort to achieve an objective . . . The Negro riots are in fact expressive acts—that is, actions which are either intrinsically satisfying ("play") or satisfying because they give expression to a state of mind.[2]

Another influential political scientist, Edward Banfield, has described the ghetto rebellions as "rampages" and "forays for pillage" that are undertaken "mainly for fun and profit."[3]

Social scientists in the 60's similarly built on an already existing "subculture" theories to explain the *source* of riots and of the spiralling rates of violent crime in the sixties. During the fifties, sociologists began to explain crime, and particularly juvenile delinquency, as the product of a lower-class "subculture" which promoted anti-middle-class values that supported delinquent behavior.[4] In the sixties, this idea was elaborated. Crime and rioting were described as resulting from a "subculture of violence" concentrated in the Black ghettoes; a set of values common to many (especially young, male) Blacks which supposedly justified the use of violence to solve personal and social problems.[5] A more recent variant of this argues that crime and violence (as well as much poverty) stems from the "culture of the lower class," defined as

> an outlook and style of life which is radically present-oriented and which therefore attaches no value to work, sacrifice, self-improvement, or service to family, friends, or community.[6]

The corollary to this was that, since crime, violence, and other urban problems were mainly due to "subcultural" values rather than economic deprivation or political oppression, political and economic change could have very little effect on them. According to many social scientists, the problem was steadily being aggravated because of the increasing concentration of "lower-class" people in the central cities. Overall, according to this argument, American society is becoming *less* rather than more violent, as the relative size of this "lower class" diminishes and more and more people take on the attitudes and life-style of the middle class. But in the inner cities themselves, this process is being reversed, as the more "stable" and "restrained" middle class people move out and are replaced by "an increasingly large proportion of persons who value a

lower-class life style."[7] In the crowded conditions of the urban slum, it is argued, these supposed "lower-class" tendencies toward criminality and violence are aggravated. In the city, Wilson writes,

> Those who are emotionally immature or possessed by explosive personalities and a desire for the immediate gratification of impulses will be more likely to encounter others who share these urges and thus who will reinforce them and reward their expression. What was once a habit of violence may become a subculture of violence.[8]

LEGITIMACY AND SOCIAL CONTROL

Since these social scientists deny the possibility of major social change and insist that the existing class structure is both necessary and relatively permanent, they assume that the presence of a "violence-prone" population in the cities must be taken as a fact of life. Because of this, sensible policy makers should forget about futile efforts to change broad social conditions and concentrate on ways of putting a lid on the predictable violence of the poor. As Wilson puts it, we must "learn to live with crime"; the crucial question becomes "what constitutes an effective law-enforcement and order-maintenance system?"[9]

This pessimism about the possibility of change is similar to that underlying the military-corporate model of police work, discussed above. Both emphasize increased social control, rather than social change, as the way to deal with crime. But behind the new "pacification" approach is the conviction that the control of urban crime and violence must become far more subtle than the military model suggests. For many U.S. social scientists, a key lesson from the riots of the 1960's was that purely repressive or overly mechanical and distant forms of official control were usually counterproductive, tending to aggravate the already volatile nature of the urban poor.

In an important paper originally written in 1968, for example, the University of Chicago sociologist Morris Janowitz showed how the

"counter-measures" used by police and National Guard during many of the ghetto riots had not only failed to stop the "spread of contagion," but had often led to the "escalation" of minor "outbursts" into major ones, and of major riots into more explicitly political forms of confrontation. According to Janowitz, the ineffective and blatantly unjust behavior of law-enforcement officials in the "lowest Negro income areas" had weakened the legitimacy of law enforcement as a whole among Blacks, thus feeding the growth of more militant politics and more strategic forms of violence in the ghettoes.[10] Similarly, many U.S. social scientists in the late sixties looked overseas for confirmation of the point that official violence and ineffectiveness could have disastrous results. One study, for example, done as a consultant paper for the Violence Commission, compared the response of the Batista regime in Cuba to that of Betancourt in Venezuela to revolutionary insurgency in their respective countries. The

inflexible and repressive response of the Batista government was found to have helped weaken the legitimacy of the whole regime and increased that of the revolutionaries, thereby helping to pave the way for the victory of the Cuban Revolution.[11]

This sense of the crucial role of law enforcement in strengthening or weakening the overall legitimacy of the political and economic system is a key theme in the "soft" approach to the police. It is assumed that the basic task of the police—handling and "managing" the conflict and violence coming from a hostile, permanent, and increasingly "strident" poor—is unlikely to change much in the near future. The pacification strategists are very much aware that a new factor has entered the picture: the increasing militancy and resistance to the police in poor and Third World communities. They therefore give most of their attention to ways in which the organization and routine street practices of the police can be modified in order to maximize their effectiveness at "order maintenance," while trying to avoid aggravating potential conflict or providing "fuel" for militants.

In addition to their criticism of over-reliance on technical "hardware,' these strategists also are wary of many other panaceas often offered as part of the simplistic "professional" approach to policing, such as "upgrading" police personnel. Instead, they emphasize small-scale, carefully designed experiments with such things as new techniques of patrol, special training programs in "sensitivity" and "conflict management," and various forms of police-community relations that stress citizen "input" into the police system. In line with this experimental emphasis, some pacification strategists call for the development of regional criminal justice research centers (either connected with universities or law-enforcement agencies, or as RAND-like private research centers), and for a Federal "demonstration and dissemination center" for new police techniques.[12] To date, the most important agency for putting this emphasis into practice is the Ford Foundation-sponsored Police Foundation, headquartered in Washington, D.C.

THE POLICE FOUNDATION

The Police Foundation was launched in 1970 with a $30 million grant from the Ford Foundation. It is presently headed by the liberal former police commissioner of New York, Patrick V. Murphy, and has a board of directors composed of many academic and professional police experts, including Harvard's James Q. Wilson. The Foundation's programs are mainly devoted to developing small-scale projects that affect the interaction between police and people on the street. One of the Police Foundation's earliest and most heavily funded projects, for example, was an experiment in "community sector team policing" (ComSec) in Cincinnati. This involved assigning small teams of police officers to operate in close contact with the residents of specific communities on a permanent basis. Instead of specialized officers being sent out from a central headquarters to perform various police functions, the community team would take care of all police functions (except murder investigations) in its neighborhood. The team's emphasis is on developing more intimate relations with people in the community than was normally possible under the usual centralized policing patterns, with the aim of developing "a feeling of trust and closeness" on the part of local residents toward the police (see "Team Policing," below).[13]

Another important Police Foundation project, in Kansas City, was designed to evaluate the effectiveness of different police patrol strategies. One Kansas City patrol division, for example, tested three kinds of patrol in three different neighborhoods. One was the standard form of neighborhood patrol; the second was a more aggressive kind of "preventive patrol"; and the third dropped the usual police patrol function completely, coming into the neighborhood only in response to citizen complaints. Preliminary findings from this study seem to show that the type of patrol made little difference in terms of rates of crime. The Kansas City Department is now testing what they call "inter-active patrol," which tries to

129

gain closer ties to the community by such devices as having citizens ride in patrol cars.[14]

Another Kansas City division is developing a procedure for identifying officers whose repeated mistreatment of community residents might "not only induce ill-feeling and uncooperative attitudes among citizens, but also provoke incidents involving violence against the police." Still another division is experimenting with a special unit to operate in neighborhoods with high levels of crime and police-community conflict. This unit is designed to increase the level of personal contact between the police and community people, to refer people to "appropriate community agencies" if necessary, and generally to develop "neighborhood mechanisms for dealing with social problems" in order to get at the "root conditions" underlying crime and social conflict in the community.[15]

Other Police Foundation programs include experiments in "diversion" of drug offenders from the criminal justice system, evaluating the special uses of women and minority people in police forces (see "Women on Patrol," below), and setting up joint police-citizen "task forces"

to study and make recommendations abou specific police policies. In all of these areas, th Police Foundation encourages small, experi mental programs aimed at discovering ways t integrate the police more closely with th community, and vice versa, in order to achiev an acceptance of the police function that th more centralized, super-"professional" polic style was not able to gain.

CONCLUSION

As this suggests, the new community pacif cation strategies do not involve a real transfe of control of police work from the polic themselves to the communities they affect. Th architects of these strategies explicitly reje the idea of community control of the polic They usually argue that community contr would lead to a kind of "local tyranny" i which the benevolent "neutrality" of the polic would be replaced by the rule of "the rawe emotions, the most demagogic spokesmen, an the most provincial concerns."[16] From the perspective, it is useful to decentralize polic *functions* without decentralizing police *autho ity:* that is, the police should have clos contact with the community, but the commu nity should not be allowed to have any re influence on the police.[17] The aim of this kin of decentralization is to enable the police t integrate some citizens into the lower levels the police system itself, on police term thereby blurring the distinction between th police and the people they control.

A prime example of this is the growing us of "citizen's auxiliaries" who will in effect d much of the police department's work fo them, by self-policing their communities in manner dictated by the police and designed t lend legitimacy to the whole police functio Several cities, including Los Angeles and Ne York, have adopted this idea in some form: i New York, auxiliary police help patrol Centr Park, on foot, bicycle, and horseback. A city wide "Citizens Patrol Program" has trained ove 6,000 civilians to engage in observing an reporting crime in 25 precincts. In Dayto Ohio, a LEAA-funded "Neighborhood Assi tance Program" involves over 100 civilians, dressed in a* uniform of blazer and slacks, dealing with a variety of minor complaints, service calls, and traffic duties. And the Los Angeles County Sheriff's Department has trained over 37,000 Boy Scouts to help local police departments across the country in various kinds of minor police work. But police strategists explicitly warn of the danger that such citizens' auxiliaries might come to see their role as "not to police the neighborhood, but to police the police by reporting on official misconduct."[18] From the police point of view, this would be a disaster, since the aim of this kind of "citizen participation" is not to increase the accountability of the police but to enable them to penetrate the community more cheaply and more effectively.

The pacification strategists are interested in the community's response only to the extent that it helps the police more effectively "manage" the community's problems. Particular police policies are to be weighed on a "cost-benefit" scale, balancing "gains in public safety against the costs in police-community relations."[19] Although their impact in the long run is hard to judge, these new "soft" strategies of policing must be regarded as some of the first feelers in an emerging set of sophisticated strategies of penetration and control of the ghettoes, barrios, and other "explosive" communities—strategies in which a certain amount of carefully controlled 'community "input," token channels for complaints and popular review of official practices, and other techniques are used to gloss over the fact of continuing repression. It's important to understand that such strategies are not confined to the police alone. Similar approaches are increasingly evident in the prison system, for example, where various kinds of "community treatment" programs are flourishing which have a veneer of citizen participation while actually extending the range of control of the prison authorities. And in industry, various schemes of strictly limited "worker participation" have increasingly been used to help ward off workers' demands for real control of their workplaces.

In the following chapters, we will take a closer look at two illustrations of the pacification approach: the recent drive to recruit women police, and the development of the concept of "team policing."

1. For a discussion of this tradition, see Jerome H. Skolnick, ed. *The Politics of Protest*, New York, Bantam Books, 1969, Chapter 9.
2. James Q. Wilson, "Violence," in Daniel Bell, ed., *Toward the Year 2000: Works in Progress*, Boston, Beacon Press, 1969, p. 288.
3. Edward Banfield, *The Unheavenly City*, Boston, Little Brown, Inc., 1971, Chapter 9.
4. See, for example, Richard Cloward and Lloyd Ohlin, *Delinquency and Opportunity*, New York, Free Press, 1959.
5. Marvin Wolfgang and Franco Ferracuti, *The Subculture of Violence*, New York, Universities Press, 1967.
6. Banfield, op. cit., p. 211.
7. Wilson, "The Future Policeman's Role," in American Justice Institute, *Project Star*, Los Angeles, 1972, p. 5.
8. Wilson, "Violence," op. cit., p. 285.
9. Wilson, "Crime and Law Enforcement," in Kermit Gordon, ed., *Agenda for the Nation*, Washington, Brookings Institution, 1969, pp. 199, 204.
10. Morris Janowitz, "Social Control of Escalated Riots," in Ted Gurr and Hugh Graham, eds., *Violence in America*, New York, Bantam Books, 1969.
11. Edward Gude, "Batista and Betancourt: Alternative Responses to Violence," in Gurr and Graham, op. cit., pp. 731-748.
12. Wilson, "Crime and Law Enforcement," op. cit., pp. 201-202.
13. Police Foundation, *Experiments in Police Improvement: A Progress Report*, Washington, D.C., November 1972, p. 28.
14. Ford Foundation, *Criminal Justice*, New York, Ford Foundation, 1974, p. 9.
15. Police Foundation, op. cit., p. 30.
16. Wilson, *Varieties of Police Behavior*, Cambridge, Harvard University Press, 1968, p. 289. For a similar point of view, see Albert Reiss, *The Police and the Public*, New Haven, Yale University Press, 1971.
17. Wilson, *Varieties of Police Behavior*, op. cit., p. 290.
18. Wilson, "Crime and Law Enforcement," op. cit., p. 186.
19. Ibid., p. 188.

12. WOMEN ON PATROL

In 1967, the President's Crime Commission pointed out that there was a serious "manpower" crisis in police forces, and a great need to begin to attract new kinds of people to police work. The Commission especially pointed to the need for police departments to recruit college-educated people, minorities, and women. In the late 1960's, many departments undertook fairly serious efforts to hire more college-educated and Third World people. But for a variety of reasons—including the internal racism of most departments and the unattractiveness of police work for many college graduates—these efforts were largely a failure. The *New York Times* pointed out in early 1971 that on many forces, the percentage of Blacks was the same as it had been 10 years before, and had actually declined in some departments.[1] In the face of this failure, police strategists began casting about for alternative sources of personnel, and they focused on the source that had been largely ignored in the recruitment drives of the late 1960's—women.

In 1971, the Police Foundation inaugurated a study of the feasibility of using more women for regular police patrol work. The Foundation candidly noted that the main reason for the sudden interest in attracting women to police work was that the other two categories of potential recruits suggested by the Crime Commission—minority people and college graduates—had not responded in significant numbers to recruitment efforts. As then-Chief Bruce Baker of the Berkeley department put it in a proposal to the Foundation, "We realized that the department would have a wider selection of officers, especially minority officers, if we recruited women. This is very important, since we have had a good deal of difficulty in attracting qualified Blacks."[2] The Foundation singled out hostility to the aims and practices of the police as a major reason for the inability to recruit Third World people. At the same time, police departments were having little luck enticing college-educated people onto the forces, and in general the effort to upgrade the educational level of the police was no succeeding. The Foundation pointed out that i New York City, for example, the average IC level of rank and file police officers wa dropping, rather than rising.[3]

THE SOFTER TOUCH

In the absence of significant participatio by Third World and college-educated people the Police Foundation argued, the increased us of women in regular police work had becom vitally important. The interest in using wome in policing was based not on an authenti concern for women's rights, nor on polic concern over sexist attitudes and practices i their routine operations. Women, the Found tion suggests, had a number of special chara teristics that might make them especially usef on patrol duty. Most importantly, wome could serve to "cool out" the potential fo violence in conflict situations that polic officers faced on patrol. The Foundatio presented the findings of several studies pu porting to show that women in various pos tions of authority—presumably because of the gentler touch—tended to lessen the violence o encounters between authorities and subjec populations. Women attendants in mental ho pitals, for instance, were found to have marked cooling effect on patients in violen wards.[4] This suggested that women police coul provide just what the police had been lookin for: effective "order maintenance" without th overt use of force. More subtly, the presence o women would tend to "humanize" the polic forces, breaking down the "squadroom set o values" emphasizing aggressiveness and insular ity.[5] There were also some very specifi functions that, according to the Police Founda tion, women were particularly good for. The were considered especially good at elicitin information from suspects, for example, an they made excellent decoys. And unlike many male police officers, who tended to disdain th more "service-oriented" aspects of police wor such as family dispute settlement, youth counseling, and so on), women, the Foundation argued, tended to be *attracted* to the idea of service as an integral part of police work.

But perhaps most important of all the advantages of using more policewomen, according to the Foundation, would be its general impact on the public's image of the police themselves. "The public," they wrote, "may begin to see the police as public servants who care about those who need assistance and are motivated to help others."[6]

For all these reasons, women, according to the Police Foundation, were a vast reservoir of potential talent. But so far that reservoir had been shamefully untapped, mainly because of traditional resistance of male-dominated departments against using women, and doubt about their ability to handle the tougher and more dangerous kinds of police work. In 1960, the Foundation noted, there were only about 5,600 women police in the country, and most of them served mainly in clerical positions or in certain areas that had become defined as women's assignments, such as matron duty or work with juveniles. In New York City in 1972, there were about 350 policewomen, less than 1% of the force; and while that number was an increase of 0 since the early 1960's, the number of men on the force had increased by 5,000. Few policewomen in New York were used on patrol, and when they were, it was to patrol areas where women and children congregated.[7] The Foundation pointed out that most forces had a quota for women of about 2% or less.[8] In other words, most departments were turning away women at the same time that they were unable to find suitable men. Most departments had long waiting lists of women, and police-science courses were filled with them. (Among other reasons, women were attracted to police work, according to the Foundation, because it was one of the few areas where the pay for women was generally equal to that for men.)

The opportunity to test some of the Police Foundation's assertions about the value of women on patrol came in 1972, when the District of Columbia Police hired a number of new women specifically for patrol work, and reassigned several others to patrol duty. The Police Foundation sponsored a study of the effectiveness of 86 women officers matched against 86 men, and generally concluded that their earlier assumptions were correct. The women turned out to be as effective as the men (although they had a lower rate of making arrests). In addition, they did show a tendency to "cool" violent situations, and they turned out to be, as the Foundation put it, "less likely to become involved in serious unbecoming conduct which can damage community relations."[9] Moreover, hiring more policewomen would tend to overcome some of the racial imbalance of the police forces, since it turned out that although few Black *men* joined the police force, a substantial number of Black *women* did. A final advantage, according to the study, was that since citizens "generally support" the idea of equal employment opportunity for women, adding more women to the force would help improve relations with the community.[10]

RESISTANCE TO WOMEN

There is still considerable resistance to the use of women, especially for patrol duties, among rank-and-file police officers and some police officials. Fifty percent of police officials questioned as part of the Police Foundation's Washington study thought that women should not become a regular part of the patrol force; 88 percent believed that having women assigned to their districts made their own jobs harder, on the grounds that women are not sufficiently strong or aggressive, are hard to supervise and discipline, and are indecisive and undependable, among other faults. Complaints have also been voiced by the Patrolmen's Benevolent Association in New York and by the Citizens Organization for Police Support (COPS), a group composed mainly of policemen's wives, which has organized demonstrations against women police in New York.

Despite this resistance, the drive to recruit women gained momentum during the mid-seventies. According to the Ford Foundation, in 1974 there were 900 women doing regular

133

patrol work across the country, where in 1972 there had been only *seven.* By early 1974, there were women on uniformed patrol in over 40 cities and towns in the U.S., and in some state police forces, including New York's and the California Highway Patrol. Overall, the number of women in sixteen police departments covered in a recent LEAA study doubled between 1972 and 1975. Even the FBI had gradually increased its number of women agents (to 47 out of a total of 8,000) by early 1976.

Many resistant police departments—including those of Chicago, Philadelphia, Pittsburgh, and Memphis—have been forced to open their hiring and promotion practices to women in the face of court orders or threats by LEAA to withhold funding if they failed to comply with affirmative action guidelines.

These changes represent a real, if partial, victory for women's demands for democratic representation on police forces. And it's possible that women police may prove more sympathetic or supportive than men in certain kinds of individual situations—such as rape investigations. But hiring more women, by itself, does not challenge the fundamental sexism of the criminal justice system. The new push to recruit women does not attempt to shatter oppressive stereotypes about women; on the contrary, it builds on them. And the tone of the Police Foundation's reports makes clear that their concern for hiring more women is based more on the need for effective social control than on a real concern for women's rights.

The precarious position of women in police forces is shown dramatically by the impact of the economic crisis of the mid-seventies on affirmative action hiring in police departments. Though police departments have been the city agencies least affected by budget cuts, in some cities they have been forced to trim their payrolls. Where this has happened, new policewomen have been among the first casualties; lacking seniority, they are the first to be laid off in a budget crisis. In New York, layoffs in July 1975 threw over 2,800 police out of work, including 400 of the 618 women on the force. Though most of the men were back on the job within a few weeks, most of the women, since they had the least seniority, stayed off. In early 1976, these policewomen initiated a class action suit charging that layoffs based on seniority were discriminatory because the reason for the lack of seniority lay in the restrictive hiring policy of the past. Although the suit was upheld in a Federal appeals court, these layoffs show how tenuous women's job gains remain in the face of a widespread fiscal crisis.

Still, some degree of increased representation of women in police departments seems to be the wave of the future. From the point of view of the more sophisticated police departments, the recruitment of women is an almost ideal strategy, for it achieves several different things at once. It helps solve the key problem of a shortage of personnel, simplifies the recruiting process, softens the public image of the force and helps diminish problems of internal discipline and control. It is a prime example of the new "soft" approach to police work, playing on established stereotypes about the gentler nature of women to help sell the police as a whole to the public as a sensitive, concerned institution, determined not only to maintain order with the least possible damage, but also to place itself in the forefront of the struggle for women's rights. But whether these women will prove to be as manageable and docile as the police strategists hope is another question.

1. *New York Times,* Jan. 25, 1971.
2. Quoted in Catherine Milton, *Women in Policing,* Washington, Police Foundation, 1972, p. 4.
3. Ibid., p. 6.
4. Ibid., pp. 27-32.
5. Ibid., p. 38.
6. Ibid., p. 37.
7. Ibid., pp. 73-74.
8. Ibid., p. 35.
9. Peter B. Bloch and Deborah Anderson, *Police-women on Patrol: Final Report,* Washington, Police Foundation, 1974, pp. 2-3.
10. Ibid., p. 3.
11. Ford Foundation, *Law and Justice,* New York, Ford Foundation, 1974, p. 12.
12. See *Christian Science Monitor,* Feb. 4, 1974; *New York Times,* August 5, 1973.
13. *Washington Post,* July 10, 1973.
14. *New York Times,* July 15, 1974.

"... and they got away with everything. Took their TV, their stereo, all their records—I mean they even took things like their toaster. And all right there in broad daylight—probably half their neighbors sitting at home."

The chairs had been arranged in classroom fashion. The 'teachers' for the evening were a couple of off-duty cops, spiffed up as though going to a cocktail party. The 'students' were from a large apartment complex in a working class area of West Los Angeles. Most were in their late twenties, maybe early thirties. Some worked in nearby factories, a couple were raters for an insurance company, a few more were secretaries, one was a taxi driver.

"So you see people have got to help us with our job. We can't do it without you, 'cause you're our eyes and ears. You've got to take an interest in everything that goes on around here. I'll tell it straight: you've got to be downright suspicious. If you see something strange, report it—see a car you don't think belongs there, call it in. You all have to become your own little police force—your own little branch of the LAPD—'Cause I'll tell you folks, we sure can't do it by ourselves."

Since the late 1960's, there has been a steady growth in the number and variety of police-initiated programs falling under the general heading of "community relations" (CR). These programs differ in important ways from the one or two person community or public relations bureaus of the past. Basically, the old programs were one-way lines of communication: a few chosen police explaining their problems and methods to the community. No one really took these programs seriously, least of all the police.

But the new CR projects are much more sophisticated attempts at trying to persuade people that the police really do "serve and protect." The programs generally have two qualities in common. One is to give people more responsibility in policing themselves—to bring people into active participation in the policing process. The other is to encourage greater daily contact between the police and the neighborhoods they patrol. The police want to foster a "new relationship" between the community and themselves—to be seen as people who can be trusted, as *part* of the community, getting back to the image of the good old cop on the beat. Theoretically, with people's trust and participation, the job of the police will be less difficult. More people will report crimes, take preventive measures, and vote tax dollars for law enforcement. "There is an obvious need to turn the citizen on to the criminal justice system through citizen action programs,"[1] said former Law Enforcement Assistance Administration head Donald Santarelli. "The LEAA effort to help citizens—to bring them into the system, to meet their needs—is going to be a high priority item for LEAA."[2]

And indeed, these "citizen action programs" are springing up in every part of the country, often with LEAA assistance and encouragement. For instance, in Dayton, Ohio, volunteer Neighborhood Assistance Officers (NAOs) conduct commercial and residential security checks, patrol parks and playgrounds, and investigate traffic complaints and the like. Though not paid, they get to dress up in uniform and handle many duties formerly reserved for fulltime cops. According to the Dayton police, the NAOs have saved the city over three-quarters of a million dollars in the last three years.

In the predominantly Chicano Hollenbeck area of Los Angeles, the police—with the help of local businessmen—have opened up a storefront police station, dubbing it Operación Estafadores (Operation Swindlers). The police want the community to bring them their problems about consumer fraud, phony immigration counselors, robberies, and other crime-related concerns. Spanish-speaking officers are recruited for this detail in hopes that the community will more easily identify and co-operate with them.

In New York, the police have developed what they call a Blockwatchers system. This,

The Velvet Glove

like similar programs throughout the country, is designed to get community people organized as a crime reporting network. This network, the department claims, is a way to "involve people who want to help but don't want to get involved."[3] Short training courses are given in which people learn how to spot criminal or "suspicious" activity. However, the police emphasize that they don't want people reporting air pollution, noise, or health code violations, crimes most often committed by corporations and large landlords. Presumably, they feel it might be a bad precedent to define vigorous profit-making as criminal activity.

One of the most sophisticated of these new community relations programs is known as "Team Policing." In this chapter, we will take a close look at the development of team policing in one city—Venice, California, a beach community within the sprawl of Los Angeles.

TEAM POLICING: THE BACKGROUND

These new programs run counter to the "professional" model of policing adopted by most urban police departments, whose outlines were laid down in the Progressive era. Great stress has been laid on specialization of different police functions, rigid hierarchy, efficiency, and development of a centralized bureaucracy.[4] Most police departments gradually abolished the foot patrol in favor of putting cops in patrol cars. Local station houses were closed down and both command decisions and radio dispatching became centralized. Under the guidance of Chief William Parker, the Los Angeles Police Department became a leader in this new "professionalization" of the police. The Jack Webb "Dragnet" model of the humorless, efficient, spit and polish, physically fit expert became the ideal for what a cop should be.

Community Relations programs were non-existent in the LAPD of the 1950's and early 1960's. As Parker said, "I'm a policeman, not a social worker."[5] In fact, even the one or two youth programs the Department did have were abolished. Parker died about a year after the

Watts revolt of 1965. The new chief, Thomas Reddin, increased the community relations section from four persons to more than one hundred; he ordered police to fraternize with Blacks and Chicanos and to wear name tags for easy identification. The Department initiated sensitivity sessions in training programs and returned some cops to foot patrol. Reddin also instituted a wide range of youth programs and used Black ex-cons in police-community liaison work.

Beset by internal dissent, Reddin quit to take a TV announcer's job in 1969, and Edward M. Davis was appointed chief. Davis' hatred of fundamental social change was never a secret to anyone. ". . . the Bolsheviks are bound and determined to overthrow our government . . . But by God we're to have peace in this city. revolution isn't going to start here."[6] Even Chief Davis, however, was quickly able to perceive the value of CR programs. By 1971 the Department had seventy separate community relations programs underway. Besides Operación Estafadores, storefront stations were opened in other Third World communities, citizen watch patrols were encouraged by the police and groups such as the 77th St. DAMES (Desire to Affirm Motivate and Encourage Support for the police) flourished under the wing of the LAPD.

But Davis' real coup in community relations was the Basic Car Plan (BCP). This program was instituted in March 1970 to "bring the police and the community face to face," making the cops "sensitive" and "the community appreciate the policeman."[7] The city was divided into ninety-five districts with one "basic" car assigned to each district to remain in the area and be staffed consistently by the same police officer. Large-scale community meetings were held once a month in each district and attended by the cops who manned the basic car. The people of the area were invited to "Talk shop with your neighborhood cop."

The LAPD bragged that over 1000 community meetings were held a year. Nevertheless, there were problems. Despite the massive publicity, police complained about low attendance at meetings, especially in Chicano and

136

lack areas, and even stooped to raffles of TVs nd turkeys to attract people. One Black ommunity leader referred to the Basic Car lan as "Basic Bullshit" and many described the eetings as "intimidating," "impersonal" or useless verbal confrontations." It was difficult or the dispatcher to keep the basic car in its wn area, and as a result cops never really eveloped the intimate knowledge of the ommunity hoped for by police administrators. more far-reaching plan was needed to create a al community-police alliance. That plan was am policing.

Although team policing has meant different hings in different places, common elements recur. The main idea is that each small region will be policed continuously by one team made up of detectives, patrol officers, and supervisors, rather than cops roaming across huge areas in their patrol cars. Ostensibly, this means that the police get to know the neighborhood and its problems and develop a kind of paternal concern for the people in their assigned "turf." The increased contact with the same people on a daily basis is also aimed at increasing the community's trust in and cooperation with "their" police. "In small cities, or in closely knit neighborhoods, information passes swiftly from neighbor to neighbor. If the people accept the police as part of the community, they share the information with

them."[8] One last component of team policing is an internal restructuring of police decision-making, with an expansion of the individual cop's participation and responsibilities.

In 1967 the President's Commission on Law Enforcement and the Administration of Justice recommended that "Police departments should commence experimentation with a team policing concept. . . ."[9] In 1970-71 LEAA discretionary grants made specific provisions for team policing. The Police Foundation has also been particularly active in its development. By 1973, many cities, including Dayton, Cincinnati, New York, Syracuse, Detroit and Richmond, California, had begun experimenting with it in one form or another. One of the cities which had a comprehensive program was Venice.

VENICE: SETTING THE SCENE

Essentially, this is a community of poor people who happen to live on a very valuable piece of real estate.

A Venice Resident[10]

In looking closely at the team policing program in Venice, we wanted to provide an analysis which would be useful to other communities facing similar police strategies. Although our conclusions are based on the specific conditions in Venice, the questions we asked and how we went about answering them are transferrable to other organizing situations.

We wanted to know: what factors went int team policing being initiated in Venice a opposed to other communities in L.A.? Wha has been the response to it from different socia groups within the community, from the polic actually involved in team policing, and from th Department as a whole, and why? What kind of political possibilities does team policin create through its impact on people's consciou ness? And, does team policing make radica organizing more difficult, or are there ways t organize in response or as alternatives to th program?

Venice is the most densely populated com munity on the L.A. coast, and the poorest i terms of per capita income. Along its 2.8 mi coastline and eastward toward L.A. live distinc communities of Blacks, Browns, elderly, Whit working class, counterculture, and smal pockets of wealthy people. Despite their diffe rences and potential divisions, *most* of Venice i described by residents as having more of a sens of community than other areas of L.A. Much c that spirit has developed through Venice' history of struggle to control its own affairs i the face of the forces of profit.

On July 4, 1905, Venice opened as a seasid resort, built in the style of the Venetia Renaissance complete with canals and gond liers imported from Italy.[11] Failing dismall the resort was converted into an amusemen park, later nicknamed the Coney Island of th

West Coast. From the beginning, the quest for profit was a factor undermining the quality of life in Venice. In the hasty process of construction, many engineering mistakes were made along with deliberate cost-cutting measures. The canals, shoddily planned and constructed, gradually became stagnant until they were declared a menace to public health in 1912. Oil drilling began in 1929 in residential areas of Venice. The middle class which had lived in Venice during its history as an amusement center moved out rapidly, and there began a slow influx of the poor Whites, elderly, Blacks, and Browns that today comprise most of Venice's population. There was already a small stable Black community in Oakwood, a few blocks inland, most of which had been employed by the early amusement company. Now this community started to grow. Also during the depression, Mexican-Americans, forced out of housing elsewhere, moved into abandoned bungalows near the oil fields. During World War II nearby aircraft industries, such as Hughes and Douglas, gearing up for military production, brought in White workers who settled in new homes in the eastern part of Venice.

In the forties many older Jews, originally immigrants from Eastern Europe, came to settle in Venice. They arrived from other parts of Los Angeles and from the East Coast. Many of them were socialists or communists. Like others, they were attracted by the fresh air and available housing. In the fifties "beatniks" came and later, the new counterculture arrived, seeking freedom to practice their own lifestyle.

Over a period of time after World War II large real estate speculators, like Hughes Tool Company, Tenneco, Kaiser, Metropolitan Life, and Coldwell Banker Company, anticipating long-term profits, bought up large parcels of land at low prices. In 1969 about 70% of all the land in Venice was owned by absentee landlords. Their interest was and is in holding the land until the housing and financial markets are favorable enough and until the value of the land is high enough to make "development" really profitable. "Development" in their terms means that "every neighborhood in Venice would be uprooted and something more expensive substituted for what is there." [12]

Tax dollars of the tenants and small homeowners have been enlisted to remove and replace them with the upper middle class. The L.A. City Council, in pursuit of the increased tax revenues "development" would bring, has been eager to serve the real estate companies' interests. They have implemented housing code regulations (one of which forced out 25 percent of the poorer residents along the beach), planned freeways, and spent over a million dollars developing a master plan for Venice, which would displace at least 25,000 people. A city planning commissioner told the *Los Angeles Times* that it makes little difference what the people of Venice think about the plan "because 90% of them won't be living there when the plan is complete." [13]

In response to this, the people of Venice have not been passive. Bulldozers were fire-bombed in 1971 when Radford Realty tried to clear out residents for a shopping center. Thousands of dollars worth of damage resulted when plate glass windows were shotgunned out at a restaurant in a flashy new plaza. There has been so much arson against construction sites that insurance companies have threatened to lift all coverage in Venice and realtors have had difficulty renting out office space in their new buildings. The battle has included strategies ranging from petitions to tenant unions and struggles for rent control to storming city council meetings and has given birth to a long process of self-education about class society.

One way that people feel the force of the developers is through the actions of the police. In the struggle against master plans and absentee landowners, the police have frequently been the agents of repression, aiding in such actions as arrests and evictions during demonstrations and code enforcements. Relations with the community were so bad that the police commonly referred to residents of the Canals, a particularly tight and militantly anti-developer area, as the "Viet Cong."

The beachfront counterculture community has also suffered constant harassment since the mid-sixties. In 1969, 10,000 people attended a free concert on the beach. The police declared it an unlawful assembly and two hundred people were arrested and many beaten as cops with rifles watched from the tops of nearby apartment buildings. Some people have also suspected the police of sanctioning gang activity on the oceanfront in an effort to drive away the residents who so tenaciously cling to their homes. In addition, police "protection" against the rapes which plagued the community was ineffectual.

The Black and Chicano communities (like most poor Third World communities) suffered even more from the repressive tactics of the police. Community workers told us that almost every kid on the streets had at some point either been "rousted" or busted by the cops. Throughout the sixties it was common to see chains of police cars driving through Oakwood with shotguns pointing out of the windows. On two December days in 1969 the Metro Squad carried out a massive roundup and street sweep operation involving hundreds of Oakwood residents. Ostensibly, it was a narcotics bust, but as one resident put it, "Suddenly, everyone was a drug addict." Houses were entered and searched, people dragged out and beaten and others arbitrarily stopped, lined up against the wall and frisked. On the first day of the roust all community workers known to the police were arrested. When not harassing the community, police tended to stay out of Oakwood. Burglaries there were not a priority for the police, and the all-pervasive heroin was ignored or encouraged.

In response to consistent harassment of different segments of the community and calculated neglect of its problems, organizing against the police took many forms. Starting in the Black and Chicano communities in 1967, a group of street workers called the "Gang-busters" patrolled in vans attempting to deal with Chicano-Black and gang fights before the police could intervene, and documenting police brutality. The Venice Defense Committee and the Venice Survival Committee organized police observation patrols along the beachfront, took complaints about police behavior, helped victims file suits and educated people about their legal rights. There were frequent demonstrations and vigils at the Venice Division Headquarters in response to instances of brutality. At various times demands were made for police

foot patrols, community police forums, civilian review boards and participation in deciding the priorities of policing.

Venice has been politically active for many years. The founding of the Peace and Freedom Party there, the Venice Five—arrested for refusing to testify on the activities of the Weathermen—and institutions such as the Midnight Special, a leftist bookstore, made Venice renowned as the "home of radical politics in L.A."

Free Venice, a community political collective, has spawned many other community projects including a newspaper, the *Venice Beachhead*, and has played a leadership role in anti-war and anti-developer organizing. Perhaps the most significant political institution is the Venice Town Council. Consisting of representatives from each of six neighborhood councils, it has become a focal point for community struggles and a forum for working through divisions among groups who share long-term interests in radically changing this society. The Town Council has confronted the issue of the immigration of Mexican nationals, which has long divided Blacks and Browns. Strategy around fighting freeway and development plans and tax and rent raises has also been coordinated through the Council.

TEAM POLICING IN VENICE

[With team policing] we want to mobilize every neighborhood into a common front—police and public—against the criminal element.
　　　　　　　　　—Chief E. M. Davis

Team policing first began in Venice in 1972 aided by LEAA funds under the Crime Specific Burglary program. The program initially began in a 95% White, "law and order" district of Venice guaranteed to show results. It was quickly expanded to the entire Venice Division of the LAPD, which takes in 180,000 people. Plans called for the entire city of Los Angeles to be "team policed" by 1975.

In most places, team policing includes specific programs aimed at soliciting active community participation in policing and inculcating in citizens a sense of responsibility for prevent ng crime. For example, in Venice people were rovided with a variety of ways they could Team up with Team 28" (28 being one police istrict in Venice).

"Operation Identification," which under arious names is now found in thousands of ommunities across the country, is one of the est known of their programs. In Venice, police ent door to door with an electronic pen ffering to mark people's valuables so that they ould be identified if stolen. There were also at ast 9,000 house-to-house inspections in which eople checked locks and advised people on ow best to secure their homes against the criminal element." Through both programs, olice appear as the allies and protectors of eople frightened and threatened by un-xplained waves of crime.

The police also initiated block meetings, dubbed "coffee klatches." Each meeting focuses on a problem particular to that area, such as burglary, auto theft or juvenile delinquency. Much more informal than basic car meetings, "coffee klatches" are held with small groups in people's homes. Cops come dressed in street clothes to show that "we're just like everybody else." Much of the meeting's content consists of reinforcing people's fears and their dependency on the police. Statistics on crime in the neighborhood and scare stories about cat burglars, peeping toms and "hypes" are recounted. The solution offered by the police is called Neighborhood Watch. People are urged to be "nosey, learn who your neighbors are, know who's supposed to be in the area and who isn't and report anything suspicious to the

police." In the all-White meetings which we attended, almost all the anecdotes the police used to scare people had criminals who were "colored gentlemen," "little Mexican kids" or transient renters. One woman said that she'd seen "two colored guys visiting a White girl" and was encouraged to report "things like that."

Although the meetings are supposedly held to deal with the community's concerns, these concerns are defined by police within the framework of how best to reduce crime. The "communication" is frequently a one-way lobby for the police and *their* concerns. The cops voiced constant complaints about the shortage of manpower and equipment, and the dangers of their jobs.

To facilitate the "coffee klatches" and other activities, block captains are recruited. Officially, these "captains" act as liaison with the police, organizing and distributing information in their areas. Many people suspect that the "responsibilities" of a block captain also extend to spying on neighbors. At one point there were 350 block captains within one small area of East Venice, but police told us it was hard to maintain enthusiasm and sustain contact.

Team policing also involves more conventional community relations efforts, such as school programs on traffic safety and boxing programs for kids. About the latter, one police lieutenant said, "There are kids in Venice who start running the moment they see a cop car. We want that to stop. We are trying to show the kids we are regular guys." [15]

The significant changes which team policing requires in departmental organization make it much more important as a trend than the more limited community relations programs. Before there were rigid hierarchies governing the relationships between different ranks of policemen. With team policing, the big emphasis is on the team. Recognizing that "genuine commitment is seldom achieved when objectives are externally imposed," [16] the program in Venice was designed so that the team as a whole sets its own short-range objectives in team meetings. Rank and file cops participate actively in decisions about such things as scheduling and what equipment and patrol methods should be

used. The rationale behind this is similar to th.. of the new trend towards involving restles workers in limited decision-making in the fa tory. As one report put it, the cops' "participa tion creates a self-respect and a sense o responsibility for the activities and goals the help to construct." [17] Of course the decision the team members are allowed to make are a within the framework of how best to kee order and maintain the status quo. Althoug perhaps *feeling* more motivated, the individu cop has no more real control over the nature the job than was ever had.

Another aspect of the new emphasis on th team is an attempt to break down the specia zation which has previously divided detective traffic cops and accident investigators. The id is that "the sharing of information among tea members [will allow them to] use their creased knowledge to decide upon bet strategies." [18] In Venice, all officers spend o week being trained by detectives and are mo actively involved in the follow-up investi tions. Team conferences are periodically held share information. The aim of all this cro training is to create cops who will each capable of and responsible for a whole range duties, rather than merely one specialized fu tion. These changes in the definition of police role require whole new training pro dures which are designed to foster new a tudes. Efforts are made to break up special based cliques and to discourage hierarchi relationships. Training includes such topics understanding the community, crisis interv tion, and public speaking. All of this new fo is aimed at preparing officers for the ways they will be expected to relate to e other and to help ease them into their relationship with the community.

The emphasis on developing this "n community/police relationship is not inc patible with the trend by police departme towards greater reliance on sophisticated te nology. In fact, much of the recent CR strat takes advantage of new technical developme In Venice, for example, the team makes us computer systems such as PATRIC, AWWS NCIC for information on suspects and st property. The LAPD is in the process of bu

600 shoulder radios so that cops can get out of their cars and into the streets.

Nor does the attempt to recruit the community imply that the state gives up its ultimate weapon: physical repression. In L.A., alongside the neighborhood teams, there is the Metro Squad, of which SWAT is one component. Metro patrols "high crime" areas, works "labor disputes," and provides crowd control in riots and demonstrations. Metro Squad cops go through extensive training in military techniques and are known for their brutality. They are dispatched to various places around the city where they will flood an area, operating independently of the local police.

WHY TEAM POLICING?

Our study of Venice helps to indicate why the team policing strategy was adopted when and where it was. The crisis of the 1960's forced a change in the conventional "professional" approach of many police departments. Urban ghettoes throughout the country were erupting in massive street battles and the looting of businesses. In Watts alone at least thirty-four persons were killed, 4,000 arrests were made and $40 million in property damage was incurred during the 1965 conflagration in which the state was forced to resort to massive repression. (As the riots were quelled, Chief Parker declared, "Now *we're* on top, and *they're* on the bottom."[19]) Time and again blame fell on the nation's police departments for exacerbating, if not actually igniting, the spontaneous revolts. In Watts, it had been a couple of California Highway Patrolmen arresting two Blacks for a traffic violation which had sparked the uprising. Before Watts, L.A. Mayor Yorty had boasted that "Harlem-type riots could not occur here."[20] That "it *could* happen here" pointed up the lack of information the police had of the Third World communities. With such limited intelligence, the strategies which they were capable of developing for policing those communities would be severely curtailed. In addition, the nationwide reaction of many groups against the police—demonstrations, demands for community control and organizing for self-defense—was re-flected in Venice, where the police had consistently brutalized the Black, Brown, and counterculture communities, and anti-police organizing had been active.

Moreover, the 1960's saw an enormous increase in street crime. In Los Angeles, rising crime rates were calling the police's ability to maintain "law and order" into question. Between 1962 and 1972 crime had risen over 102%.[21] In Venice, residents were experiencing waves of burglary and rape. Merchant delegations tramped off to Division Headquarters to complain about inadequate police protection. Meanwhile, the corporations and real estate developers were having their tremendous potential for profits from their Venice landholdings threatened by "criminals and other undesirables." The sabotage of developers' buildings and building sites, the profusion of a counterculture, people living "illegally" on developer-owned land and all the street crime made for an uneasy investment climate. As well, rental profits would be threatened. Many people would no longer be willing to pay $800 a month to live in a neighborhood constantly under seige by burglars, rapists, and those "hostile poor people."

Given the unwillingness and inability of the status quo to deal with the social roots of all these problems, it was logical that either new police strategies be tried or more money poured into the existing methods of control. But in L.A., for example, between 1960 and 1970, police appropriations had shot up 114%,[22] and fiscally squeezed city councils were reluctant to beef up an already failing strategy. And the disastrous results of the strict reliance on technology and overt repression in Vietnam had further discredited those methods to police higher-ups as *the* strategy for their brand of social control.

At the same time, the rising crime and the unwillingness of city governments to shell out vast amounts of money meant that the police would have to use their funds more efficiently and look for new sources of support. Moreover, the disrespect for, and lack of confidence in the police was obstructing their ability to control crime and continue building a political base of support for themselves as an institution.

143

Team policing, along with other new community relations programs, represents *one* response of city police departments and the Law Enforcement Assistance Administration to the problems born out of the contradictions of class society in the 1960's. Ostensibly, the police would develop closer ties with communities by involving them in policing activities, increasing their non-confrontational contact with people and generally transforming their image. Crime, according to the theory, would be cut down as a result of more intimate knowledge of the community and an increased vigilance and awareness by community people. Because the community doesn't have to be paid, it wouldn't entail great expenditures of police money. And if the programs didn't work, much of the blame could be shifted onto the shoulders of the communities themselves.

In addition to the sweeping social changes of the 1960's was a change occurring within police departments. The phenomenon of police unions and rank and file militancy was developing. Demands for higher wages, better pensions, fewer hours, and more control over working conditions threatened to inflate the cost of operating the department and to disrupt administrative efficiency. It bothered L.A.'s Chief Davis so much that in early 1970 he pleaded with the city council for an anti-union and organizing order.

Upset with militancy, high turnover, absenteeism, and a generally disgruntled police officer, many police departments looked to team policing as one remedy. The friendlier contact with the community and the ability to have a role in making decisions which affected their jobs would serve to diffuse the dissatisfaction of the rank and file. One police official in Venice said it clearly: "While other cops are turning to the Protective League [the police union], our men have never been more satisfied." [23]

THE RESPONSE

To the extent that they are successful in enlisting community participation, team policing and similar programs might reduce community-police antagonisms and perhaps even result in more "criminals" being apprehended, goals articulated by the police. However, because the programs do not deal with the underlying social conditions which cause crime, they cannot offer the possibility of a society without it. Crime, so the police explanation goes, is caused by bad people or unfortunate circumstances which are beyond our control; crime is not viewed as a product of specific social conditions which can be changed. Therefore, people are encouraged to treat crime as an isolated problem to be solved within the confines of the "criminal justice system," rather than through a radical restructuring of society.

Though they emphasize "citizen participation," the new police projects do not offer real control over the priorities of policing or a real choice of what interests should be protected by the police. So long as the society as a whole remains geared towards the accumulation of profit and not truly democratically controlled, the police will function in the interests of maintaining private property. Community relations programs offer merely the illusion of popular control.

The approach embodied in CR programs may make sense to the individual cops involved whose whole jobs are defined in the narrow framework of repressing crime and not calling the social structure into question. While many of them are sincere in wanting to "involve" people, the programs still *function* to direct people away from really changing the conditions of their lives. Citizen action programs such as Blockwatchers and Neighborhood Assistance Officers perpetuate the myth that institutions under capitalism are designed to meet people's needs and aspirations. People's energy is channelled into treating the *symptoms* of social problems, thus improving the security apparatus of the state through their alliance with the police. The roots of the problem remain untouched.

In spite of these limitations and danger many people will probably be receptive to the new overtures from the police. People in this society clearly lack opportunities to make decisions which really affect their lives, to work collectively with other people to solve problems and to live without the ever-present fear

crime. In the absence of clear alternatives offered by radical organizing, many people may be attracted to the limited participation and security the police offer.

The receptivity of specific social groups to the team policing programs varies greatly, depending on a whole range of factors. Those factors include, but are certainly not limited to: what their job experience is, what the relations are like between the different groups, what prior political organizing has occurred, how they experience crime, what the history of their experiences with the police has been, and what sort of alternatives they might have to team policing. Various combinations of these conditions will lead different groups to very different perceptions about their stake in the status quo and the possibilities for change. This in turn affects how they relate to team policing. For example, two groups with similar kinds of jobs but entirely different experiences with crime or past political organizing might respond very differently to police initiatives. Thus, it's crucial for organizers to analyze the circumstances in their particular communities in developing strategies around crime or other issues.

* * *

No social order is held together solely by physical coercion. The United States is no exception. Every day, in jobs, schools, advertising, and entertainment, we are encouraged to accept the legitimacy of this society and the impossibility of a different one. To various degrees people have come to internalize a capitalist world outlook which provides them with explanations for why things are as they are. Team policing is but one means by which people acquire this outlook. As such, it becomes crucial to understand the effects of this and other institutions and to develop alternative explanations and strategies which point to the necessity and possibility of radically restructuring this society.

145

1. *LEAA Newsletter*, Vol. 3, No. 11, (March, 1974), p. 9.
2. Ibid.
3. Quoted in "Police Enlist 'Blockwatchers' to Get Instant Tips on Crime," *New York Times*, Nov. 18, 1972.
4. See above, Section II, on "Transformation of the Police."
5. Quoted in untitled manuscript on the history of the LAPD by Gerald Woods. (Copy obtained through the Urban Policy Research Institute) (hereafter *Woods*).
6. Quoted in "There's More to Chief Davis Than Meets the Ear," by William J. Drummond, *Los Angeles Times*, Jan. 10, 1971.
7. Television program on police harassment of Blacks and Browns with Jerry Dunphy, Channel 2 (L.A.), Jan. 20, 1970, and "Billboard campaign begins for police Basic Car Plan," *Los Angeles Times*, Nov. 11, 1970, respectively.
8. Lawrence W. Sherman, Catherine H. Milton, Thomas V. Kelly, *Team Policing, Seven Case Studies*, a Police Foundation publication, 1973, p. 75.
9. Quoted in *Team Policing*, p. xiv, in the foreword by James Q. Wilson.
10. "Venice Speaks," *Venice Beachhead*, July, 1973.
11. The information for this section is based on interviews with community residents from different areas, also a draft on *A History of Population Settlement and Movement in Venice, Ca.: Causes and Effects*, by Larry Dully, (Dept. of Urban and Regional Planning, USC, April, 1970); "Save The Canals," a research paper by Jeremy Strick; "Help Build the Venice Community Center," a pamphlet by the Save the Canals Committee, "The Fifth Annual Venice Canal Festival," a pamphlet by Free Venice; and various issues of the *Venice Beachhead* and the *LA Free Press*.
12. Editorial, *Venice Beachhead*, Jan. 1969.
13. "Special Election," Rick Davidson, Dec., 1969.
14. Editorial endorsing team policing in Los Angeles, *Los Angeles Times*, Nov. 18, 1973.
15. "Venice Police Trying to KO Gap with Kids," *Santa Monica Evening Outlook*, Oct. 12, 1972.
16. From the *Final Evaluation of Team 28*, prepared as an intra-departmental document by the Planning Section of Advanced Planning Division, LAPD, April, 1974, p. 23.
17. *Final Evaluation*, p. 25.
18. *Team Policing*, p. 5.
19. *Woods*.
20. *Woods*.
21. Figures obtained from the FBI's Unitorm Crime Reports, *Crime in the United States*, for the years 1962 and 1972.
22. Thomas Bradley quoted in *Los Angeles Times*, Sept. 5, 1972.
23. Interview with Jay Downen, Civilian Administrator with the Venice Division of the LAPD.
24. *Team Policing*, p. 52.

VI. EXPANDING FOR BUSINESS

INTRODUCTION

So far we have described the historical development of the U.S. police and analyzed in depth the particular forms of policing that have emerged during the last decade. We have limited our analysis, however, to the role of the so-called "public" police within the United States. In this section of the book, we will attempt to broaden the conventional perspective on the police by examining their functions in the private sector as well as outside the United States. Chapter 14 looks at the booming private security industry and evaluates the increasingly important role played by "rent-a-cops" in protecting business interests. Rather than viewing "public" and "private" police as separate and even antagonistic entities, we will suggest that they perform similar class control functions within the overall apparatus of repression.

In chapter 15, we examine how the business community attempts to protect its interests abroad. The U.S. government is not only concerned with the development of domestic police forces, but has extended its domain to include the police forces of countries throughout the world. The apparatus and technology that have been developed for criminal justice work inside the United States are steadily finding their way into the police and other security forces of Third World countries, as the United States has taken upon itself the task of organizing, training, equipping, and indoctrinating these forces. Even domestic agencies such as the Law Enforcement Assistance Administration (LEAA) are taking on an international role, and private U.S. corporations are beginning to train military and police forces around the world. At the same time, various skills and tactics acquired by U.S. personnel operating in other countries are brought back for use in the United States.

14. RENT-A-COP: The Private Security Industry

In 1969, the National Commission on the Causes and Prevention of Violence painted this picture of the future American cityscape:

> —Central business districts in the heart of the city ... will be partially protected by large numbers of people shopping or working during daytime hours ... and will be largely deserted except for police patrols during nightime hours.
> —High-rise apartment buildings and residential compounds protected by private guards and security devices will be fortified cells for upper-middle and high-income populations living at prime locations in the city. ...
> —High-speed, patrolled expressways will be sanitized corridors connecting safe areas [and] armed guards will "ride shotgun" on all forms of public transportation. [1]

One year later, the Philadelphia Branch Manager of Pinkerton's, Inc., Francis J. Mayr, told reporters that the prophecy was "100 percent correct," and that, with the spectacular growth of private security firms, "We don't have to talk about five years from now" to see fulfillment of the Commission's prophecy, since "a lot of it is here already." Noting that in Philadelphia—as in other big cities—private security guards outnumbered the public police by a hefty margin and were expanding at a faster rate, Mayr predicted that "It should be a good decade coming up" for Pinkerton's and the other private police agencies. [2]

Mayr's optimism is characteristic of the private security industry, which is growing, according to a RAND Corporation report, "at a recession-resistant average rate of 10 to 15 percent annually." [3] Expenditures on private guard services doubled between 1963 and 1969, and spending on other security services (alarm systems, armored car services, etc.) also soared. [4] According to U.S. government statistics there was a total of 290,000 regularly-employed private guards and detectives in 1969 (some estimates placed the figure as high as 800,000), and the private security industry was a thriving 3.3 billion business. [5]

Today, the private police officer (or "rent-a-cop," as he/she is sometimes known) has become a ubiquitous feature of urban life, guarding apartment buildings, office buildings, stores, factories, hospitals, universities, sports arenas, etc. In New York City there are an estimated 40,000 private guards—compared to 30,000 municipal policemen—and in some parts of the city (Wall Street, midtown) rent-a-cops outnumber the regular police by a factor of 10 to 1. [6] Private guards now screen visitors to most large offices and stores, and some corporations have established checkpoints with armed guards on every floor. "A quasi-military atmosphere has taken hold at many places," The New York Times reported in a survey of corporate security programs. [7]

With the rise in urban violence and crime against business, the demand for police protection has risen enormously and existing law enforcement agencies have not expanded fast enough to satisfy it. As a result, many companies and institutions have turned to the private security industry for added protection. Many companies doubled or tripled their spending on security over the past few years, and the resulting demand for guards and protective devices has proved a "windfall" for the large security firms like Pinkerton's which dominate the industry. The revenues of the "Big Four" private guard companies (Pinkerton's, Burns, Walter Kidde & Co., Wackenhut Corp.) more than tripled between 1963 and 1969, rising from $93 million to $312 million, and this high rate of growth continued into the 1970's. [8] Pinkerton's reported revenues of $175 million in 1973 (compared to $120 million only four years earlier), and told its stockholders: "Record growth in all areas—revenues, income, employment, customers and services—marked your company's performance. ... These achievements were attained despite generally adverse conditions, including rising prices and taxes, growing regulation and cost-cutting by industry and business." [9] And William J. Burns International Security Services, which reported revenues of $154 million in 1973, told stockholders: "We believe the Company's greatest period of growth lies ahead. ..." [10]

149

THE DEMAND FOR PRIVATE POLICE

While many of the security firms, like Pinkerton's and Burns, were formed over 50 years ago, it is only in the past decade that they have become a conspicuous feature of everyday urban life. In looking more closely at this sudden demand for guard services, there seem to be many causes. But we believe they can be grouped into three categories: political violence, crime against business and street crime.

(1) Political Violence

The 1960's was a period of great social upheaval in the United States, which sometimes took the form of violent attacks (bombings, lootings, hijackings, vandalism) on overt instruments of repression and exploitation—banks, corporations, courts, etc. These assaults (there were 4,330 bombings in the United States between January 1969 and April 1970, according to one government report)[11] in turn generated a tremendous demand for expanded security services. After every bombing in New York City, Peter O'Neil of Wackenhut reported in 1970, "the phones are ringing off the walls" from clients asking for additional coverage."[12] After a series of bombings in Manhattan, *The New York Times* reported that "companies of all sizes are hiring guards, issuing photo identification cards to employees and sending executives to Army bomb detection school or plant security seminars."[13]

In discussing their phenomenal growth of the past few years, most security companies are frank in their acknowledgement of the role played by political and social turmoil: "All you have to do is read the papers," David Goode of Burns told the *Washington Post* in 1970. "Look at what's happening today. The headlines are enough to tell you. There's all kinds of civil strife and turmoil, bombings and disruptions. Isn't that enough of an indicator of why businesses want protection?"[14]

Banks and corporations were the major customers for added guard services in the late 1960's and early 1970's, but other institutions also contributed to the booming demand for protection. Many colleges and universities

150

There's a difference between protection and pro-tection.

Pinkerton's. The professionals.

doubled or tripled their spending on security measures after the wave of campus rebellions in 1968-1970,[15] and the crackdown on airline hijackings generated an estimated $57 million in new business for the guard companies in 1973.[16] And, more recently, there has been an upsurge in demands for *personal* guard services. "Since the [Patty] Hearst kidnaping," Wackenhut spokesman reported in 1974, "we have had a large number of inquiries about our executive protection service." Wackenhut, which already has an "executive protection" service in Latin America for resident U.S. businessmen, is thinking of launching such a service in the United States.[17]

(2) Crime Against Business

Almost all forms of crime have increased over the past decade, but none as rapidly as crimes against business—burglary, robbery, vandalism, shoplifting, employee theft, etc. The losses caused by business crime "are increasing at an astronomical rate," *Justice* magazine reported in 1972,[18] and a U.S. Senate report noted: "thievery and vandalism have reached such proportions that survival of the small businessmen in high crime areas has reached the crisis point."[19] The Federal Bureau of Domestic Commerce estimated that the direct costs of ordinary business crimes totalled $15.7 billion in 1971, and industry sources indicated that when indirect costs (lost business and profits, higher insurance premiums, time devoted to processing claims, etc.) were added, the losses would be tripled.[20]

In a desperate effort to reduce their losses, many companies have spent millions of dollars on added guard services and protective devices. Many department stores have hired dozens of guards and installed elaborate surveillance and alarm systems in an effort to discourage shoplifting, while undercover agents seek to expose thefts by employees. "Crime is growing faster than the statistics," Norman Eisenstat of Defensive Instruments observed in 1969, "and companies in this business are making sinful amounts of money."[21] In defense of their work, security personnel argue that protective services should be designated a "loss prevention department" and "treated as a *profit center* where an investment in people and equipment, especially the new electronic technologies, can bring in a much greater savings than the cost of the original investment."[22]

3) Street Crime

To most inhabitants of America's decaying central cities, street crime (mugging, holdups, rape, etc.) has become a common feature of everyday life, creating a "climate of fear" in many communities. Street crime has generated an unprecedented demand for protective services that cannot be fulfilled by existing public police agencies, and as a result, many people have turned to the private security firms. In some areas, apartment dwellers have staged rent strikes to dramatize demands for building guards, and in others people have formed block associations to hire street guards. In New York City's Upper West Side, for instance, many families contribute $5 or more per month toward the salary of private block guards, who carry nightsticks and walkie-talkies (for communication with police or roving patrol cars).

Faced with an alarming increase in mugging and rape, many urban universities have hired additional guards in an effort to halt campus crime (the University of Chicago, for instance, spent $1,343,000 on security in 1973)[23] while in some cities merchants' associations have hired private guards to reduce losses caused by the sharp decline in evening trade. Thus when a group of New York firms announced its decision to flood the midtown business district with 300 additional uniformed guards, the Executive Vice President of Rockefeller Center Inc. (which houses many restaurants and specialty shops), explained: "What we are trying to do is to create life in the area. We do not want the area to start going dead after sundown. We want people to come to the area to walk through it at night."[24]

All of these factors have, of course, generated demands for increased *public* police services—and, indeed, public spending on law enforcement services increased by 90% during the 1960's, from $2.0 billion in 1960 to $3.8 billion in 1969.[25] But the expansion in public law enforcement has not satisfied all the demands for increased security, and many firms have turned to private police agencies for added protection. Thus while much of the growth in private guard employment can be seen as supplement to public police services, other factors have also influenced the choice of private sector services:

—Private police devote all their attention to the protection of their client's property, whereas public police normally patrol a large area with many establishments.

—Private detectives are accountable to their clients exclusively, and thus never publicize any damaging or embarrassing data (e.g., disclosures of employee theft or wrongdoing) produced by their investigations. Public police, on the other hand, are officially obliged to divulge all data obtained in the course of their work.

—Private guards can be hired and fired at will in response to changing corporate needs, while public police employment is governed by strict civil service regulations.

—Private police services are much less expensive than public police services: in San Francisco, for instance, rent-a-cops receive an average of $2-$2.50 per hour, while a rookie cop on the San Francisco Police Department receives a minimum of $6.46 an hour.[26]

In general, private guards are employed when a firm wants plentiful, cheap, flexible and *personalized* security. Public police officers, on the other hand, have always had more complex

151

and varied law enforcement responsibilities, including riot control, regulation of public morality, narcotics control, race relations, protection of visiting dignitaries, etc. As a result, public cops are expected to perform a much wider range of tasks than rent-a-cops and over a much wider geographical area, and thus cannot provide continuous protection at any given site. "People would naturally rather have a regular policeman patrolling an industrial plant or shopping center," Clarence M. Coster of the Justice Department's Law Enforcement Assistance Administration (LEAA) noted in 1973, "but the local police generally don't have the manpower to give constant attention to a particular private property. Private security thus plays an important role, complementing the work of public law enforcement agencies."[27] Indeed, as police officers are increasingly transformed into elite urban troubleshooters, private guards can be viewed as a "security proletariat" that is staffing the ramparts of private property in a desperate effort to resist social turmoil and chaos. This characterization of the private police function becomes increasingly valid when one studies the organization and composition of the private security industry.

A PROFILE.
OF THE INDUSTRY

Although private police employment now exceeds that of public law enforcement agencies in most cities, very little systematic research has been devoted to private security forces. Furthermore, the *only* major study of the private police industry—a 16-month study conducted by the RAND Corporation in 1971-72 under a $171,000 LEAA grant—is replete with apologies for incomplete or insufficient information. Nevertheless, until further research is undertaken, the five-volume RAND report must constitute the basic source of data on this industry.

According to the RAND study, private police forces in the United States in 1969 (the last year for which reliable statistics are available) encompassed 222,400 "in-house" guards and detectives (i.e., security officers who work

152

exclusively for the company or institution which hires them), and 67,500 contract guards and detectives who work for Pinkerton's or one of the 3,500 other private guard firms in the United States.[28] (It should be noted that these figures are considered very conservative, and that the addition of part-time and occasional employees would boost the total by a considerable percentage.) Employment of in-house guards has declined slightly over the past decade, while contract guard employment has been growing at a steady rate of 11-12 percent per year, and was expected to double between 1969 and 1975—to an estimated force of 150,000 or more guards.[29] Among reasons cited for the shift from in-house to contract guards is that in-house employees are more likely to be unionized and thus tend to benefit from company-wide pay hikes, while the contract guards are largely unorganized and generally receive much less pay than in-house personnel. RAND estimates, for instance, that in-house guards receive $0.50-$1.00 more per hour than their contract counterparts.[30]

Within the contract security industry itself, the share of business going to the "Big Four" guard firms has been rising steadily. In 1963, for instance, these firms accounted for 36 percent of contract guard revenues, while by 1969 they received 50 percent of all such revenues.[31] While the contract guard industry as a whole has been growing at a rate of 11-12 percent per year, the revenues of the Big Four have been growing at an average annual rate of 20 percent.[32] Because of the obvious importance of these four firms, a brief profile is provided of each (see boxes, pages 157-58).

On the basis of the scanty data available RAND in 1972 indicated that the "typical private guard" is "an aging white male, poorly educated, usually untrained, and very poorly paid."[33] Contract guards, according to RAND earn a marginal wage—between $1.60 and $2.25 an hour in 1969—and often work 48-56 hours or carry two jobs in order to make ends meet.[34] Typically, the private guard is a retired policeman or civil servant seeking to earn a few extra dollars to supplement retirement pay, a chronically-unemployed worker, or an ex-serviceman (Although security work is normally an all-male profession, some of the large contract guard firms indicate a rising demand for female "guardettes"—or, in one case, "Lady Pinkerton's.")[35] Fully 40 percent of the guards who answered a RAND questionnaire reported that they had been unemployed before obtaining their current jobs and that guard work "was the best job they could find."[36]

Recently, as the demand for protective services has skyrocketed, guard pay has risen slightly and the security firms have been able to attract younger and better-educated personnel. In a 1970 survey of corporate security measures, *The New York Times* reported that "the newly hired guards are former policemen, firemen, or servicemen—young men in their prime. . . . The day of the night watchman in his 60's and 70's is rapidly disappearing."[37] Although no statistics on the racial background of guard personnel are available, any visit to the stores, hospitals, and colleges of a larger northern U.S. city will suffice to demonstrate that many of the younger guards are Black. And, despite the slight increase in guard pay, it is clear that security work is still a poorly-paid, low-status job. As noted by Margaret Hughes of *Security World* magazine (the industry's professional journal), "These are enormously underpaid men considering the nature of their work. Some agencies pay only the minimum wage and force their guards to work overtime to make an adequate income. The wonder is that these men don't steal on the job, considering their wages."[38]

The low-status nature of guard work is further indicated by the RAND data on private security training procedures. Unlike public policemen, who normally receive several months' training before being sent out on patrol, rent-a-cops typically receive minimum training of no more than 8-12 hours duration. And two-thirds of all security officers who answered the RAND questionnaire reported that they had received no pre-work training whatsoever, and only perfunctory on-the-job training. Furthermore, while almost half of the respondents were armed, less than one-fifth reported having received *any* firearms training.[39] RAND also reported that 97 percent of the guards who responded to its questionnaire

failed to pass a simple examination designed to test their knowledge of basic legal practice in typical job-related situations.[40] RAND, which labeled these findings "shocking," called on the states to pass strict licensing regulations in order to insure adequate pre-work training for private guards. (In 1969, private security employment was virtually unregulated in 10 states, while in only 10 of the remaining 40 states was there any comprehensive code governing private security practices. And, according to RAND, *no* state has yet adopted a code with "adequate scope and quality.")[41]

While guards and watchmen constitute the unskilled proletariat of the private security industry, a small number of private detectives and undercover agents form the elite ranks. In fact, many of the large security firms like Pinkerton's and Burns started out as private detective agencies and only gradually shifted into other forms of security work. Pinkerton's, for instance, was at one time the *only* national detective agency in the United States, and the firm performed many interstate investigations for local police agencies until the FBI was established in 1924.[42] Later, in the early 1900's, "Pinkerton's" became synonymous with "labor spy" and "goon squad" as business chiefs hired private guards to sabotage and suppress union organizing drives. These practices were exposed in a series of Congressional hearings chaired by Senator Robert La Follette, Jr. in 1936, and Pinkerton's subsequently announced that it would not provide detectives for labor espionage or strike-breaking operations.[43] While today most of the large firms have foresworn undercover work of this sort, and investigative work generates only about 10 percent of their revenues, many security firms still supply detectives for undercover investigations. Undercover agents, according to Burns, are available to investigate one or more of the following "management problems": inventory losses, pilferage, theft, fraud, falsification of records, forgery, poor employee morale, willful neglect of machinery, waste of man-hours and materials, theft of tools, unreported absenteeism, supervisory incompetence, inadequate surveillance and what it calls "delicate investigatory matters."[44]

In its Annual Report for 1972, Burns tells how a typical undercover investigation works: "A frequent procedure is to have the investigator obtain work in the company in a normal manner. . . . He works full days, fills an actual job and draws a regular paycheck, arousing no suspicion among fellow employees. The person who arranged the investigation is kept informed by means of secret reports. When the work is completed, the operative leaves the job in a normal way so that no one ever need know his true identity."[45] In this way, an employer can obtain "internal intelligence" on employee behavior while avoiding the bad publicity that might result from a regular police investigation. And, while most security firms indicate that their undercover operatives are only available for investigations of employee theft and other criminal activities, there is some evidence that private detectives continue to report on political beliefs, union activities and other non-criminal matters. Thus, in an article on "The Value of Internal Intelligence," Eugene V. Allen of Taskpower Services, Inc. suggested that "besides theft and dishonesty," undercover agents can report on other problems including:

—*How effectively and thoroughly new employees are indoctrinated.*

—*General employee attitudes and morale.*
—*Excessive loitering and malingering contributing to unnecessary overtime situations.*
—*Whether production "breakdowns" are truly accidental or intentional.*
—*Whether company "cliques" have a desirable or undesirable effect on new employees.*[46]

And, since the agents report exclusively and secretly to top company officials, there is no way to determine whether data on "general employee attitudes" includes information on political or union associations. Indeed, in 197- IBM issued a confidential handbook for "Instruction in Corporate Protective Services" which called for the formation of a global intelligence system to provide top company officials with confidential data on "extremist" political organizations.[47] (When the text of this report was later reproduced in the *Berkeley Barb*, a Bay Area "underground" newspaper, IBM hurriedly announced that the handbook did not represent "company policy."[48]) These undercover operations are supplemented by an assortment of other "investigation services." Burns advertises that its staff can perform any of the following services: "pre-employment investigations and personal security checks including polygraph examinations; financial responsibility investigations; electronic sweeps for hidden listening devices; surveillance of business and residential premises, hotels and employees to prevent larceny or manipulation of products, merchandise and supplies; investigation of potential contest winners for compliance with contest rules; fingerprint and document analysis and shopping tests of all kinds to determine the honesty of employees and dealers."[49] And one firm, Universal Detective, Inc. of Newton Centre, Mass., advertises that its "Rent-a-Narc" service is available for undercover investigation of schools and other institutions.[50]

Some of these activities would appear to be of questionable legality even if performed by public law enforcement officers, and may involve outright invasion of privacy. Indeed, the pursuit of background data on job applicants has led to the arrest and prosecution of top officials of several prominent security firms: 1971, six security executives—including office of Pinkerton's, Burns and Wackenhut—pleaded guilty to charges that they had bribed New York City police officers to obtain confidential police records on prospective employees of American Airlines and Trans-Caribbean Airlines.[51] (The defendants pleaded guilty to the misdemeanor charge of "giving an unlawful gratuity to a public servant" rather than face trial on bribery and conspiracy.) The invasion of privacy issue was also raised in Florida, where in 1967 Governor Claude Kirk hired the Wackenhut Corporation to constitute an unofficial state investigative force because official agencies, he felt, were doing an inadequate job; the Wackenhut operation was cancelled nine months later amid charges of "police state" tactics arising from the firm's "aggressive compilation of dossiers on Florida citizens."[52] And, while state and Federal criminal records and other personal data systems are coming under increasing legislative and judicial scrutiny, no one has yet investigated the contents of the millions of personal dossiers kept by the private security firms. According to the RAND study, Wackenhut maintains files on 2,500,000 persons, Pinkerton's on 1,500,000 persons, and Burns on at least 50,000.[53] The contents of these files are made available to clients on a contract basis, usually without the person involved ever being informed of the transaction.

Operating on a still more exalted level of detective work are the private intelligence agencies like Intertel which employ the latest spy techniques to provide confidential intelligence for their corporate clients. Many of these firms have been set up in the past few years to constitute a sort of "private CIA" for the large multinational firms which have expanded their operations in troubled Third World areas.[54] Indeed, many of these firms are staffed by ex-CIA agents and other former government operatives who, in many cases, retain informal access to privileged government files. Intertel (International Intelligence, Inc.), for instance, is headed by the former chief of the Justice Department's Organized Crime Strike Force, Robert Peloquin, and its employees include men who formerly served as: Deputy Director of Security, National Security Agency; Supervisor, Espionage and Internal Security Investigations, FBI; Director, Intelligence and Internal Security Divisions, Internal Revenue Service; and chief, Market Surveillance Section, Securities and Exchange Commission.[55] Intertel has been described as "nothing less than the legal incorporation of an old-boy network whose ganglia reach into virtually every nerve cell of the federal investigative/intelligence community."[56] Among its more noteworthy exploits: managing Howard Hughes' dramatic 1970 flight from Las Vegas and the establishment of his new resort empire in the Bahamas, and the identification of Clifford Irving as the author of the Hughes autobiography hoax.[57]

THIRD WORLD RENT-A-COPS

The globe-ranging activities of Intertel and other private intelligence firms bring to mind another facet of the private security industry: its recent and rapid expansion into Third World areas. As the U.S.-based multinationals have

built refineries and other costly facilities in Third World areas, they have naturally turned to the established U.S. security firms to provide security for their new overseas operations. Thus Wackenhut do Brasil, established in 1970, already had 1,200 guards at work in 1972 and had branch offices in Brasilia, Curitiba, Porto Alegre, Rio de Janeiro, and Sao Paulo. Wackenhut—the most aggressive security firm in the overseas market—also has subsidiaries or affiliates in Belgium, Italy, France, the Dominican Republic, Ecuador, Venezuela and Colombia. Its Colombian affiliate, the 59%-owned Wackenhut de Colombia, S.A., has 1,200 employees and its 1972 revenues of $1 million placed it among that nation's top 50 companies. In Ecuador, Wackenhut's 532 guards protect "embassies, pipelines and ports."[58] Other security firms with substantial overseas operations are Burns and Brink's, Inc.[59] Many U.S. multinationals (particularly the oil giants) have established their own security corps abroad, and one firm—the Arabian-American Oil Company (ARAMCO)—even managed to have its security officers trained at the International Police Academy in Washington, D.C.[60]

THE IMPACT OF PRIVATE POLICE

As private guards and detectives assume an even larger share of the urban police function, it is important to consider both the quality of their services and their impact on the social fabric as a whole.

Since private security forces are employed primarily to *deter* crime (by their physical presence at potential crime sites), there is no practical way to measure their job performance. (Public police effectiveness, on the other hand, can be at least roughly calculated through arrest and conviction data.) RAND reported in 1972 that no statistical research has been done to compare the cost of security forces to the cost of crimes they are meant to prevent, and that "the executives we contacted in the contract security business could not provide us with quantitative evaluations of the effectiveness of

156

their services."[61]

If there is no "hard" data on the effectiveness of private security services, there *is* considerable data on the industry's shortcomings and inadequacies. As noted earlier, RAND discovered in 1971 that most armed guards received little or no training in the use of firearms, and that the overwhelming majority of rent-a-cops are totally unfamiliar with the laws governing their work. And, in 1973, the National Advisory Commission on Criminal Justice Standards and Goals reported: "Limited research has revealed that private security forces have a variety of other shortcomings. These include excessive force, false arrest and imprisonment, illegal search and seizure, impersonation of a peace officer, trespass, invasion of privacy, and dishonest or subprofessional business practices."[62] In at least several large cities, moreover, private guard misconduct has spurred adoption of new licensing procedures and industry regulations. In Washington, D.C., for instance, Councilman Tedson J. Meyers introduced a bill imposing new controls on security firms after two guards were indicted for manslaughter and several others were charged with participation in illegal shoot-outs.[63]

Despite the inconclusive nature of existing data on private guard performance, RAND concluded in 1972 that the security industry provides "clear social benefits" to its customer and to the general public. "There seems no doubt," it asserted, "that crime rates would be higher if there were no guards protecting property, if there were no security men escorting the movements of large quantities of money, if there were no alarm systems or if no one investigated the background of job and credit applications."[64] RAND did not, however consider the social and political implications of growing private guard employment, and it is to this question that we turn next.

The growth in private guard employment can, as we have seen, be partly attributed to the city-dweller's sense of personal insecurity. Yet the attempted cure to this problem may in turn produce new problems that will enhance rather than lessen the "climate of fear" in America cities. We must consider, for instance, the psychological impact (especially on children) of coming under constant surveillance by uniformed guards in apartment buildings, stores, schools, buses, subways, offices, playgrounds, theaters, etc. At what point does such surveillance induce a "Big Brother" syndrome with consequent stifling of personal creativity, diversity, and spontaneity? Although it is hardly possible to even attempt an adequate treatment of this subject here, it seems fairly obvious that a ubiquitous guard presence can only contribute to the atmosphere of fear and paranoia in most communities, even though it may discourage some forms of crime. Increased guard services, after all, can only *deter* the performance of a crime—they cannot relieve any of the social and economic forces which generate criminal behavior in the first place, and thus cannot provide any lasting solution to the fear and insecurity that have come to dominate U.S. cities.

The question of expanding guard employment and community attitudes becomes particularly critical when we turn to urban race relations. Although private police are instructed to watch *everyone* for signs of suspicious behavior, any prolonged exposure to guard operations will suffice to demonstrate that Black teenagers are far more likely to be hassled by rent-a-cops than middle-class whites. The emergence of a society whose white citizens are increasingly clustered in "residential compounds" and "fortified cells," while its minority residents live in the surrounding badlands is an effect of the racist, capitalist system. Police —both public and private—in their class control functions, enforce racism which is used to divide the working class.

WILLIAM J. BURNS INTERNATIONAL SECURITY SERVICES, INC.

(Formerly Burns Detective Agency)
320 Old Briarcliff Rd., Briarcliff Manor, N.Y. 10510
Chairman: Frederick E. Crist
Chairman of the Executive Committee: D. Bruce Burns
President: Edward W. Hyde
Employees: 42,000 (1975)
Revenues: $181.3 million (1975)

The second largest contract guard service in the United States . . . Founded in 1909 by William J. Burns, a former investigator for the U.S. Secret Service, and still controlled by his family . . . For 40 years the investigative arm of the American Hotel-Motel Association . . . Primary source of revenue is uniformed guard service, although firm is moving increasingly into electronic surveillance and alarm services . . . In 1972 provided 48,900,000 hours of guard service to 18,600 clients . . . Maintains 110 branch offices in the United States plus offices in Puerto Rico, Colombia, the Virgin Islands and the Bahamas . . . A Miami subsidiary, The Burns International Investigation Bureau, conducts undercover investiga-tions and intelligence-gathering operations abroad.

PINKERTON'S, INC.
100 Church St., New York, N.Y. 10007
President: Edward J. Bednarz
Employees: 32,000 (1971)
Revenues: $201.5 million (1975)

America's oldest and largest private firm providing contract guard and investigative services. . . . Founded in 1850 by Allan Pinkerton, a Chicago detective . . . For 50 years the nation's only national detective service operating across state lines. . . . In 1892 provided armed guards to reopen struck steel mills during the famous Homestead massacre. . . . Notorious for its labor espionage activities until such practices attacked by the LaFollette Committee in 1936 . . . Today the firm's primary activity is providing uniformed guards for factories, hospitals, colleges, stores and sporting arenas . . . Also operates a K-9 Patrol Service and maintains an Electro-Security laboratory in Webster, Mass., for production of surveillance and guard devices. . . . Pinkerton's now has 98 branch offices in the U.S. and Canada.

THE WACKENHUT CORPORATION
3280 Ponce de Leon Blvd., Coral Gables, Fla. 33134
Chairman & President: George R. Wackenhut
Employees: 28,000 (1975)
Revenues: $102.4 million (1975)

The fastest growing private security firm in the United States, and the nation's third largest supplier of guard and investigative services ... Founded in 1954 by George R. Wackenhut, a former FBI agent, and three other ex-FBI operatives ... Provides uniformed guards for factories, stores and institutions as well as for government agencies like the Atomic Energy Commission and NASA ... Wackenhut's Aviation Division moved early into airport security field and captured many lucrative contracts for pre-flight screening of airline passengers ... In 1967 organized a controversial anti-crime task force for Florida Governor Claude Kirk ... Has expanded rapidly into the Caribbean and Latin America, and in 1973 overseas operation brought in an additional $6.9 million in revenues ... Provides "executive protection" for U.S. businessmen in Latin America, and guards many overseas facilities of U.S. multinational corporations ... Compound annual growth rate in revenues during 1965-69 was an impressive 28.4 percent ... High growth rate achieved through aggressive acquisition of smaller guard firms.

WALTER KIDDE AND COMPANY
9 Brighton Rd., Clifton, N.J. 07012
Chairman & President: Fred R. Sullivan
Chairman of the Executive Committee: John F. Kidde
Employees: 35,000 (1975)
Revenues: $1.156 billion (1975)

The largest U.S. company in the safety, security and protection business as a whole, with a host of subsidiaries producing locks, vaults, fire-detection systems, surveillance devices, etc. ... GLOBE SECURITY SYSTEMS, a 100%-owned subsidiary, is the fourth largest supplier of guard and investigative services in the United States ... Globe was founded in 1913 and acquired by Kidde in 1966 ... Globe's 1972 revenues were $48.1 million ... A Globe subsidiary, Interstate Security Services, provides guard services in the United Kingdom.

1. National Commission on the Causes and Prevention of Violence, *Violent Crime*, New York, George Braziller, 1969, pp. 69-70.
2. *The Philadelphia Evening Bulletin*, January 26, 1970.
3. James S. Kakalik and Sorrel Wildhorn, *The Private Police Industry: Its Nature and Extent*, Vol. II of the RAND Corporation study for the National Institute of Law Enforcement and Criminal Justice of the Law Enforcement Assistance Administration, U.S. Department of Justice, Washington, D.C., Government Printing Office, 1972, p. 4. (Hereafter cited as *Private Police II.*)
4. James S. Kaklik and Sorrel Wildhorn, *Private Police in the United States: Findings and Recommendations*, Vol. I of the RAND study, p. 14. (Herein cited as *Private Police I.*)
5. Ibid., pp. 10-13.
6. *The New York Times*, April 8, 1973.
7. *The New York Times*, October 2, 1970.
8. *Private Police I*, p. 14.
9. Pinkerton's Inc., *Annual Report 1971*, p. 2.
10. William J. Burns International Security Services, Inc., *Annual Report 1972*, p. 3.
11. Cited in *The New York Times*, October 2, 1970.
12. Quoted in *The Washington Post*, May 12, 1970.
13. *The New York Times*, October 2, 1970.
14. Quoted in *The Washington Post*, May 12, 1970.
15. See: James S. Kakalik and Sorrel Wildhorn, *Special-Purpose Public Police*, Vol. V of the RAND study, pp. 17-28.
16. "Private Police Forces in Growing Demand," *U.S. News & World Report*, Jan. 29, 1973, p. 55.
17. *Berkeley Gazette*, March 9, 1974.
18. Elliot H. Goldman, "Economic Impact of Security," *Justice*, May 1972, p. 28.
19. Cited in Goldman, "Impact of Security," p. 28.
20. Cited in "Growing Toll of Crimes Against Business," *U.S. News & World Report*, Oct. 2, 1972, p. 39.
21. Quoted in Margaret D. Pacey, "Quest for Security," *Barron's*, March 10, 1969.
22. *The New York Times*, July 8, 1971.
23. *The New York Times*, April 22, 1974.
24. Quoted in *The New York Times*, June 8, 1973.
25. *Private Police I*, p. 11; *Private Police II*, pp. 14, 24.
26. *San Francisco Chronicle*, Dec. 26, 1972. For further discussion of these points, see *Private Police II*, pp. 55-56.
27. Quoted in "Private Police Forces," p. 55.
28. *Private Police I*, p. 11.
29. Ibid., p. 13. See also *Private Police II*, pp. 19, 21.
30. *Private Police I*, p. 30.
31. Ibid., p. 14.
32. "Private Police Forces," p. 54.
33. *Private Police I*, p. 30.
34. Ibid.
35. Pinkerton's, Inc. *Annual Report 1971*, p. 4.
36. *Private Police I*, p. 31.
37. *The New York Times*, October 2, 1970.
38. Quoted in "Private Police Forces," p. 55.
39. *Private Police I*, pp. 34-35.
40. Ibid., p. 35.
41. Ibid., pp. 38-39.
42. *Private Police II*, p. 45.
43. Ibid., p. 46. See also *Violations of Free Speech and Rights of Labor*, Hearings Before the Committee on Education and Labor, United States Senate, Washington, D.C., U.S. Government Printing Office, 1936.
44. Burns, *Annual Report for 1972*, p. 8.
45. Ibid.
46. Eugene V. Allen, "The Value of Internal Intelligence," *Industrial Security*, August 1971, p. 28.
47. See "The IBM Papers," *Berkeley Barb*, Nov. 15-21 and 22-28, 1974.
48. *The New York Times*, November 18, 1974.
49. Burns, *Annual Report for 1972*, p. 8.
50. See advertisements in *Justice* magazine, 1973.
51. *The New York Times*, January 26, 1971.
52. *National Observer*, October 30, 1967. See also Jim Hougan, "A Surfeit of Spies," *Harper's*, December 1974, p. 53.
53. *Private Police II*, pp. 45-47.
54. Jim Hougan, op. cit., pp. 52-53.
55. Ibid., pp. 54, 56.
56. Ibid., p. 56.
57. Ibid., pp. 64, 66. See also *Los Angeles Times*, April 1, 1972.
58. The Wackenhut Corporation, *Annual Report 1972*, pp. 5-6.
59. "Increase in Security Services," *U.S. News & World Report*, Feb. 7, 1972, p. 58.
60. *Los Angeles Times*, June 7, 1974.
61. *Private Police I*, p. 25.
62. National Advisory Commission, *Police*, p. 147.
63. *The Washington Post*, June 13, 1972, and June 28, 1973.
64. *Private Police I*, p. 24.

15. POLICING THE EMPIRE *[1]

INTRODUCTION

As U.S. capitalism developed from a competitive to a highly concentrated monopoly system, and corporations were forced to expand their profit-making ventures to other countries, an entire system of repression and class control also had to be exported in order to protect them. This rise of U.S. imperialism was signalled by the Spanish-American War, through which the United States gained economic and political control of Cuba, Puerto Rico and the Philippines. Since that time, giant U.S. corporations, supported by the military and other government agencies, began to increase their control over the economic resources and political life of many countries. The United States emerged from World War II as the most powerful imperialist country in history, carrying out economic and political control through large-scale investment, trade and loans to foreign countries; CIA-led covert

operations including the manipulation of political parties, bribery, and assassination of leaders; military assistance, and finally military intervention itself by U.S. forces.

The function of U.S. military, police and other repressive agencies throughout the world is an extension of the class control tasks we have discussed within the United States. In order for imperialism to survive, particularly within Third World countries (Asia, Africa and Latin America), U.S. corporations must maintain control over large sectors of those countries' economies.

However, one of the most important political trends in the world since World War II has been the struggle by many countries for national liberation—independence from U.S. domination (direct or indirect) and the process of constructing socialism. Examples include the Chinese, Korean, Vietnamese and Cuban revolutions, and more recently, the national liberation struggles in Angola and southern Africa. Many attempts at liberation have suffered temporary setbacks due to U.S.-backed repression.

This chapter shows how the U.S. government and the multi-national corporations are opposing all these struggles. The most important agent of repression, short of military intervention, is a strong internal police force. Nelson Rockefeller, after returning from a trip to Latin America, expresses the importance of U.S. support of foreign police:

> . . . In view of the growing subversion, mounting terrorism, and violence against citizens, and the rapidly expanding population, it is essential that the training program which brings military and police personnel from other hemisphere nations to the United States be continued and strengthened. . . . The United States should respond to requests for assistance of the police by providing them with the essential tools to do their job.[2]

There are many links between political struggles in other countries and those in the United States. Both oppose the exploitative

* Copyright Nancy Stein, 1975

nature of monopoly capitalism; both confront the police, whose primary task is to protect the capitalist system from attack. The U.S. government and corporations have provided millions of dollars worth of weapons, equipment, training and indoctrination to the police forces of other countries. And as the struggle in the United States intensifies, these U.S.-sponsored techniques of repression are brought back for domestic use. A study of U.S.-supported police throughout the "free world" will provide a better understanding of the U.S. police and its functions.

OFFICE OF PUBLIC SAFETY

U.S. funds, granted through the Office of Public Safety (OPS) of the U.S. Agency for International Development (AID), have been used to construct the National Police Academy in Brazil, to renovate and expand the South Vietnamese prison system, and to install a centralized "war room" for the Caracas police. AID estimates that over one million foreign policemen have received some training or supplies through this "public safety" program—a figure which includes 100,000 Brazilian police and the former 120,000-man National Police Force of South Vietnam. Such local forces have received training not only in routine police matters, but also in paramilitary and counterinsurgency techniques developed in response to the threat of revolutionary war.

The Office of Public Safety (OPS) was established by President Kennedy in 1961 in response to a growing threat of insurgency around the world, exemplified by the triumph of the Cuban Revolution with its impact on the rest of Latin America, and by the continuing national liberation struggle in the southern part of Vietnam. At that time, a shift occurred in U.S. military strategy, from an emphasis on preparing for wars with advanced industrial countries (primarily the Soviet Union) to the development of a counterinsurgency apparatus that could deal more effectively with the growing revolutionary ferment in the Third World.[3]

The policy-makers were aware that the United States needs a stable environment

around the world to guarantee the continued growth and profits of private U.S. corporations that increasingly "see the world as their oyster." In addition, the U.S. government seeks to reduce the possibility of the rise to power of groups not firmly aligned with the capitalist system. Therefore, while publicly concerned with the development of an organized, humane, civil police force that conduct routine police business, the Public Safety program, along with other counterinsurgency measures, in fact has allowed the United States to intervene in the internal affairs of other countries by developing repressive forces to combat opposition movements that threaten the interests of the United States and its foreign supporters.

The Public Safety Program received a blow in December 1973 when the U.S. Congress voted to phase out its foreign operations because the program caused the United States to be identified too closely with repressive regimes and the practice of torture. However, the conditions that generated this program have not changed and the goals of the U.S. government remain the same. One way or another, the United States will continue to advise and supply local police forces as an important element of the counterinsurgency apparatus that was developed to repress popular move-

161

ments and to maintain regimes friendly to the United States.

Since the late 1950's, the principal instrument used by the United States to maintain stability in its Third World domain is the Military Assistance Program, which is designed to improve the counterinsurgency capabilities of the local armed forces. In dealing with urban discontent and political unrest, however, it was thought that the police would be more effective. The police force, as Professor David Burks testified before a Congressional Committee, "is with the people all the time carrying on the normal functions of control or apprehension of ordinary criminals and can, therefore, move very quickly whenever an insurgent problem develops."[4] This argument was shared by AID, whose chief officer declared in 1964: "[T]he police are a most sensitive point of contact between government and people, close to the focal points of unrest, and more acceptable than the army as keepers of order over long periods of time."[5]

Another reason advanced for the support of police forces (and one which is rarely mentioned in public), is that the police constitute a highly trained and indoctrinated force, whereas the rank and file of the armed forces are often filled with relatively undisciplined and unmotivated draftees—many of whom are Indians, peasants, or members of other oppressed groups.

At the core of these arguments is the hope that an effective police force, backed by massive U.S. aid, can prevent or postpone the need for direct military intervention by the United States or its allies—as was required to salvage the Saigon regime. At the 1965 graduation ceremonies of AID's International Police Academy, General Maxwell Taylor told Third World police cadets:

The outstanding lesson [of the Indochina conflict] is that we should never let another Vietnam-type situation arise again. We were too late in recognizing the extent of the subversive threat. We appreciate now that every young, emerging country must be constantly on the alert, watching for those symptoms which, if allowed to develop unrestrained, may eventually grow into a disastrous situation such as that in Sout. Vietnam. We have learned the need for strong police force and a strong polic intelligence organization to assist in identify ing early the symptoms of an incipien subversive situation.[6]

Acting on the premise that police force constitute the "first line of defense again subversion," the United States flooded th Third World with anti-riot equipment an police advisers under AID's Public Safety pr gram. During hearings on the Foreign Assi tance appropriations for 1965, AID Administr. tor David Bell described the rationale behin U.S. police assistance programs as follow

Maintenance of law and order includir. internal security is one of the fundament. responsibilities of government. . . .

Successful discharge of this responsibilit is imperative if a nation is to establish ar maintain the environment of stability ar security so essential to economic, social, ar political progress. . . .

Plainly, the United States has very gre interests in the creation and maintenance c an atmosphere of law and order und. humane, civil concepts and control. . . Where there is a need, technical assistance t the police of developing nations to me. their responsibilities promotes and protec these U.S. interests.[7]

The United States Government, throug AID's Office of Public Safety (OPS), h assisted Third World police forces in these thr. ways:

(1) By offering advanced training to seni. police officers at the International Police Aca. emy (IPA) in Washington, D.C., and at oth. institutions in the United States. By mid-197 more than 7000 Third World police officia received training in the United States, of who about 60 percent were Latin American. Th training of police officials from countries whi. carry out the systematic use of torture has be. the target of popular forces within the Unite States that want all such training to ceas Though IPA spokesmen maintained that the categorically condemn the use of torture as police tactic, recent disclosures of reports pr pared by IPA graduates indicate an ambivale

and often supportive attitude toward its use.

"As a last resort ..." wrote a Nepalese inspector, torture is "practical and necessary." A South Vietnamese policeman wrote that "threats and force can put out any truth in a minimum time." A Zaire officer agreed "force or threats" will expedite an investigation but warned: "This tactic must not be known by the public." And a Colombian officer stated that "It is undeniable that in innumerable cases, the interrogator is forced to use moral or physical coercion to obtain truth that the person knows."[8]

The IPA lesson plan itself included a course on "Interviews and Interrogations" which provides instruction in such techniques as "emotional appeals," exaggerating fears, and psychological "jolts."

After a struggle, Senator James Abourezk [D-S.D.] introduced legislation that was passed by the Congress in the Foreign Assistance Act of 1974, which would "prohibit the use of foreign assistance funds to provide training, advice or financial support for police, prison or other law enforcement forces of a foreign country." As a result of this action, the International Police Academy closed its doors on March 1, 1975, representing a significant victory for popular forces that had worked to eliminate this institution.

Foreign police officers receive further training in psychological operations (PSYOPs) at the U.S. Army Institute for Military Assistance at Ft. Bragg, North Carolina. A Security Assistance Symposium conducted in 1972 for the instructors of such courses developed the ground-rules for pacification programs involving the participation of the police and the military, under the rubric of Population Protection and Resources Management. The objectives of this program are to: 1) sever the supporting relationship between the population and the insurgent; 2) detect and neutralize the insurgent apparatus and activities in the community; and 3) provide a secure physical and psychological environment for the population. Techniques employed to carry out these tasks involve establishing a national identity card system, frequent search operations, checkpoints, curfews and block controls to monitor the movement of the people and goods. The Symposium concluded with a discussion of the role of the mass media and propaganda in building support for the government "since by their nature most [of these] measures are rather harsh ... [and] they should be coordinated with an intensive PSYOPs campaign to convince the population that these harsh methods are for their own good."[9]

(2) *By stationing U.S. "Public Safety Advisors" in selected Third World countries to provide training for rank-and-file police officers and to advise top police officials at the country's national police headquarters.* In 1973, 309 U.S. advisors were on duty, half of them in Vietnam. Most Public Safety Advisors were recruited from the FBI, the Special Forces, Military Police, domestic law enforcement agencies and the CIA. The Advisors normally maintained offices in the national police headquarters of the host country and they frequently participated in the repressive activities of the

163

local police (see below). The kidnaping and execution of Advisor Dan Mitrione in Uruguay in 1970 brought to public attention the various activities of OPS and the extent of U.S. involvement with the police of other countries. The film *State of Siege* is based on this incident, and has been "blamed" by AID officials for contributing to the public pressure which led to the termination of the Public Safety Program. OPS advisors were also instrumental in developing and carrying out Operation Phoenix in Vietnam, which involved the routine use of torture and assassination to wipe out all levels of government opposition.

(3) *By making direct grants of specialized police equipment, including riot gases, pistols, shotguns, gas masks, radios and walkie-talkies, patrol cars, jeeps, and computers.* About half of OPS's total spending was allocated to this supply effort. In an emergency, AID was empowered to make emergency shipments of riot equipment and other police material to support a favored regime. A less explicit aspect of this type of police assistance was the psychological warfare function. Police equipment supplied to Third World forces is designed not only to aid in the suppression of existing threats to the status quo, but also to intimidate

the public and thus prevent future disturbances. Large numbers of patrol cars, a cop on every corner, visible machine guns and shotguns, helicopters and checkpoints—are all part of the effort to create a climate of fear and hopelessness in the general population. This sense of hopelessness is perhaps best described in Frantz Fanon's study of the Algerian independence struggle, *The Wretched of the Earth*, though the people were able to overcome this feeling and gain their freedom:

> *In the innermost recesses of [the Algerian's] brains, the [French] settlers' tanks and airplanes occupy a huge place. When they are told, "action must be taken," they see bombs raining down on them, armoured cars coming at them on every path, machine gunning and police action . . . and they sit quiet, they are beaten from the start.* [10]

EXAMPLES OF "PUBLIC SAFETY" IN THE THIRD WORLD

Total aid provided by OPS between 19[ ] and 1972 amounted to $308.6 million, [ ] which some two-thirds was allocated to South[ ] east Asia, primarily South Vietnam and Tha[ ]land. U.S. assistance has been concentrated in[ ] handful of countries in each region, most [ ] which have experienced insurgent uprisings [ ] the past decade, and most of which are no[ ] characterized by repressive regimes.

The available documentation on U.S. Publ[ ] Safety programs abroad suggests that OP[ ] focused its efforts on certain key elements [ ] the local police system—particularly trainin[ ] intelligence, communications, riot-control an[ ] counterinsurgency—in order to gain maximu[ ] influence in areas of greatest concern to t[ ] United States. By concentrating its efforts [ ] these strategic aspects of police work, OPS w[ ] able to exert considerable influence over t[ ] direction of the local police apparatus despi[ ] the modest size of the funding input. Th[ ] AID's presentation to Congress on the Fisc[ ] Year 1967 OPS program in the Dominic[ ] Republic, notes that while the proposed gra[ ] of $720,000 represents but 4.7 percent of t[ ] Dominican police budget, *"for U.S. objecti*[ ]

153,000 people in 1970 as part of the CIA-funded Operation Phoenix.[13]

In South Vietnam, U.S. aid to the Saigon police apparatus extended all the way to the prison system, which was partially subsidized by OPS funds. Top Vietnamese prison officials have received training in correctional techniques at U.S. expense, and AID funds have been used to expand Vietnam's prison facilities. AID's involvement in the Saigon prison system was highlighted in 1970, when Congressmen visiting the Con Son prison complex were shown the notorious "Tiger Cells" for political prisoners.[14]

OPS, DEATH SQUADS AND THE CIA

Police participation in clandestine right-wing terrorist organizations is quite prevalent in Latin America. These groups, such as "La Mano Blanca" (the White Hand) in Guatemala, "La Banda" in the Dominican Republic, the "Death Squad" in Uruguay and Brazil, and the new Argentine Anti-Communist Alliance generally operate, in practice, with unofficial government approval. They are largely composed of off-duty policemen who attack and assassinate political activists and other public figures feared by the regimes, and do so without directly implicating the uniformed services. The *New York Times* estimates that in Brazil, more than 1000 people have been executed by the Death Squads in the past six years; and according to the *Miami Herald*, the chief criminal judge of Sao Paulo, Brazil, told newsmen in 1970 that "the members of the Death Squad are policemen . . . and everyone knows it."[15] In Argentina there has been nearly one murder a day attributed to right-wing terrorists during the first two months of 1975.

U.S. involvement in the organization, training, and equipping of Uruguay's Death Squad is described in the testimony of Nelson Bardesio, a police photographer and death squad member who was kidnaped and interrogated by the Tupamaro guerrillas in 1972.[16] Bardesio affirmed that a Uruguayan government agency which provided an official "cover" for the death squad was set up with the advice and

it provides the necessary leverage.''[11] (Emphasis added.) Not surprisingly, AID's "program objectives" in the Dominican Republic, as in other Third World countries, stressed the suppression of civil disturbances and revolutionary activity —i.e., those aspects of police work which provide protection for U.S. diplomats and business interests—rather than the reform of brutal and corrupt police administrations.[12]

In many countries, OPS funds were used for "improving records and identification facilities," and for the development of "national police command centers." Clearly, AID's intention in these efforts was to establish centralized data banks on political activists and to upgrade the anti-riot and paramilitary forces. In Venezuela, OPS funds were used to create a unified operations center in Caracas to coordinate riot-control activities. In South Vietnam, OPS launched a national identification campaign designed to register every inhabitant over 15 years of age. All citizens were to be provided with an unbreakable ID card which they must show to police officers on request; anyone caught without one is considered a "Vietcong suspect" and subject to arrest. By the end of 1970, South Vietnam's National Police command had amassed a full set of fingerprints, biographical information, photographs and data on the political beliefs of nearly 12,000,000 people. With the help of this information plus an elaborate system of roadblocks and checkpoints, the National Police detained over financial assistance of U.S. Public Safety Advisor William Cantrell. In his testimony, which served as the basis for several scenes in the film *State of Siege*, Bardesio identified other U.S. Embassy and Public Safety personnel who worked with the members of the death squad, as well as Uruguayan police officers and military officials who participated in assassinations and bombings against opponents of the government.

The connection between the United States and these terror squads became more pronounced when the existence of an OPS "bomb school," located in Texas and staffed with CIA instructors, was made public by Jack Anderson in October 1973.[17] Since 1969, OPS had offered a Technical Investigations Course at this school to at least 165 foreign police officers from Africa, Asia, and Latin America. The students were instructed in the design, manufacture and employment of homemade bombs and incendiary devices, as well as given courses in assassination weapons and booby traps. *State of Siege* depicted various training exercises from this program, which is now being conducted at Edgewood Arsenal in Maryland.

In a memorandum to Senator James Abourezk, Matthew Harvey of AID said that this program was developed in response to requests from U.S. Embassies, as acts against U.S. personnel and property were increasing.[18] He explained that the course "does not teach the student to be a bomb disposal technician" but rather enhances his investigative skills. The program was supposed to help police develop countermeasures to homemade explosive devices, but there is no way of preventing these techniques from being used offensively against government opponents—as they have been in several countries. The Department of Defense refused to provide instructors for this sensitive course—but the CIA assumed this responsibility instead.

The CIA had other ties to the Public Safety program as well, most notably through their collaboration in conducting Operation Phoenix in Vietnam. Bardesio speculated in his testimony that Public Safety Advisor Cantrell was working for the CIA—which is highly possible

given the fact that ex-AID official David Fairchild has revealed that the CIA used the Public Safety program in the Dominican Republic for six of its agents.[19] Further information comes from an inside account of the CIA by ex-agent Philip Agee, who describes how the CIA used the Public Safety program as a cover for agents, and how the Agency arranged for various police officers to receive training by the CIA in the United States.[20]

The Director of the CIA, William Colby, offered a direct account of CIA-OPS connections in a letter to Senator Fulbright, expressing his concern over Congressional action that would end U.S. support for foreign police programs (the Abourezk amendment). Colby asserted that the relationships built up with policemen through these programs have been highly useful in "obtaining foreign intelligence" from police officers in other countries. The CIA receives vital information on illicit narcotics traffic, international terrorism and hijacking, through internal intelligence programs of foreign countries and from internal security forces of foreign governments.[21]

PHASING OUT OPS

The Office of Public Safety had come under increasing attack for its activities abroad, including its connections with death squads, torture and the CIA. AID officials made some revealing statements back in 1965, when criticism of the program was just beginning. They affirmed that Public Safety assistance was "not given to support dictatorships."

This rule, however, had been violated periodically: Administrator Bell told a Senate Committee "it is obviously not our purpose or intent to assist a head of state who is repressive. *On the other hand, we are working in a lot of countries where the governments are controlled by people who have shortcomings.*"[22] (Emphasis added.) Not wanting to embarrass the U.S. government or any of its friends, Mr. Bell did not identify the rulers with "shortcomings"—but he did go on to justify our support of them by insisting that "The police are a very strongly anti-communist force right now. For that reason it is a very important force to us."[23]

166

A quick look at any breakdown of OPS expenditures will provide ample information on the flow of U.S. funds to authoritarian regimes. Thus Brazil, the major recipient of OPS funds in Latin America, has been condemned by the International Commission of Jurists and other humanitarian organizations for its brutal treatment of political prisoners. And regimes in Guatemala and the Dominican Republic, both large recipients of U.S. aid, have been condemned by the Organization of American States as violators of human rights.[24]

As information about AID's support for repressive police forces became more abundant, protest and criticism increased. In 1971, after holding a series of hearings on repression in Brazil, Senator Frank Church commented:

> . . . the U.S. aid program to Brazilian military and police agencies . . . serves mainly to identify the U.S. with a repressive government. The hearings revealed an altogether too close identification of the U.S. with the current Brazilian government, and they raise a serious question about the wisdom of assistance to the Brazilian police and mili-

tary.[25]

Largely due to these hearings and strong public opposition, the Public Safety program in Brazil was terminated in 1972. Programs in other countries were ended at the local government's request, as in the case of Chile, under President Salvador Allende.

The Public Safety Program suffered its greatest defeat in December 1973, when the U.S. Congress passed an amendment to the 1973 Foreign Assistance Act (FAA), prohibiting AID from conducting police training and related activities in foreign countries. Under this provision, existing programs were allowed to continue until their expiration date, which for most programs was by mid-1974, and no new in-country programs could be initiated. The amendment **did not** cover continued training at the International Police Academy or other U.S. institutions, did not abolish activities in the area of narcotics control, and did not prohibit the continuation of this program in countries that *pay* for these services, such as Saudi Arabia. The majority of the programs,

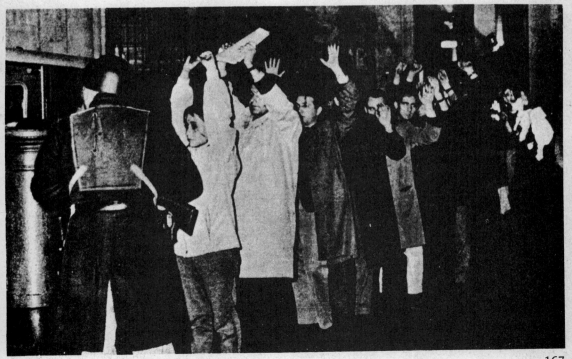

however, have been conducted on a grant basis, and the intent of the amendment was to eradicate all grant public safety activities in foreign countries by any U.S. government agency. Furthermore, this Act stated that no additional funds could be used for support of the police or prison system in South Vietnam.

The Foreign Assistance Act of 1974 carried this intention even further by prohibiting the use of funds to conduct *training* of foreign police in the United States or abroad, including a specific reference to the South Vietnamese police.

ALTERNATIVES TO OPS

In spite of the 1973 prohibition, OPS had an active program for Fiscal Year 1975, including training at IPA and other U.S. institutions, assistance in narcotics control, and programs which are totally paid for by the host country.

By looking more closely at the narcotics control program, it becomes clearer how the U.S. government can subvert the intent of the 1973 amendment, as activities carried out under this cover are far-reaching and structurally similar to those prohibited by the Congressional action. For example, the narcotics control program provided for training at IPA, assigning advisors to foreign countries to develop narcotics control capabilities, and supplying necessary equipment. In Fiscal Year 1975 there will be 15 advisors in 7 countries under this program.[26]

Under the guise of narcotics control, OPS or any other U.S. government agency can continue to relate closely to foreign police forces for many purposes, because the tactics used to locate narcotics traffic can easily be adapted for use against political opponents (i.e., surveillance, wiretapping, use of informants, etc.). An AID directive stated that "narcotics management support courses provide overseas police with training, knowledge and information to effectively coordinate civil police matters with military organizations in internal security matters and narcotics control."[27]

Drug Enforcement Administration

One possible alternative to the Office of

Public Safety which could continue to fulfill its goals, is the Drug Enforcement Administration (DEA), created in 1973 by an executive reorganization plan under which DEA absorbed the functions of other agencies concerned with narcotics control. As OPS declined in size and budget, narcotics control programs have increased. Five years ago, the U.S. overseas narcotics force was 26; as of 1974 it was 293, and for Fiscal Year 1975 DEA will have over 400 agents abroad, who will be housed in American Embassies in 42 countries. In addition, Congress is not reluctant to authorize funds for narcotics control and the budget request for DEA rose from $112.7 million in 1974 to $140.8 million in 1975.[28]

Furthermore, an in-house study of OPS written in December 1973, examined various options for continuing police training, given the Congressional restrictions of the program.[29] While it concluded that the Office of Public Safety, as an element of AID, was the best mechanism to carry out this task, the most viable alternative was to transfer the police training functions to the Department of Justice, of which DEA is a member.

DEA has an Office of Enforcement and an Office of Intelligence which maintain field offices in foreign countries, and an Office of Training which has programs open to foreign law enforcement officers. This organizational structure is very similar to that of the Office of Public Safety. DEA would be able to adequately channel money for other types of training and equipment as well as provide advisors to local police and a cover for CIA operatives, as did OPS. In fact, in February 1975, Jack Anderson revealed a number of connections between CIA and DEA, including the fact that 13 narcotics agents trained at a super-secret CIA counter-espionage school are still working for the DEA, and that 64 former CIA employees now work for DEA, half of whom are assigned to the Intelligence Unit in Washington, D.C.[30]

According to the Pentagon Papers on U.S. involvement in Vietnam, the acting director of the Special Operations and Field Support Section of the DEA's International Intelligence Division, Lt. Col. Lucien Conein, was a senior

operative of the CIA in Saigon in 1963 and served as liaison officer between the U.S. government and the forces that deposed President Ngo Dinh Diem. In May 1974, Col. Conein was briefed for three hours on electronic assassination techniques by representatives of the B. R. Fox Co., a now defunct manufacturer of wiretapping and bugging equipment. The equipment included a telephone that could be blown up by remote control, as well as explosive devices for use in cigarette packs, flashlights, and rifle ammunition clips. It was reportedly the first time law enforcement officials and Senate investigators had seen evidence that a domestic federal agency would even look at assassination techniques. Col. Conein found the material "fascinating" but said that he only purchased $500 worth of bugging equipment for DEA's foreign operations.[31]

Law Enforcement Assistance Administration

Another Justice Department agency that has recently moved into the international field is the Law Enforcement Assistance Administration (LEAA). The Crime Control Act of 1973 authorized LEAA to provide technical assistance, and coordinate information and intelligence for international agencies particularly in the areas of narcotics control, hijacking and terrorism. LEAA was granted an international role at the same time that the Foreign Assistance Act of 1973 was greatly reducing other U.S. activities related to foreign law enforcement agencies, and the three areas that LEAA will emphasize in its international work were also important elements of the Public Safety program which by their nature involve very close ties with the police of foreign countries. The nature of LEAA's international role is still in the formative stage. In its own statement before Congress on October 2, 1973 LEAA said there would be "no assistance to local [foreign] police departments for problems which are domestic in nature,"[32] but the line between investigating international narcotics and terrorist activities or hijacking and interfering in the internal affairs of other countries is very fine.

LEAA has already awarded two grants to the United Nations Social Defense Research Institute, located in Rome, for a project on "Economic Crisis and Crime," ($77,925), and the development of an international clearinghouse for criminal justice information ($136,978), which would assist in the international exchange of information regarding terrorism, skyjacking, narcotics interdiction and other criminal justice areas. A request for $175,000 to continue this project in FY 1975 was studied by LEAA, along with a proposal for a study of the nature of terrorism and possible responses to it.[33] The $150,800 grant request for this study was submitted by Pieder Konz, Director of the UN Institute and an official in the Drug Enforcement Office in the U.S. Embassy in Rome. In reference to the debate in the United Nations about defining terrorism, the project proposal states that

> ... acts of violence committed under the color of government authority should not be considered in this particular series of studies; although it is recognized that they can also be defined as terrorism, it is evident that their prevention and control involved intervention mechanisms different from those appropriate for terrorist action by individuals or groups of individuals.[34]

LEAA has also awarded $350,000 to the University of Maryland to assist the International Centre for Comparative Criminology at the University of Montreal, in setting up an international forum for the discussion, study and exchange of information on criminal justice problems.

LEAA has tentatively allocated one million dollars towards the International Assistance Program for FY 1975, which would include, in addition to the above mentioned programs, studies of: 1) Terrorism-Problem Analysis, Program Design, and Implementation—to assess current research and development and/or training needs ($500,000); 2) Foreign International Airport Security Assistance—to support the conduct of airport security surveys by technical advisory teams ($150,000); 3) Foreign Aviation Security Officers Assistance—to support the training of aviation security officers from selected foreign countries in advanced aviation security techniques ($20,000).[35]

LEAA money has already enabled 65 international trainees to complete a Federal Aviation Agency Security Training Program in Oklahoma. LEAA also cooperates with the Interagency Committee on Civil Aviation Security, which consists of representatives of Treas-

170

ury, Justice, Defense, State Departments and the Federal Aviation Agency; and the Cabinet Committee to Combat Terrorism, which is chaired by the Secretary of State and composed of the secretaries of Treasury, Defense, and Transportation, the Attorney General, the U.S. Ambassador to the UN, and the Directors of the CIA and FBI. This Cabinet committee is charged with considering the most effective means of preventing terrorism in the United States and establishing procedures to ensure the government takes appropriate action in response to terrorism.[36]

One of the effects of the Public Safety program has been the transfer of systems and programs developed in Third World countries back to the United States. For example, experiments in creating a centralized national police force in Vietnam or Brazil are being studied for application here. The national identification system developed in Vietnam may be looked at as a prototype of a similar system for the United States. As LEAA proposed, a mobile task-force trained in counter-terrorist methods would be composed of qualified personnel from various law enforcement agencies, and would complement LEAA's work in the international arena.[37] An LEAA study shows this.

Law enforcement situations also will arise in foreign countries which can with profit be studied in anticipation that similar situations may develop in the United States. For example, many foreign governments have had more extensive experience with terrorism than has this country. A properly developed research program might well detect techniques that are effective and which were suitable for application domestically. [38]

EXECUTIVE MERCENARIES—THE CASE OF SAUDI ARABIA

A former U.S. Army officer, hired by the Vinnell Corporation to train the Saudi Arabian National Guard, said: "We are not mercenaries because we are not pulling the triggers. We train people to pull triggers." Another officer laughed and said: "Maybe that makes us executive mercenaries." [39]

Using a private corporation to train the police of other countries would also be a convenient way to continue the work of OPS without directly involving the U.S. government. There are already situations where former OPS advisors have remained in their host country to continue providing training on a contract basis, as in Nicaragua. Private consulting firms and corporations that produce military and police equipment can also provide conduits for training and equipping foreign police. These contracts are often negotiated directly between foreign governments and U.S. corporations, bypassing the Pentagon. For example, Bell Helicopter International has a contract to provide a 1500 member force to train the newly created Iran Sky Cavalry which will use 500 Bell combat helicopters. The training group is headed by a retired U.S. Army Major, and is composed of other retired officers. [40]

The Vinnell Corporation of Los Angeles recruited several hundred former members of the U.S. Special Forces and other Vietnam war veterans to train the Saudi Arabian National Guard, a 26,000-man internal security force, to protect the country's oilfields and petroleum export facilities. The United States will provide the military equipment, but Vinnell will provide the training, all of which will be paid for by the Saudi government at a cost of $103 million. As of 1974, 9,535 U.S. citizens worked under commercial Pentagon contracts (40 percent in South Vietnam and 48 percent divided between Saudi Arabia and Iran). This arrangement with Vinnell could provide some glimpses into how the question of police training will be handled in the future. The Pentagon tried to keep secret the details of the Vinnell contract, which represents the first time a U.S. corporation that does not produce arms itself has been hired to train sizeable military combat units to use U.S. weapons.

Vinnell's general manager, Robert Montgomery, provided some insight into why the Pentagon would contract out a major training job to a private corporation: "Maybe this contract has come about because the political climate of the day might be against the U.S. military sending such a big team." [42]

Another aspect of Saudi Arabia's drive to improve its security forces was being carried out by OPS under the provision that the country pay for the service. An eighteen-man team of U.S. police was sent to Saudi Arabia to conduct an eight-week survey to help modernize the national police. [43] The team included Captain Louis Feder, director of the San Francisco Police Department's bureau of criminal information, and they focused on improving the criminal records and identification system.

OPS has been operating in Saudi Arabia since 1968, with the Saudi government reimbursing the United States for all costs of the program. As of August, 1974, there were seven advisors working for the Ministry of the Interior, providing training in such areas as telecommunications, fingerprinting, narcotics control and modern prison construction. Two advisors were also working for the Coast/Frontier Forces, which involved assisting the Saudis in providing better security for the oil pipeline which runs along the northern border. In addition, about 50 police officials per year had received training at the International Police Academy. Private police, working for ARAMCO, the Arabian-American Oil Company, have also been trained at IPA at Saudi expense. [44]

In expressing his concern that the Abourezk

171

amendment to the 1974 Foreign Assistance Act would close down the IPA and deprive the Saudis of their training, Alfred L. Atherton, Jr., of the State Department's Bureau of Near Eastern and South Asian Affairs urged the Senator to reconsider his proposal. He wrote that the inability "to continue this advisory relationship with the Ministry of the Interior would have detrimental effects on Saudi-U.S. relations." In light of the disclosures about the Vinnell corporation, it is interesting to note that he went on to say:

> AID does not feel at this time that the possibility of establishing a private corporation to meet Saudi public safety requirements would be a viable one. And in any case, we know from experience that in an area of such sensitivity, the Saudis would necessarily want to deal with our government and not a private company.[45]

MILITARIZATION OF THE POLICE

Finally, the role of the U.S. military in developing foreign police capabilities could be greatly expanded with little public knowledge. The military is already responsibile for training and equipping special forces and para-military troops for various countries, including the Imperial Iranian Gendarmerie. In addition, under the Military Assistance Service Funds provision of the Department of Defense Appropriations, the Pentagon provided training, arms, advisors, etc. for South Vietnam's paramilitary National Police Field Forces, responsible for carrying out Operation Phoenix.

The counterinsurgency program developed by President Kennedy in the early 1960's was based on the importance of maintaining a democratic facade while carrying out repressive actions against government opponents and guerrilla movements. In a democratic society, the police, not the military, are supposed to control domestic insurgency and crime. However, in the 1970's, many regimes could no longer maintain democratic forms, as socialist and nationalist movements continued to develop. Particularly in Latin America, the United States has been forced to rely almost exclusively on the military to guarantee U.S. investments and stability. The military, in turn, has taken over the command of the police in various countries. The militarization of the police has been one more result of the continued resistance of the people to repressive governments that do not serve their interests.

CONCLUSION

Even though the Office of Public Safety was phased out, its tasks are merely being shifted to other agencies. Whether through the military, or private corporations, or U.S. government agencies such as LEAA, the United States will continue to maintain a worldwide counterinsurgency apparatus. As long as people everywhere continue to demand the right to determine their own future and to develop their own resources, the United States will attempt to police the Third World.

1. Background portions of this article are based on Michael Klare and Nancy Stein, "The U.S. Public Safety Program," The U.S. Military Apparatus, published by NACLA, August, 1972. NACLA has published extensively on this subject, including the following articles: "How U.S. AID Shapes the Dominican Police," NACLA Newsletter, April, 1971; "AID Police Programs for Latin America," NACLA Newsletter, July-August, 1971; "Command and Control—U.S. Police Operations in Latin America," NACLA's Latin America Report, January, 1972; as well as other recent articles referenced below.
2. Nelson Rockefeller, "Quality of Life in the Americas," Report of a U.S. Presidential Mission for the Western Hemisphere, Department of State Bulletin, December 8, 1969.
3. For more on U.S. military strategy see Michael T. Klare, War Without End, New York, Alfred A. Knopf, 1972.
4. U.S. Senate, Committee on Foreign Relations, Subcommittee on American Republics Affairs, Compilation of Studies and Hearings, 91st Congress, 1st Session, 1969, p. 414.
5. U.S. Senate, Committee on Appropriations, Foreign Assistance Appropriations, 1965, Hearings, 89th Congress, 2d Session, 1964, p. 7. (Herein referred to as Foreign Assistance 1965.)
6. Maxwell D. Taylor, Address at Graduation Exercise, International Police Academy, Washington, D.C., U.S. Department of State press release, December 17, 1965.

7. *Foreign Assistance 1965*, p. 72.
8. Jack Anderson, "Questionable Means of Interrogation," *Washington Post*, August 3, 1974.
9. *Security Assistance Symposium*, December 12-13, 1972, The Military Assistance Officer Command and Staff Course 1-73, United States Army Institute for Military Assistance, Fort Bragg, North Carolina.
10. Frantz Fanon, *The Wretched of the Earth*, New York, Grove Press, 1961, p. 63.
11. U.S. Agency for International Development, *Project Data Summary FY 1966: Dominican Republic*, Washington D.C., 1965.
12. Ibid.
13. U.S. AID, *Program and Project Data Presentation to the Congress for FY 1972*, Washington, D.C., 1971. See also: U.S. AID, *The Role of Public Safety in Support of the National Police of Vietnam*, Washington, D.C., 1969.
14. *Project Data Presentation 1972*. See also: *The New York Times*, July 7, 1970.
15. *The Miami Herald*, July 24, 1970.
16. "Uruguay Police Agent Exposes U.S. Advisors," *NACLA's Latin America Report*, July-August, 1972.
17. Jack Anderson, *Washington Post*, October, 1973. See also: Michael Klare and Nancy Stein, "Police Terrorism in Latin America," *NACLA's Latin America Report*, January, 1974.
18. Correspondence to Senator James Abourezk from Matthew Harvey, Director of AID, September 25, 1973.
19. See interview with David Fairchild, former AID administrator in the Dominican Republic, in *NACLA Newsletter*, November, 1970.
20. Philip Agee, *Inside the Company, CIA Diary*, Harmondsworth, Middlesex, England, Penguin Books, 1975. See also: Victor Marchetti and John Marks, *The Cult of Intelligence*, New York, Alfred A. Knopf, 1974.
21. Jack Anderson, "CIA Admits Using Foreign Police," *Washington Post*, August 19, 1974.
22. *Foreign Assistance 1965*, p. 82.
23. Ibid., p. 75.
24. "U.S. to End Police Aid to Brazil," *The New York Times*, July 15, 1971.
25. *The Washington Post*, July 25, 1971.
26. Memorandum from Matthew Harvey, Director of AID, May 30, 1974.
27. Report from AID, June 6, 1974.
28. U.S. Congress, Senate, Committee on Appropriations, Subcommittee, *Departments of State, Justice, and Commerce, the Judiciary, and Related Agencies, Appropriations for F.Y. 1975*, Hearings, 93rd Congress, 2d Session, 1974, Part pp. 300-335.
29. Ernest W. Lefever, *U.S. Public Safety Assistance An Assessment*, prepared for USAID under contract cds-3361 with the Brookings Institution December, 1973.
30. Jack Anderson, "Closer Look at CIA Dope Link, *San Francisco Chronicle*, February 19, 1975.
31. *International Herald Tribune*, January 24, 197.
32. Quoted in *International Role and Objectives LEAA, Relations with other Federal Agencies an Recommendations*, prepared by the Executi Management Service, Inc., July, 1974, p. 18.
33. Letter to Representative John Conyers, Jr., fror Richard W. Velde, Administrator, Law Enforc ment Assistance Administration, November 1974.
34. Application for grant, No. p 74-029, *Terrorism Nature and Responses*, submitted by the U Social Defense Research Institute to LEAA January 11, 1974.
35. Conyers letter, op. cit.
36. Ambassador Lewis Hoffacker, "The U.S. Govern ment Response to Terrorism: A Global Ap proach," remarks made before the Mayor's Ad visory Committee on International Relations an Trade and the Foreign Relations Association, a New Orleans, La., February 28, 1974.
37. *Potential LEAA/NILECJ Activities Related to th International Aspects of Skyjacking, Terrorisn and Illegal Narcotics*, prepared by the MITR Corporation, March 8, 1974, pp. 21-22.
38. Ibid.
39. *New York Times* February 9. 1975.
40. *International Bulletin*, Internews, Berkeley, Calif. Vol. 2, No. 4, February 28, 1975.
41. Ibid.
42. *New York Times*, February 9, 1975.
43. *San Francisco Chronicle*, February 20, 21, 22 1975.
44. U.S. corporations operating abroad are beginnin to feel that many Third World governments ar unable or unwilling to provide adequate securit and they are turning to private U.S. security firm such as the Wackenhut Corporation to provid plant security abroad. For more on corporat response to international terrorism see: "Multi nationals under Siege: Protecting the Outposts, *NACLA's Latin America Report*, December 1974.
45. Correspondence from Alfred L. Atherton, Jr., t Senator James Abourezk, August 13, 1974.

VII. CONCLUSION

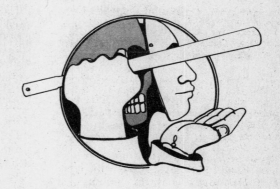

16. POLICE IN THE 1970'S

SAME FUNCTIONS, NEW FORMS

While during the recent period we have witnessed important changes in the methods and organization of policing, the general class functions of the police in capitalist society have not changed in the last 150 years. Each generation of workers has faced police repression in labor disputes, each generation of Third World people has been victimized by racist police practices, and each generation of progressive political movements has been attacked by counter-insurgent police forces and intelligence agencies. During some periods, such as the militant labor struggles of the late nineteenth century or the mass movements and labor organizing of the 1930's or the widespread revolts of the late 1960's, police repression is intensified and highly visible. But repression in capitalist society, while not always so exposed and spectacular, is day-to-day, a necessary mechanism for maintaining and reproducing exploitative social relations and a relatively stable political environment.

As we have demonstrated in the chapters on the historical development of the police, some techniques of repression are rooted in nineteenth century developments. For example, it is still "legal" for corporations to pay workers low wages and require them to work under hazardous conditions,[1] while it is "illegal" for workers who protest these conditions to block entrances to scabs. Recently, the United Rubber Workers faced repeated skirmishes with the police in their four month 1976 strike; the FBI infiltrated the striking United Electrical Radio and Machine Workers of America (UE) locals in Tampa, Florida, and Holyoke, Massachusetts, for surveillance and disruption; and court injunctions against strikes continue to provide the legal basis for arrests, as was the case with the 1976 struggle of the UE local in Minneapolis.

Similarly, old techniques of repression are being used in Third World communities. Intensified police actions against undocumented Mexican workers, who are being scapegoated

for the high rate of unemployment, have included mass deportations reminiscent of the notorious Palmer raids of 1919 (in which labor leaders, immigrants and socialists were rounded up and deported without trial) and of the notorious internment of Japanese-Americans in concentration camps in 1942. In 1974, the Immigration and Naturalization Service (INS) deported 700,000 Mexican workers and another 500,000 in the first half of 1975. In Dallas, an average of 350 workers per week are being deported by the INS.[2] During the 1970's, Indian people also have endured brutal repetition of past history. Native Americans demanding their land and treaty rights have been attacked by federal troops, state and local police, FBI agents and tribal police, especially since the 1973 battle of Wounded Knee on the Pine Ridge Reservation in South Dakota.

FISCAL CRISIS

In this book, we have focused almost exclusively on new developments in the policing apparatus. These new developments have not of course occurred in a vacuum nor are they unique. With the deepening crisis in U.S. capitalism, in which 1976 official rates of 5.5 percent inflation and almost 8 percent unemployment have become expected by government economists, the real value of workers' wages has declined severely, social services have been drastically cut back, and the ranks of the unemployed and under-employed have grown into the millions.[3] Not taking into account the more than half a million young men and women who were neither in school nor "actively looking" for jobs in 1974, teenage unemployment for 16-19 year olds was officially 16 percent.[4] But for urban Blacks and Puerto Ricans, the comparable unemployment rate hovered around 50 percent.[5]

Unemployment and inflation are part of the general fiscal crisis of the 1970's. The rapid expansion of police forces which occurred in response to the Third World and student

Federal marshals arrest 46 immigrant workers in Fort Wayne, Indiana

rebellions of the 1960's was closely tied to economic conditions. This crisis is only the current manifestation of a general decline of U.S. monopoly capitalism, accelerated by the military and political defeats that U.S. imperialism suffered in Vietnam and around the world.[6] While the struggle in Vietnam is the immediate precipitator of the economic crisis, the overall problem of the economy is not of a temporary nature but rather a permanent product of the contradictions of advanced monopoly capitalism. In times of crisis, the state assumes a more direct and visible role in regulating both the economy and social conditions. In particular, the state attempts to stabilize the monopoly sector, while maintaining a high level of profits, and to legitimate the existing political order, while cutting back on services to the working class. Since these goals are inconsistent and financial resources are limited, there is frequently a great deal of conflict over resource allocation. First priority, however, goes to the needs of the corporate state and to the repressive apparatus so that people's everyday needs (housing, health care, welfare, etc.) are sacrificed for the economic needs of big business. Thus, the burden of the economic crisis is carried primarily by the working class, as the ruling class benefits from corporate tax breaks, government subsidies, and the military-industrial complex.

During the current fiscal crisis, the reliance of the state on the police has intensified in order to back up with force the deteriorating economic situation of the working class and Third World communities. As sources of public expenditure dwindle due to unemployment and inflation, the ruling class makes repression its spending priority, while urging working people to cut back their standard of living and to demand fewer social services. At the same time, however, there has been an escalating militancy in rank and file union organizations, in Third World communities, and in many progressive political organizations. The build-up of the police, then, becomes even more necessary under conditions of growing class and political conflict. They are called upon to check working class expressions of protest and to contain popular militancy, while at the same time regulating the increase in crime that accompanies massive poverty and degradation, and creates an unstable political environment.

While the police are given priority over social services, the revenues available for repression are not unlimited and spending ceilings in

177

police departments reinforce the trend towards more business management practices and a slight reduction in the labor intensiveness of police work through technological innovation. This line of analysis may seem inconsistent with the highly publicized cutbacks of up to 20 percent of the force in cities such as Detroit, New York and Cleveland. The magnitude of these cutbacks, however, has been exaggerated by the police and media. Most urban police departments have not faced cutbacks, and rural and suburban forces have rarely been reduced. Furthermore, even where cutbacks have occurred, it is incorrect to view them as weakening the police institution.

There are three explanations for this. First, personnel cutbacks have been used to tighten departments organizationally, to increase their reliance on technology, and to eliminate "excess" personnel—that is, the proportion of a police force redundant after the introduction of new technology or the adoption of new institutional forms. Secondly, studies demonstrate that police patrol practices have little effect on rates of crime, unless they involve saturation and "cops on every corner" tactics, which are economically and politically unfeasible. And thirdly, the police are only one segment of a much larger class control apparatus. Private police, state police and the National Guard are able to reinforce departments affected by cutbacks and to do so at a lower cost because of the temporary nature of such reinforcement. When New York City, for example, was facing

imminent default in and the loss of all city services in 1975, then President Ford announced that the Federal government was prepared to provide money to keep "essential services" functioning, beginning with the police, but excluding health, education and welfare.

The most important impact of the fiscal crisis on the police is not cutbacks but rather an increased impetus to strategic rationalization. The renewed emphasis on technology and bureaucratic reform has come, not from isolated academics, but from the corporate liberal sector of the bourgeoisie. The recent wave of research projects aimed at evaluating the efficiency of police crime-control efforts, such as the Kansas City Study, has been financed by huge grants from the Ford Foundation and LEAA, and administered by the upper echelons of the police administrative and planning apparatus. Such studies, which document the ineffectiveness of police patrol in curbing crime, have been used to justify technological modernization while ignoring the social roots of crime.

The fiscal crisis has also intensified contradictions within the police institution. Beginning in the late 1960's, the hiring of Blacks and women as police officers in increasing (but still pitifully small) numbers was an important concession to popular struggles against the police. The lack of any serious commitment to ending racist and sexist recruitment practices is indicated by the fact that layoffs have fallen hardest on these groups. This undermining of affirmative action is being fought hard, especially by Black police officers' associations. Furthermore, there are increased antagonisms between rank and file police organizations and management over wages and working conditions. As one response to these internal conflicts, police administrators have compensated for cutbacks in the lower ranks by increasing the proportion of college-educated "specialists." These officers are more likely to identify with management due to their ideological training, are more isolated by their education from the communities which they patrol, and are more likely to adhere to organizational and "professional" requirements than most rank and file police.

As the economic crisis deepens and political discontent spreads to almost all sectors of this society, more repressive demands are placed on the police and their crime-control functions become even more peripheral to their class-control priorities. But the police are not the only agency of repression and they do not function without considerable support from other sectors of the state apparatus. It is in this context that seemingly disparate events become tied together in a coherent policy: the re-introduction of the death penalty; repeal by the current Supreme Court of some of the modest constitutional gains made by the Warren Court; mandatory sentences for certain adult defendants and proposals to try youths over the age of 16 in criminal courts; an increasing reliance on "adjustment centers" and "drug therapies" to pacify and intimidate militant prisoners; the resurgence of genetic theories of intelligence and reactionary proposals for containing crime;[7] the recent implementation of a 10 o'clock curfew for those under 18 in Detroit;[8] vigilante actions against Blacks in the North (for example, Boston and Chicago) as well as the South, and against Chicanos and Mexicans in the Southwest, often implicitly supported by local police forces and culturally legitimated through such movies as Death Wish; massive deportations of "illegal aliens"; and harassment and intimidation of progressive foreign students and activists (most recently, Iranians and Koreans) living in the United States.[9]

It is not surprising, then, that during the last decade there have been significant shifts in the form of policing and an intensification of the repressive apparatus. We have attempted to identify the parameters of this transformation of the police institution and examine more closely some of its internal dynamics. Under the guise of a crusade against crime on behalf of "law and order," there has been an unprecedented growth in police personnel and budgets, unprecedented efforts to rationalize and streamline the police into a nationally coordinated institution, and unprecedented use of the most sophisticated technology and weaponry. Washington, D.C., for example, nearly doubled its force from 3,000 to 5,100 within a decade, and rural and suburban areas with comparatively low crime rates not only expanded their police forces but also in some cases developed para-military approaches to police organization.[10] Greatly increased police budgets facilitated the adoption of such new technological innovations as weapons systems, modern communications operations, drug-detecting devices, snow-mobiles, infra-red lenses, and a vast array of complex electronic gadgetry.[11]

MORE FIST, MORE GLOVE

The increase in personnel and resources has been accompanied by new efforts to centralize and coordinate different components of the repressive apparatus. This is exemplified by the emphasis on central police radio and dispatch systems for metropolitan areas, integrated computer systems to permit rapid retrieval and transmission of information, and increased co-operation between different local police units and between local, state and Federal police units. Much of this work has been encouraged and subsidized by LEAA grants and training institutes. The tendency towards centralization and coordination is not limited to the "civilian" police. The military and National Guard have recently started training to assume regular police functions during "emergencies"; and private industrial and commercial police forces have been expanded, their quality improved, and their duties more closely integrated with public police agencies.

In addition to expansion and coordination, there has also been an increased diversification of the methods of policing to emphasize the development of both technical instruments of repression (iron fist) and strategies of legitimation (velvet glove). Technical innovation in policing has traditionally lagged far behind the capital-intensive sector of the corporate economy. Policing is still highly labor-intensive, with over 80 percent of all police budgets being used for wages and fringe benefits. But in recent years, patrol activity—the single most expensive component of police labor—has been repeatedly earmarked for substantial cutbacks and, while

179

they'll patrol with pride in Blauer's "NEW IMAGE" STORMWEAR

Blauer's "New Image" line projects a smart new contemporary look . . . fosters respect among the people you protect . . . sets a new standard of comfort, utility, warmth and dryness.

police spending at all levels of government increased 38 percent from 1971 to 1974, police employment increased only 13.6 percent.[12] There is a growing reliance on computer systems for record-keeping and identification, central radio dispatch systems, experiments in helicopter patrol, and "riot-control" weaponry.

The police have not only augmented their repressive capacity. Given the mass political movements of the late 1960's and the growing popular disenchantment with the existing political system, the police have made efforts to rescue their image and legitimacy through the tokenistic hiring of Third World people and women, through bogus community relations programs such as team policing, and through such gimmicks as dressing the police in blazers or giving lectures to high school students on the dangers of drugs. This "velvet glove" component of policing is not antagonistic to nor in competition with the "iron fist" approach. Rather they are integrated and complementary approaches to an overall repressive strategy. It is not paradoxical, therefore, that the Los Angeles Police Department, which prides itself on being one of the most militaristic and racist departments in the country,

180

also boasts a highly sophisticated community relations program, a specialized family crisis unit, and extensive team policing practices. Its officers are given special sensitivity training and encouraged not to use derogatory and racist language, while at the same time they are being trained how to use an elaborate range of weaponry and how to infiltrate progressive political organizations.

The police department of industrialized El Segundo, California, provides a good example of the increasing coordination of police agencies and the interconnections between the iron fist and velvet glove approaches. This department has expanded its formerly one-man Community Services Section into a large, specially trained anti-strike unit. In addition to supervising police control of strikes, the "Labor Relations" unit also coordinates the deployment of police from both El Segundo and neighboring towns whenever workers organize to prevent scabs from crossing their picket lines. This unit has also developed tight bonds with the large number of private security forces in the area. Regular meetings are held with these private agencies to foster a "personal working relationship between the police and security forces of the city." These meetings, which are also attended by private security representatives from neighboring cities, enable the police to anticipate strikes and to plan ahead to meet the needs of the aerospace industry for additional tax-supported repression.[13]

The growth and diversification of the police in the current period is not only a domestic development nor simply a manifestation of effective police lobbying. The current crisis in U.S. imperialism has necessitated the export of police technology, training and weaponry to all corners of the empire, wherever multinational corporations are faced with popular resistance movements (as in Asia, Africa and Latin America). And these same corporations have played a major role in helping to formulate and put into practice the iron fist and velvet glove strategies within the United States. Subsidized by the Federal government, the corporations have provided representatives for national commissions, generated policy guidelines from their foundations and think tanks, and actively participated in the construction of a booming police-industrial complex. Weapons and equipment industries aggressively promote their latest technology to local police officials who in turn are encouraged by federal subsidies to rationalize their operations. These sales, which generate further development of police technology and increasing reliance on corporate expertise, are a by-product of the adaptation of Vietnam era weaponry to domestic use by companies seeking new alternative markets. For example, sections of the U.S.-Mexican border are guarded by electronic sensors first used to monitor night movement by Vietnamese liberation troops.

While our analysis in this book has stressed the unprecedented sophistication and repressive capacity of the police, we do not regard these latest developments as monolithic or as so terrifying and formidable that they are immune to resistance. As we have discussed earlier, the loyalty of the police to the ruling class is not automatic and the most devastating forms of repression do not guarantee political stability. We have noted, for example, the problems posed by police militancy and unionism to the smooth functioning of the repressive apparatus. In the remainder of this chapter, we will examine another major problematic aspect of policing which suggests the complexity and vulnerability of the police as an institution, namely the ineffectiveness of the police in controlling crime.

THE FAILURE TO CONTROL CRIME

At a time when the police are being funded and armed at an unprecedented high level, it has become widely apparent that they have done little to stem the rise in serious street crime which has accompanied a deteriorating capitalist economy. The police are concerned with crime, for the crime-control ideology is deeply embedded in their training and professional mission, and they are organized to control certain kinds of crime in order to retain a minimum of popular legitimacy. But the roots of everyday crime are to be found in funda

mental economic and political conditions over which the police have no control. Aside from the vast array of bourgeois and state crimes which the police either ignore or help to reproduce, they have proved totally ineffective in protecting working class and Third World communities from intra-class crimes of personal and economic victimization. This conclusion is supported by a number of studies, financed primarily by LEAA.

In 1965, when the number of police officers on duty in the subways of New York, for example, was increased from 1,200 to 3,100, a short-term drop in crime followed. During the next five years, however, crime increased six times over the 1965 level. Some night-time

crime was prevented, concluded the Rand Institute's evaluation, at a cost of $35,000 per felony, but the rate of crime was simply displaced to the less policed day-time.[14] A "target-hardening" project in Atlanta met a similar fate. A special anti-robbery squad made 41 arrests during the year, at a cost of $26,000 per arrest, but the level of robberies increased in other parts of the city.[15]

The Kansas City Preventive Patrol Experiment (financed by the Police Foundation) found that tripling the levels of police automobile patrols had no effect upon the crime rate; a subsequent experiment in eliminating patrols and simply responding to citizen calls for assistance likewise made no difference.[16]

Another study found that there was no relationship between the level of crime and the level of police expenditures in the 166 largest urban areas in the United States.[17]

The Johnson and Nixon administrations tried to turn Washington, D.C. into a showplace of crime-control measures, largely by increasing the size of the force, improving technology, and increasing the level of street lighting. This federally controlled force reported a substantial decrease in crime each year after 1968, but a 1972 study found massive fraud in the keeping of crime statistics. Some felony property crimes had been downgraded to misdemeanors, about 40 percent of all citizen crime reports had not been recorded, and the pre-1970 increase had not been adequately studied to provide a base for comparison.[18]

Studies of foot patrol practices show that massive increases in the number of officers on patrol may lessen the level of street crime in a given place at a given time but without reducing the overall rate. When the police have refused to work, there has not, with the apparent exceptions of Boston in 1919 and Montreal in 1969, been any appreciable change in the crime rate. As the Brooklyn District Attorney explained during the 1971 New York police strike, "a patrolman on the street is only a deterrent in the place where he is standing. Muggings very seldom are committed right in front of a policeman."[19]

Recent authoritative studies, based on empirical data collected nation-wide, indicate that massive investment in the police has neither reduced the level of crime nor improved the quality of justice. According to a systematic evaluation of LEAA by the Center for National Security Studies, "the evidence is overwhelming: the Federal government has greatly increased its expenditures to combat crime, but these expenditures have had no effect in reducing crime. Not only has the LEAA program failed to halt the rising crime rates, but the program administrators haven't yet determined the steps or procedures that can be taken to achieve that goal."[20] Beginning in 1972, LEAA annually invested $160 million in eight target cities (Atlanta, Baltimore, Cleveland, Dallas, Denver, Newark, St. Louis, and Portland) with

a view to reducing serious crime by 5 percent in two years and 20 percent in five years. With the exception of two cities where there was little change, the rates of crime (according to the FBI) in the other six cities were considerably higher.[21] A more sophisticated and accurate survey of crime victims nation-wide showed no significant change in victimization rates for violent crimes and slightly higher rates for property crimes from 1973 to 1974—a period when LEAA's program was supposedly having its greatest impact.[22] "What can be said about our crime reduction capacity?," an important LEAA policy-maker recently asked. "Not much that is encouraging. We have learned little about reducing the incidence of crime, and have no reason to believe that significant reductions will be secured in the near future."[23]

The failure of the police to control street crime and the growing cynicism among government officials about the inevitability of crime serve to underscore the class-control functions of the criminal justice system. But even the repressive functions of the police do not always operate smoothly or effectively. In Atlanta, for example, a $1.5 million grant was given by LEAA for a helicopter patrol. During its first year, of a scheduled 22,000 hours of flight time, nearly 9,000 hours were lost to maintenance and weather problems. In addition, according to the Commissioner of Public Safety, "we lost three helicopters because we didn't have the best flyers in the world and the training program was not the best."[24] Similarly, experiments in police-monitored burglar alarms have been plagued by an extraordinarily high level of false alarms and technical breakdown;[25] and, in Chicago, a slippery substance used by the police to control demonstrators did an effective job on the police and on pedestrians going to work the next day, as well as on the demonstrators.[26] Even the most sophisticated computer technology has been vulnerable to the planned obsolescence and shoddy construction of capitalist commodities. In California, for example, the Alameda County Justice Information System is "bogging down under its own weight—producing poor data, slow results, gaps and duplications—is mistrusted by some of its own users, and is costing millions of dollars

183

annually," according to a recent study by the Stanford Research Institute.[27]

As we move closer to the 1980's, it is clear that the police are a formidable and increasingly dangerous institution of repression. They have become more centralized and rationalized, better equipped with complex technology and elaborate weapons systems, more sophisticated in their techniques of militarism and pacification, and better prepared to crush insurgency. On the other hand, they are faced with rank-and-file militancy from within and attacks on their racism by Black officers' associations, and their previously shaky credibility as a "crime-fighting" force has been even further eroded in recent years. But their most fundamental weakness lies in their inability to control class conflict. The development of the modern police goes hand in hand with the emergence of the industrial proletariat, the struggles of Third World communities for self-determination, and the rise of the organized socialist movement. Repression can not be understood nor analyzed in isolation from the political economy which it sustains and the resistance movements which it attempts to contain. In the concluding chapters of this book, we will examine this relationship between resistance and repression, summarize the recent experiences of political struggles, and discuss implications for future organizing.

1. Joel Swartz, "Silent Killers at Work," *Crime and Social Justice*, 3, Summer 1975, pp. 15-20.
2. "Immigration Law Attacks Mexicans," *The Guardian*, November 10, 1976, p. 8.
3. Irwin Silber, "Will the 'Recovery' End Up on the Rocks?," *The Guardian*, October 27, 1976, p. 4.
4. Robert B. Carson, "Youthful Labor Surplus in Disaccumulationist Capitalism," *Socialist Revolution*, 9, May-June, 1972, pp. 37, 40.
5. Kevin Kelley, "Poverty: Worse for Minorities," *The Guardian*, October 27, 1976, p. 7.
6. For a detailed analysis of the fiscal crisis, see *Radical Perspectives on the Economic Crisis of Monopoly Capitalism*, New York, Union for Radical Political Economics, 1975; and James O'Connor, *The Fiscal Crisis of the State*, New York, St. Martin's, 1974.
7. See, for example, Ernest van den Haag, *Punishing Criminals*, New York, Basic Books, 1975; and Jackson Toby, "Open-Ended Sentence," *New York Times*, January 15, 1976.
8. "State of Siege: Curfew in Detroit," *The Guardian*, November 3, 1976, p. 11.
9. *The Guardian*, November 3, 1976, pp. 4-5; November 10, 1976, p. 3.
10. See, for example, Robert A. Shaw, "A Tactical Operation Unit in a Small County," *Law and Order*, 24, 10, October 1976, pp. 22-25.
11. Gary Chamberlain, "IACP Shopping Center: Array of New Products Aid Police," *American City*, 88, 1, January 1973, pp. 56-57, 64-66.
12. U.S. Department of Justice and U.S. Department of Commerce, *Trends in Expenditure and Employment Data for the Criminal Justice System, 1971-1974*, Washington, D.C., U.S. Government Printing Office, 1976, p. 18.
13. James H. Johnson, "El Segundo's Industrial Asset: A Strike Detail's Challenge," *Crime Prevention Review*, 3, 4, July 1976, pp. 11-16. See also El Segundo Police Department, *Labor Relations Policy, Procedure, and Guidelines for Handling Labor Disputes*, El Segundo P.D., 1974.
14. Ian M. Chaiken et al., *The Impact of Police Activity on Crime: Robberies in the New York City Subway System*, New York, Rand Institute, 1974.
15. Center for National Security Studies, *Law and Disorder IV*, Washington, D.C., Center for National Security Studies, 1976, p. 32.
16. George Kelling et al., *The Kansas City Preventive Patrol Experiment*, Washington, D.C., The Police Foundation, 1974.
17. Thomas Pogue, "The Effect of Police Expenditures on Crime Rates," *Public Finance Quarterly*, 3, 1, January 1975.
18. Robert Seidman and Michael Couzens, "Getting the Crime Rate Down: Political Pressure and Crime Reporting," *Law and Society Review*, Spring 1974.
19. *New York Times*, January 19, 1971.
20. Center for National Security Studies, op. cit., p. 4.
21. Ibid., p. 30.
22. U.S. Department of Justice, *Criminal Victimization in the United States: A Comparison of 1973 and 1974 Findings*, Washington, D.C., U.S. Government Printing Office, 1976.
23. Gerald Caplan in testimony before the House Committee on Science and Technology, 1975.
24. Center for National Security Studies, op. cit., p. 33.
25. Ibid., p. 12.
26. Ibid., p. 133.
27. Ernie Cox, "Cops' Computers: Million-Dollar Mess," *Oakland Tribune*, October 20, 1976.

17. SUMMARIZING EXPERIENCE

Repression and changes in the organization and techniques of policing do not occur in an historical or political vacuum; rather they are inextricably connected to and shaped by mass struggles against the capitalist state. Such massive repression as we are experiencing today indicates a fundamental weakness, rather than strength, of the existing system, since it acknowledges the decreasing legitimacy of the ruling class and their need to rule by fear and force. But the history of repeated repression in the United States clearly indicates that it does not eliminate resistance. The working class movement has survived over a hundred years of repression (including dozens of massacres, mass jailings, spies, and provocateurs) of their right to engage in collective bargaining and strikes. The United Farm Workers, for example, still continue to struggle despite vigilantes, police protection of scabs, deportations, and agribusiness propaganda. Blacks, Native Americans, and other Third World people persistently struggle against institutional racism, continuing a tradition of resistance rooted in Indian warriors and rebel slaves. The socialist movement has survived thousands of arrests, the purges of 1919 and the early 1950's, and hundreds of political trials to still struggle for workers' ownership of the means of production. And, more recently, the anti-war movement prevailed in the face of massive police repression and helped to speed the victory of the Vietnamese people over U.S. imperialism.

It is true that some of these movements suffered setbacks and serious problems as a result of repression, but repression also generates increased commitment to struggle. Moreover, resistance creates difficulties for the legitimacy of the capitalist state. The mass movements of the 1960's, for example, posed a crisis for the ruling class.

This does not mean, however, that the police will automatically become the victims of their own self-destruction or spontaneously surrender to mass resistance. Only an organized working class, led by a class-conscious party

experienced in day-to-day practice, can wage a long-term struggle against the political hegemony and military superiority of the ruling class. This struggle entails a clear understanding of capitalist society, a firm grasp of strategic and tactical imperatives, and an ability to summarize and learn from the strengths and weaknesses of previous experience. It is in this spirit that we undertake an evaluation of recent struggles against the police.

REFORMING THE POLICE

In reviewing efforts to transform the police, it is important to distinguish between (1) corporate reforms, (2) liberal reforms, and (3) popular struggles.

(1) Corporate Reforms

Most efforts to reform the police have been dominated by corporate reformers since the Progressive era. As we have extensively discussed in earlier chapters, the Progressive movement was led by the most class-conscious sectors of monopoly capital who recognized the necessity for far-reaching economic, political

"I'VE LIVED HERE IN THIS CITY FOR OVER 40 YEARS!...AND NEVER ONCE HAVE I BEEN BRUTALIZED BY THE POLICE!!"

R. COBB

and social reforms. Under their leadership, laissez-faire business practices were severely restricted, the role of the state in economic planning was increased, and the modern welfare state was built. Corporate reforms were developed at the national level through the regulatory powers of an expanded Federal government and at the local level through the commission and city manager systems of government. The corporate reconstruction of the political economy, which was not achieved without conflict within the ruling class, represented a victory for the more "enlightened" wing of monopoly capital which advocated strategic alliances with urban reformers and supported a variety of concessions to the working class.[1]

The major thrust of corporate reformers, from the Progressive era to the present, has been towards rationalization, professionalism, and managerial efficiency. During the early part of this century, they advocated special training to clearly demarcate the police from the working class from which they were recruited; the development of more sophisticated techniques of pacification and counter-insurgency; and the penetration of the police into a variety of preventative and social work functions. During the recent period of institutional reform, corporate reformers have played an active role in expanding the "velvet glove" functions of the police; promoting greater coordination among and centralization of police agencies; and introducing a higher level of technological repression. Clearly, corporate reforms are not designed to increase the power of the working class and Third World communities; nor are they designed to reduce the levels of state repression. Rather, such reforms are part of ruling class efforts to contain the contradictions of capitalist society and to make the mode of punishment correspond with changes in the economy and productive relationships.[2]

(2) Liberal Reforms

During the 1960's, the increasing visibility of the police and the obvious absence of any real controls on their behavior created much concern among liberal reform organizations, such as the American Civil Liberties Union and the

American Friends Service Committee, and among individual writers who were critical of police atrocities and unchecked police power. This concern led to a number of critical studies and reports, such as ACLU attorney Paul Chevigny's *Police Power* and *Cops and Rebels*, the "Walker Report" on police violence at the 1968 Democratic convention, sociologist Jerome Skolnick's *Justice Without Trial*, and many others.[3]

Liberal reformers, though subjectively and often politically at odds with corporate reformers, accept the basic parameters of capitalist society, while working for its "enlightened" reform. This is due to a combination of their petty bourgeois* class interests, their naive view of the capitalist state, and their tendency to pursue reforms as ends in themselves. Liberal reformers, however, differ from corporate strategists in several important respects. In particular, they place greater emphasis on upholding democratic ideals of justice and equality than on the need for order and social control. The reforms most frequently proposed by this group—civilian review boards, improving the caliber of police administrators, demilitarization of the police and decriminalization of certain offenses—are designed to limit the present powers of the police system. But though these reforms raise real criticisms of the police system, they do not challenge the structure of political and economic power that lies behind it, nor do they analyze the way the police function to serve that structure of power and privilege; and they are therefore limited in their potential for fundamentally affecting the way the police work. It's important, therefore, to evaluate these reforms critically in order to understand their inherent limits.

* Although the precise composition of the petty bourgeoisie is a subject of much debate, it is most frequently seen as including professionals, small business owners, and independent craftspeople. The ideologies advanced by this sector range from a strong support for "law and order" programs to the advancement of liberal reforms of capitalism through the maintenance or expansion of bourgeois democratic rights. The specific ideology advanced by the individual members of the petty bourgeoisie are rooted in the material conditions which they experience.

The liberal reformers' main focus is on police abuses of power; in particular, their disregard of the rules of due process of law in dealing with suspects, their routine use of violence or summary justice against certain groups, and their hostility and insensitivity toward Third World people, youth, gay people, drug users, and radicals. The reformers usually see these abuses as the result of a fundamental dilemma faced by the police in modern "democratic" society—what Skolnick and others have referred to as a dilemma between "law" and "order," reducing crime rates, "clearing" crimes are supposedly required to uphold constitutional principles of due process of law in dealing with citizens—but on the other hand, they are under constant bureaucratic and social pressure to produce results in the form of "order"; reducing crime rates, "clearing" crimes by arrest, and so on. The result, according to this analysis, is a constant tendency to break the democratic rules of the game.

Another source of police abuses often pointed to by liberal reformers is the culture and attitudes of police officers themselves. The reformers stress the authoritarian or at least "conventional" values held by most policemen as a major stumbling-block to democratic policing, as well as the "police subculture" generated by the quasi-military standards, insulation from normal civilian contact, and the tense and dangerous working conditions the police routinely face. Many reformers have argued that the factors of danger and authority, inherent in police work, tend to make the police naturally suspicious and abusive in their dealings with citizens.[5]

From this perspective, then, police abuses are usually seen as resulting from problems and conflicts *within* the police bureaucracy itself—not primarily as the result of the basic job the police are called on to do in a fundamentally oppressive society. The implication of this focus on the internal aspects of police organization and culture is that police problems can be remedied by putting restraints on the bureaucracy, and/or by changing the nature of police "culture."

The typical proposals advocated by liberal reformers—such as demilitarization of the police, community relations programs and civilian review boards, and sensitivity training for recruits—are in theory reasonable demands but their limitations are fully revealed in practice. Take, for example, the civilian review board established in Berkeley, California, by a popular referendum in 1973, perhaps the only such board functioning in the country. The Police Review Commission's nine members are appointed by the mayor and the city council and are empowered to investigate complaints against the police, to review and recommend policies, and to subpoena necessary documents. Due to police non-cooperation and a lack of enthusiastic support by the city council, it took the Commission over a year to set up trial boards, its mechanism for disposing of citizens' complaints. While the Commission has redressed several grievances against individual officers and raised community consciousness through public forums, it has not been effective in challenging the institutional racism of the police, nor in altering their law enforcement priorities. Moreover, the Commission has served to coopt community militancy and channel opposition

"WE MUSTN'T DO ANYTHING THAT WILL BRING ON REPRESSION!"

to the police into an institution that is fundamentally incapable of challenging the class-control functions of the police.[6]

The proposals offered by liberal reformers are based on an image of the U.S. political system as a basically democratic one. The reformers are not oblivious to the results of a small ruling elite dominating and controlling the structures and institutions of our society. They are concerned that the economic and political realities do not measure up to the professed democratic ideals of our government and constitution. They find the sources of this discrepancy in the lack of equal opportunities for education and employment, in unenlightened bureaucrats running social institutions, and in the generally apathetic, conservative mood of society.

These reformers argue that all of these problems can be remedied given enough time and the will to do so. Thus, they argue that people must take advantage of the political

processes available to them to bring about change. Better educated administrators and better trained personnel will bring about better or more efficient, more responsive institutions. Public pressure will motivate general improvements in the socio-economic conditions.

But this picture ignores the resistance of the ruling class in capitalist society. Although many of the reforms it suggests are fundamentally humane ones, *by themselves* they do not offer any hope for significantly changing the way the police behave. First, they are not designed to challenge the larger and more basic questions of who runs the police and to what ends—and therefore, even if they work, they do so only on the level of toning down some of the worst abuses of the existing police system. Second, such reforms often don't work effectively even on their own limited terms. This, again, is because they are based on an inadequate understanding of the realities of class, race, and power in the United States. If police abuses *did* come mainly from the problems of police bureaucracy and the police "subculture," then such measures might accomplish a lot. But police abuses are more correctly seen as part of a deeper pattern of repressive police control of oppressed populations, a pattern that is tied closely to the most basic needs of the corporate economy.

While it is inaccurate to simply characterize liberal reformers as the lackeys of corporate strategists, they have historically served similar objective functions. Through their reforms, they seek to secure the existing political and economic arrangements, albeit in an ameliorated and regulated form, and they stoutly defend capitalism, while working for its enlightened reform.[7] Furthermore, some liberal reforms are on their face anti-working class and ultimately increase the level of class oppression. Professionalization, for example, insulates the police from popular control and mystifies their job by promoting law enforcement as an activity best handled by "neutral experts" who understand the science of "public order." Increased isolation, mystified authority, and improved efficiency actually facilitate the apparatus of repression.

188

3) Popular Struggles

Throughout this book, we have referred to the persistence of popular struggles and to the interconnections between repression and resistance. In chapter 4, we discussed the emergence of widespread militancy, especially in Third World communities, against the police during the 1960's. In many communities, this militancy took the form of organized self-defense against White vigilantism and racist police practices; it also included guerilla attacks on police and police stations in retaliation for police murders in Black, Chicano and Puerto Rican communities.[8] Efforts to go beyond this limited form of resistance were by and large unsuccessful. Even when community struggles had a high level of working class and Third World participation, they lacked stable organizational forms and a long-range strategy, and they become dominated by bourgeois political conceptions. This was a reflection of the low level of revolutionary political development in the left movement as a whole, the absence of organized leadership in the socialist movement, and the domination of community struggles by petty bourgeois reformers. These weaknesses in the political organization of popular resistance are revealed in two apparently different, but in fact related, programs against the police—left-wing adventurism and community control.

Left-Wing Adventurism

During the 1960's, there was an increase in attacks on the police. Some of these were the legitimate efforts of oppressed communities to defend themselves against vigilantes and lawless police. Others, however, were committed by groups and individuals who advocated armed confrontation with the police and stressed this as a *priority* in any political program.[9] Left-wing adventurism, which typically takes the form of isolated terrorist attacks or bombings, is basically an anti-working class strategy, with roots in petty bourgeois failure and frustration. Organizations such as Weatherman (in its early days) and the SLA were isolated from the broad masses of people, had romantic illusions about their own efficacy, and failed to reduce repression in poor and Third World communities. The long and difficult task of organizing a popular movement to defeat the capitalist state and create socialism is abandoned by these ultra-left groups. Rather than advancing the level of struggle, the individualism of groups such as the SLA underestimates the tenacity of the corporate state and serves primarily to legitimate repression.

Community Control

The movement for community control of the police differed from other efforts to reform the police in the 1960's because it originated out of the political initiative of the Black and student communities, and represented an effort to fundamentally transform police priorities. Unlike the isolation of left-wing adventurism, it was firmly rooted in the necessity for mass organizing; and unlike the proposals of corporate reformers and liberals, which centered on improved technology and professionalism, community control advanced the demand for a service-oriented police under local, democratic control. As an issue, the demand for community control brought together a strong, however short-lived, coalition of people and groups committed to asserting some responsibility over the actions of the police. Despite their failure, these struggles put the police on the defensive and opened up their policies to public scrutiny. Moreover, the struggles raised political consciousness and involved large numbers of people in practical political work. (For more detailed discussion of specific community control proposals, see chapters 4 and 21.)

In reflection, however, the campaign for community control made some serious political errors which we would do well to avoid in future struggles against the police. Aside from the particular shortcomings of each campaign (which partly account for its defeat), the politics of community control are strategically unsound and overall sets back the progressive movement by leading it into reformism and utopianism. The basic liberalism of community control results from the theoretical bankruptcy of the concept of "community" and a petty bourgeois analysis of the state.

First, community control is usually based on

189

a narrow conception of power, limiting struggles to the "local" area and failing to confront the interlocking, national basis of economic power. Focusing solely on the local community obscures the real nature of power in the United States and thereby fosters illusions about how the system can be changed. The most serious problem with the concept of community, however, is that it tends to dismiss or replace the concept of class. Marjaleeno Repo, summarizing comparable experiences in Canada, puts it this way: "The 'neighborhood as a community' concept assumes a classless society at the local level, in which a mysterious 'people of all classes' work towards a common goal. . . . The assumption here is that everybody is equal, that all work together for a common good, that no class conflicts exist or that the[y] can be abolished at the neighborhood leve[l] This is contrary to the existing reality."[10]

Secondly, there is an assumption behin[d] "community control" that it is possible t[o] capture a piece of the bourgeois state an[d] convert it into an instrument of popular co[n]trol. This view of the state is fundamental[ly] utopian and reformist because it assumes eith[er] the neutrality of the state or the possibility [of] legislating it out of the hands of the ruling clas[s] This is incorrect because, as Lenin pointed ou[t] the state is neither neutral nor "an organ f[or] the *reconciliation* of classes." Rather "the sta[te] is an organ of class *rule*, an organ for t[he] *oppression* of one class by another; it is t[he] creation of 'order,' which legalizes and perpet[u]ates this oppression by moderating the confli[ct] between the classes."[11] This does not mean th[at] as socialists we should not participate in ele[c]toral politics and struggle for parliamenta[ry] reforms but rather that we should be aware [of] the inherent limitations of such struggles, [al]ways keeping them subordinate to the task [of] building a revolutionary movement, and bei[ng] careful to grasp their reality so that we do n[ot] develop utopian expectations. In the fi[nal] chapter, we will explore the implications of t[his] analysis for future organizing.

1. See, for example, William Appleman Williams, *The Contours of American History*, Chicago, Quadrangle, 1966; Gabriel Kolko, *The Triumph of Conservatism*, Chicago, Quadrangle, 1967; and James Weinstein, *The Corporate Ideal in the Liberal State, 1900-1918*, Boston, Beacon, 1969.
2. Georg Rusche and Otto Kirchheimer, *Punishment and Social Structure*, New York, Russell and Russell, 1968.
3. Paul Chevigny, *Police Power*, New York, Random House, 1969; National Commission on Causes and Prevention of Violence, *Rights in Conflict*, New York, Bantam Books, 1968; Jerome Skolnick, *Justice Without Trial*, New York, John Wiley, 1967.
4. Skolnick, op. cit., chapter 1.
5. Ibid., chapter 3; see, also, William A. Westley, *Violence and the Police*, Cambridge, M.I.T. Press, 1972.
6. This conclusion is based on data and materials available on file at the Center for Research on Criminal Justice.
7. For a more extensive analysis along these li[nes] see Ralph Miliband, *The State in Capitalist [So]ciety*, New York, Basic Books, 1969.
8. See, for example, *Communique No. 12* of [the] Black Liberation Army.
9. See, for example, Hal Jacobs, Ed., *Weatherm[an]* California, Ramparts Press, 1970, pp. 84-85.
10. Marjaleena Repo, "The Fallacy of Commu[nity] Control," *Transformation*, date unknown, [pp.] 11-17, 33-34. See, also, Stanley Aronowitz, "[The] Dialectics of Community Control," and Fr[ank] Riessman and Alan Gartner, "Community Con[trol] and Radical Social Change," *Social Policy*, J[uly] 1970, pp. 47-55; and Barbara Bishop and Tho[mas] Bodenheimer, "Socialism in One Clinic: A C[lass] Analysis of the National Community He[alth] Service Proposal," *Synthesis*, 1, 3, Octo[ber] November 1976, pp. 29-43.
11. V. Lenin, *The State and Revolution*, Pek[ing] Foreign Languages Press, 1970, p. 8.

18. IMPLICATIONS FOR ORGANIZING

RACISM AND RESISTANCE

The current deterioration of the U.S. economy and the accompanying fiscal crisis of the state has had its most severe impact in Third World communities. With extraordinarily high unemployment rates, cutbacks in social programs and services, and continuous repression of progressive organizations, these communities are plagued by a very high level of individualistic victimization (street crime, alcoholism, drug use, etc.) and intensified police militarism and vigilantism. In recent years, the attacks on Blacks, Chicanos, Puerto Ricans, Native Americans, Asians and other Third World communities have increased.

In the eleven months preceding September 1976, for example, the police in the San Antonio area killed 19 Chicano youths between the ages of 16 and 19; in a period of four years, the police killed 8 Chicano, 6 Black, and 1 White youth in San José; in the South, there has been a resurgence of vigilantism, often with the complicity or acquiescence of local police; In Boston, the "anti-busing" campaign has incited many attacks on Blacks and, in Chicago,

Nazi-led racists have harassed Black families in the Marquette Park area; a group of Whites indiscriminately clubbed individual Blacks in New York's Washington Square Park in September 1976; and, in October, there was a series of firebombings of Black churches in Las Vegas.[1]

The Native American struggle, particularly the American Indian Movement (AIM), has suffered very intense repression from a combined force of FBI, U.S. Marshals, state police, military, Bureau of Indian Affairs Police and vigilantes. Since the conflict at Wounded Knee, over 200 Indians have been killed on the Pine Ridge Reservation. Moreover, Indians have the highest percentage of all types of arrests—over 200,000 in 1971 according to the International Treaty Council.

Given the present economic conditions, the tendency to scapegoat the most oppressed sectors of capitalist society in times of political and fiscal crisis, and the militaristic build-up of

the criminal justice system in recent years, it i not surprising that police brutality is also on the increase. But this repression has not gon unchallenged. Struggles against the police ar on the rise throughout the country. Many ar spontaneous reactions to outrageous incident of repression, some are matters of survival fo progressive and revolutionary organizations while others are made necessary by the routin police harassment which pervades working-clas communities. In California, for example, th Ocean Beach Human Rights Commission an Santa Cruz Citizens for Police Accountabilit were organized a couple of years ago, th former to protect citizens from arbitrary "sto and frisk" practices, the latter to block th creation of a police-directed communicatio center; in San Antonio, the Tenants Unio called for the transference of funds from a already bloated police budget to use on muc needed public housing repairs; and, in Sa Francisco, the residents of International Hote who have been struggling for many years prevent the demolition of their building by large corporation, organized against th presence of police spies and police photo raphers at their rallies and meetings.

Most frequently, however, struggles again the police are mobilized around the demand f removal or punishment of "killer cops" and end to such militarized police units as SWAT Los Angeles, STRESS in Detroit, and BOSS New York City. This was the case with t Tyrone Guyton Committee in Oakland and t Claude Reeves, Jr. and Clifford Glover Comm tees in New York. Similarly, the Nashvil Coalition Against Police Repression was form in 1972 in response to the murder of a Bla youth; in Chicago, a campaign for Communi Control of the Police was launched in 19 after several incidents of police murder a brutality in the Black, Latino and Whi working class communities; a similar campai was begun in 1974 in Milwaukee through t Citywide Coalition for Community Control the Police after the police had gone on rampage in the Latino community; more cently, in San Francisco, a coalition of Latin Black, Asian and White working class commu ty organizations has begun a campaign

"Witness Guidelines" under which citizens would have the power to observe police arrests and offer support to defendants; and in Oakland, the Chicano community responded with tremendous energy and intensity after the 1976 murder of Barlow Benavidez, leading to the formation of the Committee Against Police Crimes.[2]

In some of these struggles, the organizations have dissolved, having failed to win their immediate demands; in some, the outcome is still unclear; and in others, there is considerable internal struggle over tactics and strategy. Nevertheless, there are indications that current struggles against the police are being waged at a different level of political and organizational development. There appears to be greater participation by the working class in such struggles, less vulnerability to utopian schemes, and more awareness of the need to combat police crimes as one aspect of the capitalist state. Consider the following examples.

In southern California, several defense committees have united in a Coalition Against Police Abuse (CAPA) to "let the authorities know that we will no longer tolerate the senseless harassment, injury and murder of community people by the police and that we have resolved as our main purpose, to organize and mobilize the masses of people to eliminate police terrorism in our communities." CAPA specifically demands, among others, elimination of special tactical squads, undercover agents, and the Internal Affairs Division in Los Angeles police agencies; prosecution of "killer cops;" and a community-controlled investigation of police crimes. CAPA recognizes that "lurking behind" the rash of police crimes "lies a worsening economic and political crisis in which the government, guided by a false notion of Law and Order, has begun to legislate and order through the courts more repressive acts by the police." Similarly, in Oakland, the Barlow Benavidez Committee Against Police

Crimes is attempting to go beyond specific police crimes to "examine the contradiction" on the one hand of an increasingly repressive system of law enforcement which "discriminates against poor and low income people, while on the other hand an entire world of high crime in big business and government runs free and is in fact protected by the police establishment."[3] In both of these campaigns, there is an emphasis on pooling resources through coalitions and an attempt to go beyond single-issue struggles by focusing on the repressive and racist functions of the police in capitalist society.

GUIDELINES FOR ACTION

Struggles against the police are complex and vary according to local conditions. We do not have a programmatic agenda to fit all situations nor do we presume to tell working class and Third World communities how to fight their struggles. On the other hand, we have written this book as a stimulus to political action, so that we not only have a better understanding of the problems we face, but that we can also use this knowledge as a weapon of criticism and action. In previous struggles, we have noted several errors and weaknesses—a tendency to see the police as a *local*, and relatively *self-contained* institution; a *single-issue* approach to police crimes; and a *reformist* and *utopian* analysis of the state. Given the present fiscal crisis and intensified repression, especially in Third World communities, it is important to learn from these past errors and develop tactics which take into account the changing organization and forms of policing.

● We do not think it is possible to have a humane and "democratic" police under capitalism. Given the repressive origins of the modern police, the class-control functions of their training and professionalization, their enforcement of laws made by the capitalist class, and their interconnections with other sectors of the capitalist state—it is not possible under this system to turn the police into an instrument of working class justice or eliminate their repressive role. On the other hand, we do think it is possible to neutralize and limit the police in some circumstances. We can organize to check the growing militarism of the police by, for

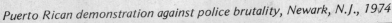

Puerto Rican demonstration against police brutality, Newark, N.J., 1974

194

example, preventing the passage of Senate Bill 1, calling for the firing and disciplining of "killer cops," supporting community investigations of police crimes, and lobbying for reductions in wasteful and dangerous police budgets. These kinds of actions make it more difficult for the police to operate.

● Working class and Third World communities organizing against the police find themselves allied at many points with liberal and petty bourgeois organizations whose long-term objective is not socialism but whose short-term goals—such as reducing police racism and brutality—are not incompatible with the struggle against capitalism. In the past, as we have pointed out, efforts to reform the police have generally been dominated by liberal organizations and individuals, resulting in innocuous changes, cooptation or cynicism. During the present period, when there is not only intensified repression but also a movement under way to reduce civil liberties, it is important to maintain such alliances. Past experience, however, indicates that it is very difficult to win even the most minimal concessions from the police and that such alliances preferably should be entered into from a position of strength—

that is, politically and ideologically led by organizations that are firmly rooted in working class and Third World communities.

● Police repression is a potent source of mass mobilization. Throughout the country, there are hundreds of defense committees and community organizations created in response to police terrorism and negligence. In this respect, the police provide a mechanism for exposing both their own specific lawlessness and their repressive functions under capitalism. Struggles against the police should emphasize that, while in themselves they are a dangerous and often unregulated force, they derive their role and legitimacy from the ruling class. It is not accidental that the police converge primarily on working class crimes and direct their intelligence operations against progressive organizations, while bourgeois crimes and the small minority which benefits from them are protected by the state. Struggles against the police should be used to raise consciousness about the political economic roots of repression, the role of the state in capitalist society, and the different forms and mechanisms of repression.

● In order to avoid the error of combating the police only as a local institution, struggles

195

against the police should take into account their increasingly national and even international character. Attention should be paid to the growing police-industrial complex, especially the relationship between law enforcement agencies, corporations, and research institutes involved in modernizing the means of repression. By focusing, for example, on how IBM, a company involved in computerizing the South African apartheid pass book system, is also a main LEAA contractor for police command and data retrieval systems here, it is possible to demonstrate the extent to which corporations benefit from and encourage the production of repressive technology.

● The police are not monolithic or invincible. We should be careful not to feed into this illusion, as it encourages cynicism and defeatism. We cannot afford to pretend that militant popular struggles can proceed unopposed by the police. At the same time, however, it is an error to think that repression makes organizing futile. In spite of waves of nearly complete suppression of democratic rights in the United States, police repression has never been able to stop the struggles of the American people for very long, partly because new forms of organ-

196

ized resistance have evolved alongside of and at times ahead of police practices. In recent years, for example, Native Americans across the country have defied the combined forces of the police, National Guard, Army and armed vigilantes to reassert their right to land and sovereignty. While pursuing every avenue of legal redress, they have also when necessary taken up arms in self-defense. Similarly, the anti-war movement was able to grow in size and militancy despite the massive police, F.B.I. and other efforts to contain its effectiveness. Also, it is important to keep in mind for strategic purposes that the police are not a monolithic institution. Aside from inter-agency rivalry and rank and file militancy, the police are often victimized by planned obsolescence and regular breakdowns in the elaborate technology which they have been sold by corporations.

● Finally, community organizing around the police must take into account the fact that crime is a real issue and a real danger. Given that the police attempt to legitimate their class-control functions as crime-control functions, it is necessary to clearly explain the material sources of crime, demonstrate that the police are unable and unwilling to control

"street" crime, and show how the "law and order" ideology is a thinly disguised rationale for racist scapegoating. In addition to educational work, positive actions can be taken to make poor and working class communities safer. Demands made on local government along these lines might include police escort for elderly people, better or free public transportation, free self-defense classes, improved building security and street lighting. But we should not rely on the police to provide these kinds of services. In addition, neighborhoods and block organizations can establish their own escort services, alarm systems, rape crisis centers, and drug control projects—as they have done throughout the country.

These "self-help" activities should not be encouraged in the spirit of community responsibility for "wayward criminals," but rather out of dissatisfaction with the criminal justice system and in order to combat the demoralizing effect that crime has on political organizing. Such programs should point out how the causes of crime are rooted in the capitalist system, particularly in its economic policies which guarantee high unemployment and job instability, and in its political policies which reproduce competitive and exploitative social relations.

As more enduring forms of organization develop that can unite workers, the unemployed, students and other progressive forces of all races, our struggles against repression and economic exploitation will be more closely linked. Such organization will give direction and strength to local work and will make it easier for local projects to link up with national campaigns. Ultimately, building a humane and decent society in the United States will depend on our ability to build a socialist movement that can put an end to all forms of exploitation. Educational and political campaigns about the police, while they are not ends in themselves, can be a crucial part of that movement. movement.

1. *The Guardian*, September 1, 1976, p. 4; November 10, 1976, p. 5.
2. Some of these examples are described more fully in the first edition of this book, others are on file at the Center for Research on Criminal Justice.
3. Coalition Against Police Abuse, *Statement of Purpose*, 1976; "Community Conference Against Police Crimes" (leaflet), 1976. Both these documents are on file at the Center for Research on Criminal Justice.

VIII. RESOURCES

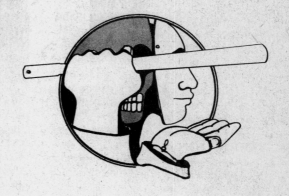

19. BIBLIOGRAPHY

There are two important sources of information available to anyone attempting to understand the police in capitalist America. These are (1) materials written about the police (and other relevant state institutions) in their social, political, and historical context; and (2) the publications of various government agencies, commissions, organizations and foundations. This bibliography gives a sampling of the first kind of materials; the second are covered below, in the *Research Guide*.

I. INTRODUCTION

For recent data on the growth and structure of the police and other criminal justice agencies, see *Research Guide*, below, on U.S. Government Law Enforcement Agencies. A general discussion of the increasing role of the police is Paul Takagi, "A Garrison State in Democratic Society," *Crime and Social Justice*, 1 (Spring-Summer 1974), pp. 27-33. In order to understand the role and function of the police in the United States today it is necessary to identify and analyze the larger apparatus of the capitalist state of which they are a part. The classical Marxist works on this subject are: V. I. Lenin, *The State and Revolution* (Peking, Foreign Languages Press, 1970); Frederick Engels, *The Origin of the Family, Private Property and the State* (New York, International Publishers, 1942—deals with the emergence of the state in pre-feudal societies); and the writings of Antonio Gramsci, most clearly summarized and discussed in Carl Boggs, "Gramsci's Prison Notebooks," *Socialist Revolution* Nos. 11 & 12 (September/October & November/December 1972). The writings of Marx on the state are synthesized in E. Mandel, *The Marxist Theory of the State* (New York, Pathfinder Press, 1973), and Paul Sweezy, "The State," Chapter xiii in *The Theory of Capitalist Development* (New York, Monthly Review Press, 1968).

One of the best works on the modern state is Ralph Miliband, *The State in Capitalist Society*

(New York, Basic Books, 1969). An economic analysis of the modern state is developed in James O'Connor, *The Fiscal Crisis of the State* (New York, St. Martin's Press, 1973). In Alan Wolfe, *The Seamy Side of Democracy* (New York, David McKay, 1973), a historical examination of the state and political repression in the U.S. is presented.

The upheavals of the 1960's made the prisons, courts, and police more visible to people in the U.S. The following books explore the way these institutions enforce patterns of class, racial, and sexual oppression. Richard Quinney, *Critique of Legal Order: Crime Control in Capitalist Society* (Boston, Little Brown & Co., 1974), and (Ed.), *Criminal Justice in America* (Boston, Little Brown, 1974) deal with the criminal justice system in general. Anthony Platt and Lynn Cooper, Eds., *Policing America* (Englewood Cliffs, New Jersey, Prentice-Hall, 1974) is a collection of radical essays on all aspects of the police. The courts and the reflection of racism in their proceedings are analyzed quantitatively and qualitatively in Isaac Balbus, *The Dialectics of Legal Repression: Black Rebels Before the American Criminal Courts* (New York, Russell Sage Foundation, 1973). A comparative analysis of U.S. police practices with those of four Western European countries is found in George Berkeley's *The Democratic Policeman* (Boston, Beacon Press, 1969). An excellent but hard to get historical account of the development of prisons and their relation to capitalism is Georg Rusche and Otto Kirchheimer, *Punishment and Social Structure* (New York, Russell & Russell, 1968). Two other sources on prisons are the left-liberal American Friends Service Committee, *Struggle for Justice* (New York, Hill and Wang, 1971) and Erik Olin Wright, et al., *The Politics of Punishment* (New York, Harper Torchbooks, 1973), which deals primarily with California prisons.

The laws in this country serve for the most part to maintain the conditions of capitalism and the oppression of the great majority of the people. This historical development is analyzed in Mark Kennedy, "Beyond Incrimination," in Quinney (Ed.), *Criminal Justice in America* (cited above), and in Kenneth Cloke, "The Economic Basis of Law and State," in Robert Lefcourt (Ed.), *Law Against the People* (New York, Vintage, 1971). *Law Against the People* contains other valuable essays as well.

The manipulation of the "crime problem" and the effect that this has in protecting the more socially harmful criminals are discussed in David Gordon, "Class and the Economics of Crime," *The Review of Radical Political Economics*, Vol. 3, No. 3 (Summer 1971) and Frank Pearce, "Crime, Corporations, and the American Social Order," *Politics and Deviance* (Middlesex, England, Penguin Books, 1973). On official conceptions of and responses to rape, see Julia and Herman Schwendinger, "Rape Myths: in Legal, Theoretical, and Everyday Practice," *Crime and Social Justice* 1 (Spring-Summer 1974), pp. 18-26. For a general discussion of issues in analyzing street crime, see the editorial, "The Politics of Street Crime," *Crime and Social Justice*, 5 (Spring-Summer 1976), pp. 1-4.

There is nothing written that systematically compares rates of crime among different capitalist countries. Likewise, there exists nothing that compares rates of crime between capitalist and socialist countries. There does, however, exist a literature on socialist legal institutions which allows us to see what alternatives to a repressive and class-biased legal system look like. These models have been developed primarily in Cuba and China. See Michael Tigar, "Socialist Law and Legal Institutions," in *Law Against the People*, for a discussion of both these countries. Jesse Berman, "The Cuban Popular Tribunals," *Columbia Law Review* (Vol. 69, 1969, pp. 1317-1354) discusses the system of local courts that operate without lawyers with neighbors as judges. More serious offenses in Cuba are dealt with at a higher level, and these political prisoners are discussed in Fidel Castro and Lee Lockwood, "Political Prisoners," in Lockwood, *Castro's Cuba, Cuba's Fidel* (New York, Vintage, 1969). The formulation of laws that

serve the people is treated in Robert Cantor, "New Laws for a New Society," *Cuba Resource Center Newsletter* (December 1973, reprinted in *Crime and Social Justice*, No. 2, Fall-Winter 1974). This new journal is an excellent source for radical analyses and bibliographies on all aspects of the criminal justice system. Correspondence to: *Crime and Social Justice*, P.O. Box 4373, Berkeley, Ca. 94704.

The Chinese system is described with a great deal of data, but a weak liberal analysis, in Jerome Alan Cohen, *The Criminal Process in the People's Republic of China* (Cambridge, Harvard University Press, 1968). The operation of People's Courts is described in Felix Greene's pamphlet "A Divorce Trial in China" (New England Free Press). A useful discussion of one aspect of the Chinese approach to crime is Annette T. Rubinstein, "How China Got Rid of Opium," *Monthly Review*, Vol. 25, no. 5 (October 1973), pp. 58-63.

II. THE ORIGINS AND DEVELOPMENT OF THE POLICE

The history of the U.S. police is still mainly unwritten. Most historical works are either contemporary "house histories" done from a totally uncritical point of view during the 19th century or, more recently, liberal historical accounts that almost never go deeply into the political and economic functions of the police.

The contemporary accounts can be interesting, though, because they show the police mentality of the time very clearly. Two typical ones are J. J. Flinn, *The Chicago Police* (Chicago, Police Book Fund, 1887), and August E. Costello, *Our Police Protectors* (New York, C. F. Roper & Co., 1885). Among the recent standard histories, probably the best are James Richardson, *The New York Police* (New York, Oxford University Press, 1970), and Roger Lane, *Policing the City* (Boston, Harvard University Press, 1963). Allan Silver, "The Demand for Order in Civil Society," in D. Bordua (Ed.), *The Police* (New York, Basic Books, 1968) is useful on the rise of the police in England and the U.S.

For the earliest police and the rise of slave patrols, see Selden Bacon, *The Early Development of American Municipal Police* (Ph.D. Dissertation, Yale University, 1939); Eugene Genovese, *Roll, Jordan, Roll* (New York, Pantheon Books, 1974); Herbert Aptheker, *American Negro Slave Revolts* (New York, International Publishers, 1962). A recent radical analysis of the development of an urban police force in response to working-class agitation is Sidney L. Harring, "The Buffalo Police, 1872-1900: Labor Unrest, Political Power, and the Creation of the Police Institution," *Crime and Social Justice*, 4 (Fall-Winter 1975), pp. 5-14. See also the same author's "Development of the Police Institution in the United States," *Crime and Social Justice*, 5 (Spring-Summer 1976), pp. 54-59.

The rise of the U.S. police can't be understood without looking at the history of class conflict in the 19th century. Good sources for labor-capital conflict in this period are Jeremy Brecher, *Strike* (San Francisco, Straight Arrow Books, 1972); Richard Boyer and Herbert M. Morais, *Labor's Untold Story* (New York, Cameron Associates, 1955); Vincent Pinto, *Soldiers and Strikers* (San Francisco, United Front Press, 1973). Useful general histories dealing with this period are William A. Williams, *The Contours of American History* (Chicago, Quadrangle Books, 1967), and Robert Wiebe, *The Search for Order, 1877-1920* (New York, Hill and Wang, 1967).

III. PROFESSIONALIZING THE POLICE

Even less has been written about the development of the police in the first half of this century. The best sources are the writings of the Progressive police writers and the various commissions they created to study the police.

Among writings in the first category, the standard Progressive work for many years was Raymond Fosdick's *American Police Systems* (New York, The Century Co., 1920). Also interesting is Arthur Woods, *Policeman and Public* (New Haven, Yale University Press, 1919), written by the Progressive Commissioner of the New York police. The various writings of August Vollmer, the so-called "father of police professionalism," are important; see especially his "Aims and Ideals of the Police," *Journal of Criminal Law and Criminology*, (Vol. 13, No. 2, August 1922), and *Police and Modern Society* (Berkeley, University of California Press, 1936). Among the many commissions created in the early 20th century, probably the most important are the Lexow Commission on Corruption in the New York police; the Cleveland Foundation Survey of Criminal Justice (Cleveland, 1922, several volumes), especially the volume on "Police" by Raymond Fosdick and the Summary by Roscoe Pound; and the National Commission on Law Observance and Enforcement (Wickersham Commission), Washington, D.C., Government Printing Office, 1931, in 14 volumes, especially the volumes on Police and on Causes of Crime.

For a general perspective on the Progressive approach to criminal justice, the many writings of Roscoe Pound are essential; especially the Summary Volume of the Cleveland Foundation Survey, and *Criminal Justice in America* (New York, H. Holt & Co., 1930). On the Progressive Movement generally and the political and economic situation in which it grew, the book above by Wiebe is interesting, as is Gabriel Kolko's *The Triumph of Conservatism* (New York, Free Press, 1963) and James Weinstein, *The Corporate Ideal in the Liberal State* (Boston, Beacon Press, 1967).

On the politics and makeup of the various criminal justice commissions, see Anthony Platt, Ed., *The Politics of Riot Commissions* (New York, Macmillan, 1971); for the commission reports themselves, see *Research Guide*, below, under Commissions. For the fate of civilian review, see Leonard Ruchelman, Ed., *Who Rules the Police* (New York, New York University Press, 1973).

There is increasingly more information available on the ideology and practice of community control. Some of the best works on the general issues are: Stanley Aronowitz, "The

Dialectics of Community Control," *Social Policy* (May-June 1970), Milton Kotler, "Theories of Neighborhood Organizations and the Radical Politics of Local Control," *Neighborhood Government* (Indianapolis, Bobbs-Merrill, 1969); Frank Riessman and Alan Gartner, "Community Control and Radical Social Change," *Social Policy* (May-June 1970); and Paul Sweezy, "Afterword: The Implications of Community Control," in Annette Rubinstein (Ed.), *Schools Against Children* (New York, Monthly Review Press, 1970).

Some of the basic books on Third World community control efforts are: Rodolfo Acuña, *Occupied America: The Chicano's Struggle Toward Liberation* (San Francisco, Canfield Press, 1972)—see especially Chapters 9 and 10; Robert Allen, *Black Awakening in Capitalist America* (New York, Doubleday Anchor Books, 1970); Alan Altschuler, *Community Control: The Black Demand for Participation in Large American Cities* (New York, Pegasus, 1970); and Mario Barrera, et al., "The Barrio as an Internal Colony," in Harlan Hahn (Ed.), *People and Politics in Urban Society* (Beverly Hills, Sage Publications, 1972); and James Boggs, "The City Is the Black Man's Land," *Racism and the Class Struggle* (New York, Monthly Review Press, 1968); Antonio Camejo, *La Raza Unida in Texas* (New York, Pathfinder Press, 1970); Edward Greer, "The Liberation of Gary, Indiana," *Transaction* (January 1971); José Angel Gutiérrez, "Mexicanos Need to Control Their Own Destinies" (New York, Pathfinder Press, 1969 pamphlet); and Marjorie Heins, *Strictly Ghetto Property* (Berkeley, Calif., Ramparts Press, 1971).

The major articles and books dealing specifically with community control of the police are: Jeffrey Freund, "Neighborhood Police Districts: A Constitutional Analysis," *California Law Review*, 57 (1969); Harold A. Nelson, "The Defenders: A Case Study of an Informal Police Organization," *Social Problems*, 15 (Fall 1967); Huey P. Newton, "A Citizen's Peace Force," *Crime and Social Justice*, Vol. 1 (Spring-Summer 1974); David Riley, "Should Communities Control Their Police?" *Civil Rights Digest* (Fall 1969); Arthur Waskow,

"Community Control of the Police," *Transaction* (December 1969).

Political groups which have been actively involved in community struggles for controlling the police have produced various pamphlets and articles on their efforts. These include: Tom Hayden and Carol Kurtz, "An Evaluation of Community Control of the Police in Berkeley"; Nashville Coalition Against Police Repression, *December Offensive* (November 1973); National Committee to Combat Fascism, "Community Control of the Police" (Berkeley, California, January 1971); "Northside Campaign for Community Control of the Police" (Chicago, Illinois, August-September 1973); "Campaign for Community Control of the Police" (Milwaukee, Wisconsin, 1974); Police Information Committee, *Newspaper* (Spring 1974); The Red Family, *To Stop a Police State: The Case for Community Control* (Berkeley, California, 1971). Copies of all these materials are on file at the Center for Research on Criminal Justice, P.O. Box 4373, Berkeley, Ca. 94704.

On the development and performance of LEAA, in addition to the sources cited in the *Research Guide* under U.S. Government Law Enforcement Agencies, the following are also useful: *Law Enforcement: The Federal Role*, Report of the Twentieth Century Fund Task Force on the LEAA (New York, McGraw-Hill Book Co., 1976); U.S. House of Representatives, Committee on Government Operations, "The Block Grant Program of the LEAA," 92nd Congress, 1st Session (October 1971); Lawyers' Committee for Civil Rights Under Law, *Law and Disorder III: State and Federal Performances Under Title I of the Omnibus Crime Control and Safe Streets Act of 1968* (Washington, D.C., The National Urban Coalition, 1972); U.S. Office of Management and Budget, *Issue Paper on LEAA* (1976); Committee for Economic Development, *Reducing Crime and Assuring Justice* (New York, CED, 1972); Center for National Security Studies, *Law and Disorder IV* (Washington, D.C., Center for National Security Studies, 1976).

There is a growing literature on police militancy, most of it unsatisfactory, but useful for general historical data. See Margaret Anne Levi, *Conflict and Collusion: Police Collective Bargaining*, Technical Report No. 07-74 (Cambridge, Mass., MIT Operations Research Center, 1974); Harvey A. Juris and Peter Feuille, *Police Unionism* (Lexington, Mass., Lexington Books, 1973); and the same authors' *The Impact of Police Unions, Summary Report* (U.S. Department of Justice, Law Enforcement Assistance Administration, December 1973). The literature on minority police and their struggles is also sparse. The major work on this subject, Nicholas Alex, *Black in Blue: A Study of the Negro Policeman* (New York, Meredith, 1969), is written from a very limited work organizational perspective. There are several articles which do present a more radical, although incomplete, analysis; these include: "Anguish of Blacks in Blue," *Time* (November 23, 1970); Carol Morton, "Black Cop: Black and Blue Ain't White," *Ramparts* (May 1972); Edward Palmer, "Black Police in America," *The Black Scholar*, Vol. 5, No. 2 (October 1973); Richard E. Rubinstein and Stephen M. Kaplan, "Black and Blue in Chicago," *The New Republic* (April 6, 1968).

IV. THE IRON FIST

The best source for materials on the military-corporate approach to policing is the various commission reports and technical conferences from the late 1960's; see *Research Guide*, under U.S. Government Law Enforcement Agencies and Commissions. For an overview of related military concepts and planning in the 1960's, see Michael T. Klare, *War Without End* (New York, Random House, 1972); and for more on "bringing the war home," National Action–Research on the Military–Industrial Complex, *Police on the Homefront* (Philadelphia, American Friends Service Committee, 1971).

For the development of police technology, too, the best sources are government and foundation reports; see especially the section on Citizens and University Groups and Foundations, in the *Research Guide*. See also North American Congress on Latin America, *The*

University-Military-Police Complex (New York, NACLA, 1972).

A good discussion of the role of SWAT is "Garden Plot and SWAT: U.S. Police as a New Action Army," *Counterspy* (Winter 1976), Vol. 2, No. 4. The most complete listing of textbooks on police technology and surveillance is available from Charles C. Thomas Publishers (301-347 East Lawrence Avenue, Springfield, Ill. 62717). Some of these include: David C. Pollock, *Methods of Electronic Audio Surveillance* (1972); Robert J. Rieder, *Law Enforcement Information Systems* (1972); Malachi L. Harney and John C. Cross, *The Informer in Law Enforcement* (1968); Carmine J. Motto, *Undercover* (1971); Raymond M. Momboisse, *Riots, Revolts, and Insurrections* (1970); and Alan Burton, *Police Telecommunications* (1972). Arthur Miller, a leading critic of the growing system of federal and local police data banks and computers, has written *The Assault on Privacy* (Ann Arbor, University of Michigan Press, 1971). For a good overview of domestic intelligence, although from a strictly civil libertarian perspective, refer to Paul Chevigny, *Cops and Rebels* (New York, Pantheon Books, 1972); Paul Cowen, et al., *State Secrets* (New York, Holt, Rinehart and Winston, 1974); and Frank Donner, "The Theory and Practice of American Political Intelligence," *The New York Review of Books* (April 22, 1971, pp. 27-38). Information on the role of the agent provocateur can be found in Dough Porter, "Undercover Agents: A Profile," *CounterSpy* Vol. 2, No. 1 (Fall 1974); Andrew Karmen, "Agents Provocateurs in the Contemporary U.S. Leftist Movement," in Charles Reasons, *The Criminologist: Crime and the Criminal* (Pacific Palisades, California, Goodyear Publishing Co., 1974), and *The Glass House Tapes*, by the Citizens Research and Investigation Committee and Louis E. Tackwood (New York, Avon Books, 1973).

The Law Enforcement Assistance Administration (LEAA) publishes an extensive directory of criminal justice information systems and distributes reports prepared by contractors concerning technological surveillance systems. The Senate Committee on the Judiciary has published hearings on data banks and computer privacy. In addition, the International Association of Chiefs of Police (IACP) publishes many technical reports on police weapons and tactics. For a complete listing of all these reports, refer to the sections on federal agencies, congressional committees, and professional organizations in the *Research Guide*.

Information on the F.B.I. falls into two categories. It is either written to glorify the role of the F.B.I., or it represents a left progressive analysis. Books like J. Edgar Hoover's *Masters of Deceit* (New York, Pocket Books, Inc., 1950) and Harry Overstreet's *The FBI in Our Open Society* (New York, W. W. Norton and Co., 1969) clearly belong in the first category. William Turner's *Hoover's FBI* (New York, Dell Publishing Co., 1970) and Robert Wall's article "Special Agent for the FBI," in *The New York Review of Books* (January 27, 1972) provide a totally different and critical perspective. Both are former F.B.I. agents and testify to the repressive and counterinsurgency operations of the agency. Fred Cook, *The FBI Nobody Knows* (New York, Pyramid Books, 1965) and Pat Walters and Stephen Geis (Eds.), *Investigating the FBI* (New York, Doubleday, 1973) also supply valuable information documenting the actions of the F.B.I. An excellent documentation of inside operations is found in "The Complete Collection of Political Documents Ripped Off from the F.B.I. Office in Media, Pa., March 8, 1971," *Win*, Vol. VIII, Nos. 4 and 5 (March 1972). Max Lowenthal's *Federal Bureau of Investigation* (New York, Harcourt, 1950) is a very good historical analysis of the Bureau. For a listing of F.B.I. publications, refer to the *Research Guide*, under federal agencies.

Useful materials relating to the recent congressional investigations on political surveillance can be found in Comptroller of the United States, *FBI Domestic Intelligence Operations—Their Purpose and Scope* (Washington, D.C., General Accounting Office, 1976); House Committee on the Judiciary, *Report to the President by the Commission on CIA Activities Within the United States* (Washington, Government Printing Office, June 1975);

Senate Select Committee to Study Governmental Operations with Respect to Intelligence Activities (Church Committee), Vol. 2 (*Houston Plan*), Vol. 3 (*Internal Revenue Service*), Vol. 4 (*Mail Opening*), Vol. 5 (*National Security Agency*), Vol. 6 (*Federal Bureau of Investigation*), and *Final Report* (Washington, Government Printing Office, 1975).

V. THE VELVET GLOVE

The best source for the "soft" perspective on policing is the work of those U.S. social scientists who have been primarily responsible for developing the theory behind it. In particular, see the works of James Q. Wilson, especially *The Varieties of Police Behavior* (Cambridge, Mass., Harvard University Press, 1968) and the article "Crime and Law Enforcement," in K. Gordon (Ed.), *Agenda for the Nation* (Washington, D.C., Brookings Institution, 1969), and his more recent *Thinking About Crime* (New York, Basic Books, 1975). See also Albert J. Reiss, *Police and Public* (New Haven, Yale University Press, 1971).

For the background of ideas in U.S. social science about the conception of "subcultural" crime and violence, see Richard Cloward and Lloyd Ohlin, *Delinquency and Opportunity* (New York, Free Press, 1959); Marvin Wolfgang and Franco Ferracuti, *The Subculture of Violence* (New York, Universities Press, 1967); and for a recent, very conservative version, Edward Banfield, *The Unheavenly City* (Boston, Little, Brown, 1971).

On the need for more sophisticated handling of riots, see especially Morris Janowitz, "Social Control of Escalated Riots," in Graham and Gurr (Eds.), *Violence in America* (New York, Bantam, 1969).

Much has been written about the practices of the police in poor and Third World communities. The most current and the best political analysis is Paul Takagi's "A Garrison State in a 'Democratic' Society," *Crime and Social Justice* Vol. 1 (Spring-Summer 1974). See also, for example, books by James Baldwin, *Nobody Knows My Name* (New York, Dell,

1962); Eldridge Cleaver, *Soul on Ice* (New York, McGraw-Hill Book Company, 1968, esp. pp. 128-137); Phillip Foner (Ed.), *The Black Panther Speaks* (New York, Lippincott, 1970); George Jackson, *Blood in My Eye* (New York, Random House, 1972); Bobby Seale, *Seize the Time* (New York, Vintage Books, 1968); Angela Davis, *If They Come in the Morning* (New York, Third Press, 1971); Panther 21, *Look for Me in the Whirlwind* (New York, Random House, 1971); George Jackson, *Soledad Brother* (New York, Coward, 1970); *Autobiography of Malcolm X* (New York,

Grove Press, 1965); Armando Morales, *Ando Sangrando* (California, Perspective Publishing, Compton Co., 1971). Other books containing good community strategy and analysis include Marjorie Heins, *Strictly Ghetto Property*, cited above; a publication by the National Committee to Free Los Tres entitled "Free Los Tres" (Los Angeles, 1974); and Paul Jacobs, *Prelude to Riot* (New York, Random House, 1966). Two books written from a left-liberal, civil libertarian perspective are Paul Chevigny, *Police Power: Police Abuses in New York City* (New York, Pantheon, 1969); and Knowles and

Prewitt, "Racism in the Administration of Justice," in *Institutional Racism* (Englewood Cliffs, N.J., Prentice-Hall, 1969). The recent novel by Jimmy Breslin, *World Without End, Amen* (New York, Avon, 1973) provides excellent documentation of police practices. In addition, Robert Conot, *Rivers of Blood, Years of Darkness* (New York, Bantam Books, 1967), and John Hersey, *The Algiers Motel Incident* (New York, Bantam Books, 1968) provide descriptive studies of police racism, although they are basically apolitical. Finally, the Federal Commissions of the 1960's, particularly the *Kerner Commission,* contain much discussion of policing Third World communities and outlines of the new Velvet Glove approach; see *Research Guide,* under Commissions.

On the origins and development of the experiment in women police, see especially two reports by the Police Foundation: Catherine Milton, *Women in Policing* (Washington, D.C., Police Foundation, 1972); Peter Bloch and Deborah Anderson, *Policewomen on Patrol: Final Report* (Washington, D.C., Police Foundation, 1974).

On team policing, see Lawrence Sherman, et al., *Team Policing: Seven Case Studies* (Washington, D.C., Police Foundation, 1973). There are some revealing (and funny) insights on team policing in Joseph Wambaugh's novel about the Los Angeles Police, *The Choirboys* (New York, Dell, 1976). On police approaches to "community relations" generally, the official literature is extensive (and self-serving). For some examples, see Ralph A. Almos, *An Introduction to Police-Community Relations* (Springfield, Ill., Charles C. Thomas, 1974); U.S. Department of Justice, Law Enforcement Assistance Administration, *Improving Police-Community Relations* (Washington, D.C., LEAA, 1973); and see *Research Guide,* under U.S. Government Law Enforcement Agencies.

VI. EXPANDING FOR BUSINESS

For materials on the growth of the private police industry, see *Research Guide,* section on Private Police Agencies, and also these studies:

Milton Lipson, *On Guard: The Business of Private Security* (New York, Quadrangle, 1975); Institute for Local Self-Government, *Private Security and the Public Interest: A Pioneering Statewide Study* (Berkeley, Calif., 1974).

On the U.S. contribution to the militarization of the Third World generally, see Klare, *World Without End,* cited under section IV; good analyses of various aspects of U.S. domination of the Third World are available in NACLA's *Latin America Report* (New York and Berkeley, North American Congress on Latin America); see, especially, "U.S. Police Sales Abroad" (July-August, 1976); "Command and Control: U.S. Police Operations in Latin America" (January 1972); and also Michael Klare and Nancy Stein, "The U.S. Public Safety Program," in NACLA's *The U.S. Military Apparatus* (August 1972). There is much useful information in a publication of the Comptroller of the United States, *Stopping U.S. Assistance to Foreign Police and Prisons, Report to Congress* (Washington, General Accounting Office, 1976).

IX. CONCLUSION

There is a growing body of studies showing that the police are ineffective in reducing rates of crime. See particularly George Kelling, et al., *The Kansas City Preventive Patrol Experiment* (Washington, D.C., Police Foundation, 1974); Thomas Pogue, "The Effect of Police Expenditures on Crime Rates," *Public Finance Quarterly,* Vol. 3, no. 1 (January 1975).

General perspectives on the current economic crisis and its fiscal impact on the cities can be found in David Mermelstein, Ed., *The Economic Crisis Reader* (New York, Random House, 1975); James O'Connor, *The Fiscal Crisis of the State* (New York, St. Martins Press, 1974).

For hard-to-get material on current political struggles against the police, readers may write to the organizations listed below in our *Research Guide.* Other materials are on file at the Center for Research on Criminal Justice.

207

20. RESEARCH GUIDE

The rise of police professionalism and the competition for LEAA funds have resulted in the publication of previously unavailable information about the police. Although police departments guard their information in "sensitive" areas such as political surveillance, most information is available somewhere, in some form.

Information sources within the police framework are: the police departments themselves, the state and regional LEAA agencies, local governmental bodies (city council, board of supervisors, etc.), police rank and file organizations and their publications, and trade magazines.

Police departments publish annual reports which usually contain information on crime and arrest statistics, the organizational structure of the department, the statistical profile of the staff (race, sex, age, etc.) and general budget figures. In addition, most departments now have a full-time public relations information officer who, if approached correctly, as an ally, can provide specific information.

Local governmental records contain such things as detailed budgets, hearings on budgets and other matters relating to the department. Court transcripts may contain information on police practices that's revealed only under cross examination by a lawyer. This is particularly true of data on such subjects as surveillance.

State LEAA agencies publish a wealth of information about law enforcement operations. Every state criminal justice planning agency annually publishes a COMPREHENSIVE PLAN (called the Annual Action Plan and available on request or in public libraries) which outlines the statewide program for "improving" the criminal justice system. The PLAN contains factual data on crime in the state and programs that are to be funded in order to combat it.

Regional LEAA offices publish a regional version of the statewide plan. It is here that projects from local departments will show up. These projects, which may range from SWAT vehicles to juvenile counseling centers, are

208

described in their proposals according to objective, methodology, budget, lifespan, etc. When the regional office evaluates them, they are given a priority number and the money is stretched as far as it can go. It is easy to see exactly what LEAA is and is not funding in your region.

Projects can also be funded after the ANNUAL ACTION PLAN is published. In California, as in most states, these are listed in the state's monthly LEAA newsletter, and more detailed information is available from the regional office.

Trade magazines and police rank-and-file publications, as well as your local newspapers, also contain information that provides a starting point for further investigation.

Remember that almost all the information you are seeking is public record and cannot be withheld from you. Of course, it often helps to develop a strategy (innocence, friendliness, conservatism, aggressiveness based on prior research) to help grease the wheels of bureaucracies that can be very uncooperative in the execution of their duties. Don't overlook seemingly unimportant bits of information. It was a researcher's curiosity about the word "COINTELPRO" which appeared in one of the F.B.I. documents stolen from their Media office that led to the disclosure of those operations.

Also, don't be overwhelmed by the mass of information you will need to sift through, much of which will be useless. Research consists of a continuous process of selecting the important by systematic examination of the available. We have been led to believe that only a select few are intelligent enough to engage in serious research and that research is somehow distinct from political action. Once you start, you will discover the reasons why we have been taught those things. Research can help us identify people and institutions that wield power, suggest strategies for resistance, locate weak points in the system, and combat paranoia. As such, it is a powerful weapon when placed in the hands of the people.

Sources of Information

A. U.S. GOVERNMENT LAW ENFORCEMENT AGENCIES*

Major federal law enforcement agencies are identified and described in the annual *U.S. Government Organization Manual*, available for 3.00 from the Government Printing Office (GPO), Washington, D.C. 20402.

Department of Justice

The Justice Department (Constitution Ave. and 10th St. NW, Washington, D.C. 20530), will supply upon request *U.S. Department of Justice: Function and Organization*, which describes the principal Justice Dept. agencies. For more complete data, see *The Attorney General's First Annual Report on Federal Law Enforcement and Criminal Justice Assistance Activities* (1972), available for $5.00 from the GPO. U.S. Attorneys, Marshals, and other officers are identified in the *U.S. Government Organizational Manual*. Texts of the Attorney General's statements and other information are available from the Department's Office of Public Information.

Federal Bureau of Investigation

The F.B.I. (J. Edgar Hoover Building, Washington, D.C. 20530) will supply, upon request, the *FBI Annual Report*, and other descriptive materials. F.B.I. field officers are listed in the *U.S. Government Organizational Manual*. See also the *FBI Law Enforcement Journal*, available in most university and municipal libraries.

Law Enforcement Assistance Administration (LEAA)

LEAA (633 Indiana Ave., NW, Washington, D.C. 20530), a Justice Dept. agency, will supply on request the *LEAA Annual Report* and *Safe Streets—The LEAA Program at Work*. LEAA publications are listed in the *LEAA Reference List of Publications*, available free from LEAA's National Criminal Justice Reference System. For background on LEAA's research arm, the National Institute of Law Enforcement and Criminal Justice (NILECJ), see *A National Program of Research, Test, and Evaluation on Law Enforcement and Criminal Justice*, available for $1.50 from the GPO. NILECJ research studies are listed in the *LEAA Reference List* (most are available on request free from LEAA, or on sale from the GPO.) For a discussion of LEAA operations in support of local police, see *The Federal Criminal Justice System*, hearings before a subcommittee of the Joint Economic Committee, 91st Congress, 2nd Session, 1970 (available free from your congressional representative or GPO for $1.00). LEAA also publishes a monthly *LEAA Newsletter*, available upon request.

For basic statistical data, refer to *The Sourcebook of Criminal Justice Statistics— 1973* by Michael J. Hindelang, Christopher S. Dunn, L. Paul Sutton, and Alison L. Aumick (National Criminal Justice Information and Statistics Service, LEAA, August 1973, available from the GPO for $6.95). The 500 pages of charts and tables cover such information as characteristics of the criminal justice system, public attitudes towards crime, nature and distribution of known offenses, characteristics and distribution of persons arrested, judicial processing of defendants, and persons under correctional supervision.

For statistical data on state and local law enforcement agencies, see *Criminal Justice Agencies in the United States: Summary Report*, 1970 (available from the GPO for $6.50).

An LEAA guide to police education is

contained in *Higher Education Programs in Law Enforcement and Criminal Justice* (available from GPO for 50¢).

The *Directory of Automated Criminal Justice Information Systems (1972)* lists and details over 450 different computer systems, indexed according to State, System name, Function and Computer manufacturer. (1,000 pages)

In addition, LEAA distributes reports prepared by contractors under the Omnibus Crime Control and Safe Streets Act of 1968 and related legislation. Most of these reports are available free to the public, or are for sale through the GPO. Write the LEAA for its *Reference List of Publications.* Of particular interest are: *Project Sky Night: A Demonstration in Aerial Surveillance and Crime Control; Reports, Records, and Communications in the Boston Police Department; Police Telecommunications Systems; Detection of Potential Community Violence; The Utilization of Helicopters for Police Training; Voice Identification Research; STOL Aircraft; Higher Education Programs in Law Enforcement and Criminal Justice; The Cincinnati Police-Juvenile Attitude Project; Neighborhood Team Policing; Police Training and Performance Study; Manual for Training for Sheriffs; Basic Elements of Intelligence; Patterns of Burglary; A Look at Criminal Justice Research; The Nature, Impact and Prosecution of White-Collar Crime.*

Some of the earlier LEAA-sponsored symposia and research studies are excellent examples of the military-corporate model. Two especially interesting ones are the volume *Proceedings of the Third Annual Symposium on Law Enforcement, Science and Technology* (Chicago, IIT Research Institute, 1970), and Alfred Blumstein, *A National Program of Research, Development, Test and Evaluation on Law Enforcement and Criminal Justice* (Washington, IDA, November 1968).

B. COMMISSIONS

1. President's Commission on

Law Enforcement and the Administration of Justice, 1967

The Commission's final report, *The Challenge of Crime in a Free Society,* is available from the GPO for $2.25. (An Avon paperback edition is also available.) Commission Task Force Reports which are available from the GPO include *Corrections* ($1.25); *The Courts* ($1.00); *Crime and Its Impact* ($1.25); *Drunkenness* ($0.65); *Juvenile Delinquency and Youth Crime* ($2.00); *Narcotics and Drug Abuse* ($1.00); *Organized Crime* ($0.65); *The Police* ($1.50); *Science and Technology* ($1.25). The GPO also sells the research studies and field surveys prepared for the Commission. These include: *Studies in Crime and Law Enforcement in Major Metropolitan Areas* (2 volumes @ $3.50 per set); *The Police in the Community* (2 volumes @ $2.75 per set); and *National Survey of Police and Community Relations* ($2.00).

National Commission on the Causes and Prevention of Violence, 1969

The Commission's Final Report, *To Establish Justice, Insure Domestic Tranquility,* is available from the GPO and in a Bantam paperback edition. Other Commission reports available from the GPO include: *Violence in America—Historical and Comparative Perspectives* (2 volumes @ $2.75 per set); *The Politics of Protest—Violent Aspects of Protest and Confrontation* ($1.25); *Miami Report* ($0.50); *Shut It Down! A College in Crisis—San Francisco State College* ($1.00); *Shoot-Out in Cleveland* ($0.75); *Assassination and Political Violence* ($2.50); *Law and Order Reconsidered* ($2.50); and the Walker Report, *Rights in Conflict.* Most of the above reports are also available in Bantam paperback editions.

3. National Advisory Committee on Civil Disorders, 1968

The Committee's Report, known as the

Kerner Report, is available from the GPO and in a Bantam paperback edition ($1.25). Also, *Supplemental Studies* ($1.50).

4. The United States Commission on Civil Rights

This commission has published various reports on police and the Third World community. Some of them include: *Mexican Americans and the Administration of Justice in the Southwest* Part I, "Law Enforcement" (1970, available from GPO); *Report on California: Police-Minority Relations* (California Advisory Committee to the Commission on Civil Rights, August, 1963); *Police-Community Relations in East Los Angeles, California* (October, 1970); *Report—Justice* (1968).

5. The National Commission on Law Observance and Enforcement, 1931

This committee has published the *Report on Crime and the Foreign Born* (Vol. IX, 1931, available from GPO). Its findings were popularized in a book called *Our Lawless Police* by Jerome Hopkins.

6. National Advisory Commission on Criminal Justice Standards and Goals, 1973

The Commission's final report, *A National Strategy to Reduce Crime,* is available from the GPO for $2.55. Task Force Reports are also available from the GPO: *Police* ($6.65); *Courts* ($3.95); *Criminal Justice System* ($3.35); *Proceedings of the National Conference on Criminal Justice.*

7. President's Commission on Campus Unrest, 1970

The final report of the Commission, *The Scranton Report,* is available at the GPO for $2.50.

8. President's Commission on Crime in the District of Columbia, 1966

The Commission's final report, *Report on the Metropolitan Police Department,* is available from the GPO.

C. CONGRESSIONAL COMMITTEES

1. Permanent Subcommittee on Investigation of the Senate Committee on Government Operations

This subcommittee has published a series of hearings on *Riots, Civil and Criminal Disorders,* beginning in 1967. It is available upon request from local Congressmembers and the Subcommittee itself.

2. House Committee on Internal Security (HISC)

HISC has published a series of hearings on *Subversive Influence in Riots, Looting, and Burning, Subversive Involvement in Disruption of the 1968 Democratic Party National Convention,* and on other crime-related topics. These are available from local Congressmembers and from HISC.

3. Senate Committee on the Judiciary

Various subcommittees of this committee have conducted hearings on law enforcement issues. The Subcommittee on Criminal Laws and Procedures has published hearings on *Measures Related to Organized Crime* and *Controlling Crime Through More Effective Law Enforcement.* The Subcommittee on Constitutional Rights has published hearings on *Privacy, Federal Questionnaires, and Constitutional Rights* and on *Military Surveillance, Data Banks and the Bill of Rights.* The Subcommittee on Administrative Practice and Procedure has held hearings on *Invasions of Privacy by Government Agencies* and on *Computer Privacy.*

In addition to the above, the Appropriations Committees of the Senate and House hold annual hearings on Department of Justice Appropriations. For complete reference on these and other Congressional hearings, consult the *Monthly Catalog of U.S. Government Publications,* available in most libraries.

D. ADDITIONAL FEDERAL AGENCIES

1. The National Institute of Mental Health (NIMH)

For an overview of the Federal law enforcement apparatus, refer to this agency's publication, *The Role of the Federal Agencies in the Crime and Delinquency Field* (available from GPO for $1.25). In addition, one of its subcenters, The Center for Studies of Crime and Delinquency, has published a series of monographs on 'Crime and Delinquency Issues.' The complete listing is available on request from NIMH at 5600 Fishers Lane, Rockville, MD 20852.

2. The Office of Juvenile Delinquency and Youth Development—Department of Health, Education, and Welfare

This office published the *Juvenile Delinquency Reporter* and other publications related to juvenile delinquency. It also published reports concerning police education and training programs in the United States, including *Educational Training* (1966) and *Education and Training.* The office publishes additional data on police education training programs in *Education, Training and Manpower in Corrections and Law Enforcement* (four volumes) and *Education and Training for Criminal Justice—A Directory of Programs in Universities.*

E. STATE AND MUNICIPAL LAW ENFORCEMENT AGENCIES

Basic statistical data on the incidence of crime by city, state and region is available in *Crime in the United States—Uniform Crime*

Reports, published annually and available from the GPO for $1.50.

For general background information, see *State-Local Relations in the Criminal Justice System,* published by the Advisory Committee on Intergovernmental Relations and available from GPO for $2.25. Local planning for implementation of the Safe Streets Act is discussed in *Regional Criminal Justice Planning: A Manual for Local Officials,* published by the National Association of Counties Research Foundation and available from the GPO.

1. State agencies

Most states publish an annual yearbook or legislative manual which identifies state law enforcement agencies and names their officers. Some cities also publish a newspaper or journal which contains basic data on police promotions and hirings, budgetary affairs and contract administration (see, for example, the *City Record,* Official Journal of the City of New York). Most local newspapers also report such information. Some of the larger police departments also publish their own annual reports or yearbooks. Some departments also publish magazines.

These reports and periodicals are usually available in the larger municipal libraries. Many police agencies also maintain community relations offices which usually supply general information on the department upon request. The benevolent associations of some of the larger police forces also publish journals—see, for instance, *New York's Finest,* published by the Patrolmen's Benevolent Assn. (250 Broadway, New York, NY 10007).

F. PROFESSIONAL ORGANIZATIONS

1. International Association of Chiefs of Police (IACP)

IACP (11 Firstfield Rd., Gaithersburg, MD 20760) is the most important professional organization in the law enforcement field. It publishes *Police Chief*, the leading journal in the field, *The Police Yearbook* (proceedings of the annual IACP conference), and many other technical and procedural manuals and reports. IACP divisions include the Legal Research Section, which published the *IACP Law Enforcement Legal Review*, the Police Weapons Center, and the Professional Standards Division. In conjunction with the Northwestern University School of Law, the IACP publishes a quarterly, the *Journal of Police Science and Administration*. The annual *Buyers Guide and Directory of Members* lists police associations, police equipment, manufacturers, and individual members by city. The IACP publishes many manuals and technical reports on police weapons and tactics. Of particular interest are: *Guidelines for Civil Disorder and Mobilization Planning*, by R. Dean Smith and Richard W. Kobetz (1968, $3.00); and *Police Chemical Agents Manual*, by Thompson Crockett (1970; $3.00). IACP also publishes a series of manuals on police procedures known as the "Police Technical Series." Titles in this series include *Recognition of Explosive and Incendiary Devices* (2 vols. @ $5.00 each); and *Vehicle Theft Identification Manual* ($7.50). IACP also produces a "Police Weapons Center Data Service" which includes a directory of police weapons and periodic technical reports (available for $30.00 annually).

The annual "Directory Issue" of *Police Chief* (usually the October issue) lists all major suppliers of police weapons and other equipment in the United States. Police training programs are listed in the *Law Enforcement Education Directory*, published annually by IACP and available upon request. For a complete list of IACP publications and services, write IACP itself.

2. The American Society for Industrial Security (2000 'K' St. NW, Washington, D.C. 20006) publishes *Industrial Security* and other materials in the area of industrial security.

3. The National Sheriffs' Association (1250 Connecticut Ave. NW, Washington, D.C. 20036) publishes *The National Sheriff*.

4. The International Association of College and University Security Directors (John H. Powell, Executive House, Hamden, Conn. 06514) publishes the *Campus Law Enforcement Journal*.

5. The Military Police Association (Box 7500, Ft. Gordon, Ga. 30905) publishes the *Military Police Journal*.

G. CITIZENS AND UNIVERSITY GROUPS, AND FOUNDATIONS

1. National Council on Crime and Delinquency (NCCD)

The NCCD (Continental Plaza, 411 Hackensack Ave., Hackensack, N.J. 07601) is the principal citizens' organization concerned with crime and law enforcement. NCCD has a national headquarters in Hackensack, N.J., and branches in other large cities. NCCD publications include *Crime and Delinquency*, *Crime and Delinquency Literature*, and the *Journal of Research in Crime and Delinquency*. For a list of NCCD offices, services, and publications, write to the Council directly.

2. National Action Research on the Military Industrial Complex (NARMIC)

The National Action-Research on the Military-Industrial Complex (NARMIC) of the American Friends Service Committee (160 N. 15th St., Philadelphia, Pa. 19102) has published a study of the university role in domestic law enforcement training and research—*Police on the Homefront* (1971; $1.35).

3. National Center on Police and Community Relations

The National Center (School of Police Administration, Michigan State University, East Lansing, Michigan) publishes a bibliography on police-community relations, and other materials on this subject.

4. The Illinois Institute of Technology Research Institute (IITRI)

The Illinois Institute of Technology Research Institute (IITRI, Chicago, Ill.) has sponsored a bi-annual "Symposium on Law Enforcement Science and Technology." These symposia bring together policemen, scientists and engineers for a series of panels on police technology. The *Proceedings* of these conferences are particularly valuable sources of information on the "state of the art." *Law Enforcement Science and Technology II* and *III* (1968 and 1970, respectively) are available from IITRI (P.O. Box 4963, Chicago, Il. 60680) for $10.00 each. *Law Enforcement Science and Technology I* (1967) is available for $35.00 from the Management Development Center (148 E. Lancaster Ave., Wayne, Pa. 19087).

5. National Science Foundation (NSF)

A good source on less-than-lethal weapons is a 68-page report to the National Science Foundation (1800 G St. NW, Washington, D.C. 20550) entitled *Nonlethal Weapons for Law Enforcement* (March, 1972).

6. Police Foundation (funded by the Ford Foundation)

This foundation (located at 1015 Eighteenth St. NW, Washington, D.C. 20036) makes periodic reports about the police. The initial proposal is entitled "A More Effective Arm," and the progress report is "Experiments in Police Improvement" (Washington, D.C., 1972). Special reports include those on *Team Policing* (Washington, D.C., 1972); *Women in Policing,* by Catherine Milton; *Policewomen on Patrol—Final Report,* by Peter B. Bloch and Deborah Anderson; and *A Conference on Managing the Patrol Function.*

214

H. BIBLIOGRAPHIES, TEXTBOOKS, NEWS SERVICES, JOURNALS

1. Bibliographies

Articles on police science and criminology are indexed in EXCERPTA CRIMINOLOGICA and the *Index to Legal Publications,* available in the reference sections of law school libraries. The National Council on Crime and Delinquency (Continental Plaza, 411 Hackensack Ave., Hackensack, N.J. 07601) publishes a handy *Selected Reading List* on crime and delinquency (available on request), and *Crime and Delinquency Literature,* a comprehensive quarterly listing of recent books and articles in the field (annual subscription: $15.00). NCCD also publishes a *Bibliographical Manual for the Student of Criminology* ($1.00; 1965).

Other bibliographies on law enforcement subjects include: *International Bibliography on Crime and Delinquency* (Information Center on Crime and Delinquency, NIMH); Harold K. Becker and George T. Felkenes, *Law Enforcement: A Selected Bibliography* (Scarecrow Press, Metuchen, N.J., 1968); *A Bibliography of Police Administration, Public Safety and Criminology to July 1, 1965* (Charles C. Thomas, Springfield, Il., 1967); *A Bibliography on Police and Community Relations* (School of Police Administration, Michigan State University, East Lansing, 1966; Supplement issued 1967). These bibliographies are available in the larger university and municipal libraries, and in libraries of schools with police science programs.

2. Publishers

A number of publishers specialize in police textbooks and manuals, including: Charles C. Thomas, Publishers (301-327 East Lawrence Ave., Springfield, Il. 62703); McGraw-Hill Book Company (Technical and Vocational Education Division, 330 West 42nd Street, New York, NY 10036); Arco Publishing Company (219 Park Ave. South,

215

New York, NY 10003); Glencoe Press (8701 Wilshire Boulevard, Beverly Hills, CA 90211); and W. H. Anderson Company (Department P, 646 Main St., Cincinatti, OH 45201). Write these publishers directly for price lists. Police textbooks are most likely to be found in college libraries which service police science programs.

3. Other News Services and Periodicals

a. *Crime Control Digest* (published by Washington Crime News Series; weekly; $95 per year). Current news of interest to law enforcement officials.

b. *Criminal Justice Digest* (Washington Crime News Services, $12 per year).

c. *Law and Order* (published by *Law and Order Magazine*, 37 W. 38th St., New York, NY 10018; $7.00 per year).

d. *Security World* (Security World Publishing Company, 2639 S. La Cienega, Los Angeles, CA 90034; monthly, $10.00 per year).

e. *Journal of Criminal Law and Criminology* (Northwestern University School of Law, 357 E. Chicago Ave., Chicago, Il.).

I. PRIVATE POLICE AGENCIES

For a comprehensive study of the private police industry, see the exhaustive five-volume study prepared by the RAND Corporation and sold by the GPO. The titles in this study are: Vol. 1, *Private Police in the United States: Findings and Recommendations* ($1.00); Vol. 2, *The Private Police Industry: Its Nature and Extent* ($1.25); Vol. 3, *Current Regulation of Private Police* ($1.50); Vol. 4, *The Law and Private Police* ($1.00); Vol. 5, *Special-Purpose Private Police* ($0.50). Private police manuals include: John D. Peel, *The Story of Private Security* (Charles C. Thomas, 1971); and Richard S. Dost and Arthur S. Kingsbury, *Security Administration* (Charles C. Thomas, 1972). The two journals in the field, *Security World* and *Industrial Security*, are standard sources of information in this area. University police agencies are discussed in *Campus Law Enforcement Journal*, published by the International Association of College and University Security Directors, and available from Herbert Voye, Tufts University Police, Medford, Mass. 02155.

J. RESEARCH ORGANIZATIONS (as of 1978)

Center for National Security Studies
122 Maryland Avenue NE
Washington, D.C. 20002

CNSS conducts research on such issues as the CIA's covert operations, government secrecy, and The Freedom of Information Act. The Center recently published *Law and Disorder IV*, a critical analysis of LEAA.

Citizen's Research and Investigation Committee
1619 South Bonnie Brae
Los Angeles, California 90057

CRIC is composed of journalists, writers, teachers and citizens who came together to explore various facets of police intelligence agencies in the United States. Their best-known publication is *The Glass House Tapes*, a book about the history and operation of counterinsurgency in Los Angeles.

Crime and Social Justice
P.O. Box 4373
Berkeley, California 94704

Crime and Social Justice is a progressive, Marxist-oriented journal, published at least twice a year by collectives in Berkeley, Buffalo, and Las Vegas. The journal includes analytical and historical articles, course outlines, reports on popular struggles, and reviews of the latest literature in criminology.

National Action/Research on the Military-Industrial Complex
1501 Cherry Street
Philadelphia, Penn. 19102

NARMIC produced *Police on the Homefront*, a pioneering investigation of the police-industrial complex, U.S. police training programs abroad, and the rise of technological forms of repression.

National Alliance Against Racist and Political Repression 150 Fifth Ave., Rm. 804 New York, New York 10011	The Alliance, established by the Communist Party of the USA, is engaged in legal defense of political prisoners, organizes mass support for political defendants and prisoners, holds educational conferences and forums, and publishes a regular newsletter.
National Lawyers Guild Police Crimes Task Force 1764 Gilpin Street Denver, Colorado 80218	The PCTF publishes a "Police Misconduct Litigation Manual"; a manual for legal workers on "Police Abuse"; a resource list of attorneys involved in police misconduct cases; a bi-monthly newsletter including both legal and political articles; and a network for materials on police misconduct litigation.
New Mexico Civil Liberties Union P.O. Box 25961 Albuquerque, New Mexico 87125	A group from the NMCLU is doing research on domestic repression, surveillance, etc. They have also done research on police technology and have written "Ten Years More, 1974," a report on invasion of privacy and the technology of control.
North American Congress on Latin America P.O. Box 57, Cathedral Stn. New York, New York 10025 P.O. Box 226 Berkeley, California 94701	NACLA's primary orientation lies outside the criminal justice system but it has conducted invaluable studies of various aspects of the repressive apparatus. NACLA has produced a series of studies on the international aspects of the police and the military, especially the export by the United States of "crime control" and counterinsurgency training and equipment.
Northern California Police Practices Project ACLU Northern California 814 Mission Street San Francisco, California 94103	The Police Practices Project works to promote public accountability of California police agencies and to assist citizens who seek legal and administrative remedies for police misconduct. The Project works with local community groups and professional organizations.
Organizing Committee for a Fifth Estate P.O. Box 647, Ben Franklin Station Washington, D.C. 20044	Fifth Estate is a progressive organization involved in researching and exposing the U.S. intelligence apparatus. They are working to abolish covert intervention, domestic repression, excessive secrecy, technological control, and other illicit and dangerous practices of counterinsurgency agencies. They also publish the magazine *CounterSpy*, which documents their research and exposés.
Public Interest Law Center of Philadelphia Police Project 1315 Walnut St., 16th Floor Philadelphia, Pennsylvania 19107	The Police Project provides services to police abuse victims by pursuing strategies of redress through both judicial and non-judicial channels. They publish a bi-monthly newsletter reporting on local struggles around the police as well as information on legal cases.
Repression Research Group 5500 St. Louis Avenue Chicago, Illinois 61625	The RRG has been established in Chicago to engage in research of abuses of power by the Chicago police, FBI and military intelligence forces in the Chicago area.

217

21. DOCUMENTS

A. Excerpt from *To Stop a Police State; The Case for Community Control of the Police*, Berkeley, 1971.

In 1971, a community coalition came together in Berkeley, California, to campaign for a Community Control Amendment aimed at allowing direct control of the police by people in the community. The measure was defeated three to one, but a campaign two years later was partly successful. The following document outlines the principles behind the 1971 campaign; the 1973 measures are outlined in section B, below.

The Berkeley police are virtually independent under the present system. Legally they are responsible to the City Manager. In fact the City Manager has consistently shielded the police department from community and even City Council pressure. He has been free to do this because he himself is relatively immune to Council pressure: a two-thirds Council majority is required to replace him or direct his actions, so in reality his office has become a permanent bureaucracy with wide and flexible powers.

THREE BASIC COMMUNITIES

The Community Control Amendment would re-arrange city government to permit direct control of the police by the people in three administrative (and neighborhood) districts.

Community Control is based on a principle of self-government that is deeply rooted in American tradition. Thomas Jefferson, for instance, proposed to "divide the counties into wards of such size as that every person can attend, when called upon, and act in person. Ascribe to them the government of their wards in all things relating to themselves exclusively."

Two centuries later, similar ideas have inspired students and young people, black and brown people, to carry on struggles for control of their education, their culture, their work, their government.

In the Berkeley community, Jefferson's "wards" are the three distinct areas defined by the Community Control Amendment: the black community, the campus/youth community, and the middle-class Northside/Hill community. Of course, these are not completely distinct areas. The "black" community defined in the Amendment is actually one-fourth white. The "hill" community contains a generation gap. The "campus" community contains students, freaks, and many long-time Berkeley residents. Nevertheless, the communities are distinct from each other, each with its common hang-outs, common life-styles, common shopping and recreation areas, common problems.

The police like to criticize the Amendment for creating divisions in the community. In fact these divisions already exist, as the police themselves recognize in their own practice, assigning different personnel and developing particular programs for each of the three areas. What the Amendment really recognizes is that the present police department only "represents" the conservative areas of Berkeley and antagonizes the majority of people who live in the black and campus communities.

The Amendment would give power to those who are now neglected or oppressed by the police, instead of perpetuating the fundamental "division" in Berkeley between powerful and powerless.

If at any time community realities change, there are provisions in the Amendment for altering the boundaries of the proposed districts.

POLICY-MAKING PROCESS

Neighborhood people would set police policy and standards of conduct in their areas through Police Councils. Based on population, these Councils would include 15 citizens elected from 15 precincts. These precincts would not be much larger than the present voting precincts. There would be two Councils of 15 in the black area and the Hills/Northside area respectively because of their size, and one

Council in the Campus area.

The Councils would choose individual Commissioners to carry out policy decisions on a day to day basis. The five Commissioners (two from the black area, two from the Hills/Northside, one from the campus) would be the administrative coordinators of the police, replacing many of the functions of the police chief.

In the words of the Amendment: "The Commissioners shall fix the policies of the police within the Department, shall punish police officers for violations of said policies and for violation of the law, shall determine qualifications of members of the police department, and shall fix compensation for all employees of said Department."

The elected Councils "shall review the policies of the Police Department and will recommend changes or modifications of such policies when such policies no longer reflect the needs or will of the Neighborhood represented by the Council." Each Council also will create grievance machinery for complaints against the police, and will have the power to "discipline members of the Department for violations of law or policy occurring within that District."

The BPD has attacked these provisions as leading to differential enforcement or avoidance of the law. Yet it is the police themselves who are selectively enforcing the law, in various areas of Berkeley on the basis of their political likes and dislikes. The new system would let the community concerned decide on the priorities for law enforcement. In the South Campus this might mean the beginning of needed social service programs instead of Avenue harassment.

GUARANTEES OF RIGHTS

The Amendment provides many guarantees of real democratic rights, thus protecting against the formation of new bureaucracy. The Commissioners must hold regular public meetings when the residents are "most able to attend," and then vote for or bring up any matter as instructed by the Councils. The Councils too must meet regularly "at a time when interested persons may attend." The

people of a precinct can recall their Council members by a petition representing 20 percent of those voting in the last precinct election. Commissioners can also be recalled by a similar process in their general district.

RESIDENCY REQUIREMENT

A final guarantee of local power is the residency requirement which would make each police officer live in the area he or she served. Although this is common police practice in many cities, in Berkeley all but 35 police now live outside the city—in Albany, Richmond, El Cerrito, Oakland, Walnut Creek and San Francisco.

The BPD now justifies its "outsider" status on three grounds. First, that housing is hard to find in Berkeley. This is hardly an insurmountable obstacle when dealing with only 200 people. Second, that it is "unfair" to govern the private living decisions of police. But the place of residence of a policeman can affect his ability to serve the public. Third, the police fear living among the people they have to arrest. But someone determined on revenge could certainly go to a policeman's house in Albany. More importantly, the Community Control proposal would lessen, not increase, the friction that now results from police acting as an outside force.

The present isolation of the Berkeley police —racially, culturally and politically—is nearly total in much of Berkeley. And this is the real reason so many officers prefer to live outside the city. Living among the people he or she serves would force the police to harmonize with the community and seek its genuine support. There is no better way for the police to become familiar with the community's problems and no better way for a neighborhood to know and control what its police are doing.

FINANCING

Under the Amendment, the police budget would still be appropriated by the City Council, but it would be disbursed to the three departments "on the basis of the number of people residing in each department district on the last preceding election." This would sever the City Manager's control of the police payroll and place funds in the hands of the people most affected.

COORDINATION BETWEEN AREAS

The decentralized nature of the proposed police system would in no way prevent necessary coordination. The Commissioners are allowed to "enter into necessary agreements with other police departments and other government agencies." The three departments "may enter into agreements with each other for the operation, maintenance and staffing of certain facilities in which there is a common interest, including, but not limited to laboratories, vehicle repair equipment, including vehicles and weapons."

In fact, the Amendment is so clear on the means of coordination that police criticism on this point (for instance, the claim that the present police building would have to be closed down) cannot be taken seriously. What the police appear to fear, really, is the threat to their present centralization which is required not to maintain "efficiency" but to better carry out policies against a hostile community. Ad-

ministrative efficiency can be accomplished i many ways; the real question is whether it achieved in the service of, rather than agains the public's expressed will.

One aspect of current coordination whic would undoubtedly come up for review is tha between the BPD and the University, the BPD and the Alameda deputy sheriffs, and the BPD and the outside government agencies—force which are tied together through "mutual aid," "integrated patrol," and numerous other arrangements. The Amendment would make i possible to cancel or alter any of these agree ments to which the City is now a party. Th public could cancel, for instance, the "right" o University police to patrol within a mile radiu of the campus; or it could begin legal investiga tions of the Alameda County sheriffs instead o congratulating them; or it could expose th undercover work done in this community b the FBI, CIA, Army and Navy.

The net effect of this Amendment would b to transform the police from an occupyin force to one which wholeheartedly serves th people of Berkeley. It would reject the tradi tional solutions of greater professionalism an control of the police by the City Manager. I would insure that the people directly affecte represent themselves and begin to find solution to their problems. In this sense, the Amend ment goes beyond the philosophy of "repre sentative government" and suggests the solutio of direct democracy.

B. The Berkeley Police Initiative and the Police Review Commission

In 1973, Berkeley citizens placed on th ballot an initiative calling for city counc control of police agreements with outside la enforcement agencies, limitations on polic weapons, a residency requirement for polic officers, and a civilian police review board. Tw of these demands passed—council control o police agreements and the creation of a polic review commission. The first document de scribes the four provisions in more detail; th second is an excerpt from the text of th ordinance establishing the Police Review Com mission.

1. Excerpts from a Newsletter by the Police Initiative Committee, Berkeley, 1973.

No. 4
COUNCIL CONTROL OF
POLICE AGREEMENTS
requires public disclosure of all secret police agreements with outside law enforcement agencies

provides for City Council approval of all agreements following public hearings

No. 6
WEAPONS REGULATION
establishes City Council control over weapons and arsenal

outlaws submachine guns, automatic pistols, dangerous chemicals and gases

provides for new weapons tests

regulates and limits police sidearms to revolvers

removes shotguns from cars, to stay at station for emergencies

No. 5
RESIDENCY
provides that police must live in Berkeley —one year for present members to establish residence, 90 days for new employees

hardship exceptions allowed

promotes affirmative action to desegregate Berkeley police

No. 7
POLICE REVIEW
creates 9-person Commission appointed by City Council

investigation of all citizen complaints required

establishes review of police practices and policies

provides for public hearings on police matters

2. Berkeley Police Review Commission Ordinance

ESTABLISHING A POLICE REVIEW COMMISSION, PROVIDING FOR THE APPOINTMENT AND REMOVAL OF MEMBERS THEREOF, AND DEFINING THE OBJECTIVES, FUNCTIONS, DUTIES AND ACTIVITIES OF SAID COMMISSION.

The people of the City of Berkeley do ordain as follows:

Section 1. The general purpose of this ordinance is to provide for community participation in setting and reviewing police department policies, practices, and procedures and to provide a means for prompt, impartial and fair investigation of complaints brought by individuals against the Berkeley Police Department. . . .

Section 10. The Commission established by this ordinance shall have the following powers and duties:

a) to advise and make recommendations to the public, the City Council, and the City Manager;

b) to review and make recommendations concerning all written and unwritten policies, practices and procedures of whatever kind and without limitation, in relation to the Berkeley Police Department, other law enforcement agencies and intelligence and military agencies operating within the City of Berkeley, and law enforcement generally, such review and recommendation to extend to, but not be limited to, the following:

i) Treatment of rape victims;
ii) Police relationship with minority communities;
iii) Use of weapons and equipment;
iv) Hiring and training;
v) Priorities for policing and patrolling;
vi) Budget development;
vii) Other concerns as specified from time to time by the City Council. . . .

221

C. LAW ENFORCEMENT COMPUTERIZED INFORMATION SYSTEMS

SYSTEM	LOCATION & POPULATION	DATE COSTS (LEAA FUNDS)	CONTRACTORS
AWDI Automated Worthless Document Index	Los Angeles 2,800,000	1972 $508,790 ($303,035)	System Sciences Development Corp. IBM
CABLE Computer Assisted Bay Area Law Enforcement	San Francisco 715,000	1972 $1,000,000	System Sciences Development Corp. IBM
CJIS California Justice Information System	California 17,761,032	1973 $8,800,000 (N.R.)**	Computer Deductions, Inc. Informatics, Inc.
LEADS Law Enforcement Automatic Data System	Ohio 10,652,017	1968 $16,000,000 ($5,790,000)	Midwest Information System IBM Ernst & Ernst
LEIN Law Enforcement Information Network	Michigan 8,875,083	1967 N.R. (N.R.)	System Sciences Development Corp.
NYSIIS New York State Identification & Intelligence System	New York 18,190,740	1969 $17,568,443 ($844,627)	Systems Development Taft Corp. United Aircraft Systech Computer Usage Corp. Touche, Ross, Bailey
ORACLE Optimum Records Automatic for Courts & Law Enforcement	County of Los Angeles 7,500,000	1973 $7,200,000 (N.R.)	Ampex
PATRIC Pattern Recognition & Information Correlation	Los Angeles 2,800,000	1974 $5,800,000 ($1,927,150)	System Development Corp.

Abbreviations:
CLETS — California Law Enforcement Telecommunications System
LEIN — Law Enforcement Information Network   NCIC — National Crime Information Center
NYSPIN — New York Statewide Police Information Network   NLETS — (not given)
RCIC — Regional Crime Information Center

COMPUTER HARDWARE	INTERFACE*	DESCRIPTION
IBM 370/155	None	Indexes all names pertinent to a worthless (forged) document investigation including identification used, addresses & phone numbers signed by the endorser, check & account numbers, etc.
IBM 370/155	NCIC NLETS CLETS	Provides access to information on persons, places, vehicles, articles and guns. It connects with digital computers in patrol cars.
2 RCA S 70/60	CLETS	Provides information on arrests-case disposition, criminal histories, licensing/registration, stolen property (vehicles, guns, etc.) and warrants.
IBM 370/155	NCIC NLETS LEIN RCIC	Provides data to about 1,000 terminals throughout Ohio regarding arrests, warrants, stolen vehicles, guns and licenses, auto & drivers' licenses and crime trend analysis.
3 Burroughs B-5500	NCIC	Three distinct files index wanted persons, stolen property (vehicles, guns, etc.) and revoked drivers' licenses. Inquiries may be made by driver's license or social security numbers, license plate, vehicle I.D. or a combination of name, age and physical description.
2-Burroughs B-6700	NCIC NYSPIN	Centralized data collector and disseminator of criminal justice information in New York including criminal histories, fingerprint verification, wanted persons. Also, a latent fingerprint file and an infrared data file to identify unknown substances.
Ampex Video File Information System	None	A television information system to speed and automate the handling of more than 18,000,000 Sheriff's Department law enforcement documents including fingerprints and photographs.
IBM 370/155	None	Aids investigative and patrol personnel by providing an index of suspects, their trademarks, physical description & personal additives, premises attacked, weapons used, date time and vehicle descriptions. The system also correlates patterns.

* refers to other computer system with which it is connected.
** N.R. — none reported

Source: *1972 Directory of Automated Criminal Justice Information Systems*, U.S. Department of Justice, Law Enforcement Assistance Administration, Washington, D.C., December, 1972.

D. "LESS-THAN-LETHAL" WEAPONS—A GUIDE

Weapon	Description	Effects	Current Use or Status	Major Problems or Issues Requiring Research
A. Kinetic Energy Impact Weapons:				
Baton, Nightstick and Billy Club	Wooden stick from 12" to 36" hanging from a leather thong.	Used to administer a physical blow to immobilize or incapacitate or as a hand-held barrier.	Standard equipment for most police and other law enforcement officers for routine patrol and disorder control.	If improperly used, can cause serious injury to victim; need for improved training.
Extensible Billy Club	Measures 6" to 7" in closed position. The three telescopic sections rapidly flick open to an extended 16" to 18".	Adaptation of billy club offering concealment and surprise for personal protection or plainclothes use.	In use in Japan; in limited use in U.S.	Need to identify possible users and user needs.
Breakaway Nightstick	Billy or nightstick made of substance that will break if used incorrectly.	Adaptation of billy club to limit severe injury from misuse.	Undeveloped. Not in use.	Needs to be developed; questionable level of acceptability by law enforcement agencies.
Stun Gun	Special stun gun delivers cartridge containing a 4" diameter bean bag loaded with 1/5 to 1/2 lb. of shot. Can be used as handgun or with an extension as a shotgun.	Bag hits victim with full force as it flattens on impact. Has effect of hard-hit baseball.	Widely advertised, but used by few law enforcement agencies.	If fired within 20 feet, force of impact may cause death or serious injury to skull, liver or other parts of body.
Broomstick Round	Wooden cylinder delivered by riot guns or by a British Army signal gun.	Normally aimed to strike at legs of rioters or at close range on ground for a ricochet effect. Produces extreme discomfort; effective dispersal agent.	Although used by foreign control forces, not used by U.S. police forces.	Possibility of serious internal injury or death because of force of impact. Field testing revealed problem of splintering.
Soft Plastic Ricochet Rounds	Polyethylene pellets 1/16" in diameter delivered from standard 12-gauge shotgun aimed to ricochet. Available in larger sizes.	Used at short ranges (but more than 10 feet), has peppering effect. Used for personal protection.	Not in general use.	No range. Can be lethal within 5-10 feet. Beyond that, insufficient kinetic energy to be effective.

Device	Description	Effect / Use	Status	Comments
Rubber Baton	Pliable rubber cylindrical projectiles delivered from the riot gun or British Army signal gun.	Used to disperse disorderly crowds and mobs. Shot at ranges of 100 feet; impact on legs or bodies causes rioters to disperse.	Extensively used by the British in Northern Ireland.	Some U.S. police forces have experimented with and indicated desire to purchase these if British manufacturer could export enough. Some risks of internal injury or death.
Blake Impact Gun	Aluminum alloy-type golf ball-sized projectile fitted to a bolt-action shotgun.	Stuns victim.	New; not now in use.	Possibility of serious injury or death.
Rubber Ball Rounds	Rubber ball fitted with a "Blake" attachment to shotgun. Ball can be solid or filled with liquid or gas. Various designs for point or area targets.	Effects depend on substance in rubber balls, shape and velocity.	Not in general use.	Possibility of serious injury or death, depending on the velocity and material.
Selector System Gun	Handgun designed to give a choice between three types of projectiles: (1) chemical agent, (2) marking dye, and (3) training round.	Varies depending on how loaded. Gives alternative nonlethal capabilities in one weapon.	Available from private manufacturer. Limited use to date.	Poor quality, easily broken. Forces officer to make difficult decision under pressure. Training round can be lethal if shot at too close a range.
Splatt Round (thixotropic)	Any caliber shotgun shells with grease or soft putty on tip; deforms on impact.	Flattens out on impact, making this projectile less lethal than some others mentioned above.	Not in general use.	Possibility of serious injury or death.
Water-filled Projectile	2"-3" spheres with a flexible polyethylene skin. Delivered from special adaptor on shotgun or handgun.	Designed to rupture with an orange peel effect on impact, making it less lethal than most projectiles.	Experimental.	Projectile is too large to be accurate.
Water Cannon	Mobile unit which projects a continuing stream of water.	Force of water, general discomfort and slippery surface aid in dispersing crowds.	Has been used abroad, but not often in the U.S.	Poor public image from highly publicized use of fire hoses in civil disorders in the South.

Weapon	Description	Effects	Current Use or Status	Major Problems or Issues Requiring Research
B. Chemical Weapons: (Chemicals can be disseminated by grenades, projectiles, cartridges or mechanical bulk dispensers. Effectiveness is determined by choice of proper delivery system to fit situation.)				
CN	Conventional tear gas—alphachloroacetophenone	Causes choking, eye tearing, difficulty in breathing. Odor of apple blossoms	In use after World War I by military and many law enforcement agencies for crowd control and flushing out barricaded persons.	Affected by weather conditions. Some temporary eye and skin injury reported when aerosol dispensers used at close range.
C. Electrical Weapons:				
Electrified Baton	Standard dimension baton which delivers an electric charge of low voltage, powered by standard flashlight cells.	Administers uncomfortable but harmless shock as a barrier or prod. Effect is like a bee sting but not as severe.	Has been used in some institutions and in a few cases for civil disorders control, but not in general use.	Poor public image. Widespread public outrage developed when it was used by control forces during early civil rights marches. Limited research on effects.
Electrified Water Jet	Mobile unit projecting a water-stream charged with high voltage, low amperage.	Proposed as barrier; also has disabling potential for crowd control or dispersal.	Concept patented but not yet developed; technology available.	Problem of public acceptance. Limited research on effects.
Taser	Fires small, barbed electrical contactors with up to 500 feet of trailing wire which snags victim's clothing. Electric charge administered through barbs.	Victim is paralyzed until electrified contacts are removed or current shut off.	Developed	Insufficient testing and research on effects. Public reaction to use unclear.

	Description	Effect	Status	Comments
Dart Gun	Modified shotgun or handgun in which the projectile is a drug-filled syringe activated by a small charge on impact. Wide variety of drugs available.	Drug immobilizes victim after several minutes delay.	Currently used only in capture of animals.	Amount needed for quick immobilization might be lethal dosage. Police skeptical of any weapon with delayed action.
E. Light Emission, Acoustical, Cold, and Stench Weapons:				
High Intensity Lights	High intensity light on a reflector-equipped hand-held candle holder.	Destroys night vision if blinked off and on to disorient a crowd.	Only used in relatively infrequent special situations.	Effective for only a short time period, as eyes become adjusted to light.
Teleshot	Cartridge projecting a powerful sonic device delivered by a 12-gauge shotgun.	Effect is to disorient and to disrupt communications between leadership and crowd in riot situation.	Only in experimental use.	Affects user as well as victim.
Sound Curdler	Mobile unit creating high intensity sound painful to ear.	Proposed use to break up communication in crowds and to create discomfort to precipitate dispersion.	Only in experimental use.	Affects user as well as victim. At physical distress levels serious risk of permanent impairment of hearing.
Cold Brine Projector	Delivers slug of liquid below body temperature.	Causes incapacitating shock to body.	Technology available, but undeveloped.	Impractical because portable weapon would not have required capacity. Further research needed to determine if cold actually arrests activity. May burn when used in very cold condition.
Stench	Pot or grenade which projects obnoxious odor.	Proposed for use to disperse crowds.	Not in use.	Problems of decontamination, public acceptance and effectiveness. May be physically harmful to persons with respiratory problems.

F. Miscellaneous Weapons:

1. Marking Devices

Paint Gun	Gelatin capsule contains a marking agent which splatters on impact leaving a 3" circle and streamers from 12" to 18".	Could indelibly mark fleeing persons for later capture.	Available for commercial marking but not as a weapon.	Police have no systems for use of such a weapon. Questionable effectiveness.
Smoke Dyes	Marking dye can be added to smoke in crowd control.	Identification of rioters. Also a deterrent for anyone anxious to avoid identification.	Available.	Not specific enough. Could mark innocent bystanders as well.
Fluorescent Marking Powder	Concept envisions a fluorescent powder sprayed onto crowds from pressurized container. Particles adhere to clothing and are only visible under ultraviolet light.	Could be used as proof of an individual's presence at an unlawful gathering.	Available.	Not specific enough. Could mark innocent bystanders as well.

2. Others

Foam Generator	Concept involves blowing air through nylon net kept wet with mixture which creates foam.	Enormous quantities of foam can be produced quickly to create a barrier which will last 5 to 10 minutes.	Available; not in use.	Difficult to control. Affects users as well as victims.
Instant Jungle, Instant Cocoon, Instant Mud	Quick-setting sticky substances delivered by projectile or from back pack container.	Inhibits undesirable action by restricting movement.	Not available.	Questionable suitability and effectiveness for many control situations.
Rapid Rope	Nylon rope dispersed by "Archolithic Gun" using compressed air mounted on truck. Thirty cubic feet per minute.	Can be used to block off small areas such as store fronts.	Available.	Police dislike most barriers because they lack flexibility and affect users as well as victims.

* From: Security Planning Corporation, *Non-lethal Weapons for Law Enforcement*, Washington, D.C., 1972.

E. CALIFORNIA INTELLIGENCE PROJECTS
FUNDED BY LEAA, 1972–1974

Recipient and Title (Project No.* and Duration)	Amount
1972	
Orange County DA (605; 2 yrs.) Intracounty Intelligence Coordination Project	$ 75,421
Long Beach Police Department (441; 2 yrs.) Analysis, Redevelopment, Upgrading of Intelligence Section	120,264
Department of Justice (174; 3 yrs.) Integrated Program to Combat Organized Crime	1,060,438
Fresno County Sheriff (458; 2 yrs.) Intercounty Information System	34,150
Santa Clara DA (1940; 1 yr.) Santa Clara County Organized Crime Task Force	27,000
Sacramento County Sheriff (861; 8 yrs.) Organized Crime Detection and Prevention Program	63,177
San Mateo County Sheriff (561; 2 yrs.) Countywide Organized Crime Unit	134,922
Fresno County Sheriff (458; 3 yrs.) Intercounty Information System	28,281
South Lake Tahoe Police Department (564; 2 yrs.) Organized Crime Intelligence Unit	35,060
Santa Barbara County Sheriff (1245; 1 yr.) Organized Crime Unit	70,937
San Diego County DA (712; 2 yrs.) Organized Crime Prevention Program	177,700
Alameda County Sheriff (1258; 1 yr.) Alameda County Organized Crime Enforcement Association	100,000
Santa Cruz County (1066; 1 yr.) Tricounty Organized Crime Information Council	56,710
Riverside County Sheriff (1458; 1 yr.) Riverside County Organized Crime Intelligence Unit	94,890
Office of Emergency Services (875; 1 yr.) Statewide Prepositioning of Riot Control Equipment	484,050
Los Angeles County Sheriff (29; 2 yrs.) Riot and Crowd Control Instruction	71,864
California Military Department (475; 3 yrs.) California Civil Disorder Management Course	423,978
Sacramento County Sheriff (1276; 1 yr.) Sacramento Area Explosive Ordinance Disposal Unit	91,210

229

Yuba City Police Department (1729; 99 yrs.)   3,308
Microfilming of departmental records in lieu of shelf and cabinet storage

Alameda County Sheriff (1292; 1 yr.)   64,839
Alameda County Hazardous Devices Squad

California Military Department (1454; 1 yr.)   626,600
Officer Survival and Internal Security Course (includes 3rd year of 0475)

1973

Department of Justice (1672; 1 yr.) $ 115,000
California Narco Information Network (CNIN) State Component

Torrance Police Department (1839; 1 yr.)   49,000
South Bay Information and Narcotics Unit

Stanislaus County (1865; 1 yr.)   250,000
Stanislaus County Drug Enforcement Unit

Santa Clara County DA (1940; 8 yrs.)   75,000
Santa Clara County Organized Crime Task Force

Santa Clara County Sheriff (1669; 2 yrs.)   38,236
California Narco Information Network (CNIN) Local Component

Sacramento County Sheriff (861; 2 yrs.)   41,892
Organized Crime Detection and Prevention Program

Stockton Police Department (1283; 2 yrs.)   63,670
Regional Organized Crime Intelligence

Orange County DA (605; 3 yrs.)   121,352
Intracounty Intelligence Coordination Project

Baldwin Park Police Department (1170; 2 yrs.)   366,323
East Valley Information System (EVIS)

South Lake Tahoe Police Department (564; 3 yrs.)   22,604
Organized Crime Intelligence Unit

Long Beach Police Department (441; 3 yrs.)   196,195
Analysis Redevelopment and Upgrading of Intelligence System

Santa Barbara County Sheriff (1245; 2 yrs.)   64,000
Organized Crime Unit

San Mateo County Sheriff (516; 3 yrs.)   94,587
Countywide Organized Crime Unit

Sonoma County Sheriff (1808; 1 yr.)   92,648
North Bay Regional Criminal Information System

Santa Cruz County DA (1066; 2 yrs.)   53,254
Tricounty Organized Crime Information Council

California Military Department (1454; 1 yr.)   0
Officer Survival and Internal Security Course (includes 3rd year of 0475)

Sacramento County Sheriff (1276; 2 yrs.)   51,273
Sacramento Area Explosive Ordinance Disposal Unit

1974

Sacramento County Sheriff (861; 3 yrs.)   20,946
Organized Crime Detection and Prevention Program

Baldwin Park Police Department (1170; 3 yrs.)   389,875
East Valley Information System (EVIS)

Santa Barbara County (1245; 3 yrs.)   32,000
Organized Crime Unit

Stockton Police Department (1283; 3 yrs.)   58,734
Regional Organized Crime Intelligence Unit

Riverside Sheriff's Department (1458; 2 yrs.)   99,591
Riverside County Organized Crime Intelligence Unit

Modesto Police Department (2040; 1 yr.)   2,599
Surveillance Kit

Conservation Department Forestry Division (2089; 1 yr.)   147,506
Computer Assisted Automatic Photographic Surveillance System

Total $6,287,885

* Office of Criminal Justice Planning Project

Source: Center for National Security Studies, *Law and Disorder IV*, Washington, D.C., Center for National Security Studies, 1976, pp. 121-123.

Picture Credits

Title page motif by Malaquias Montoya

PAGE	SOURCE
40	Bits Hayden, *The Big Strike*
41	Bits Hayden, *The Big Strike*
45	Danny Lyon, *The Movement*
48	*Liberation News Service*
92	*Liberation News Service*
104	*CounterSpy*
113	*Liberation News Service*
117	*Akwesasne Notes*
118	*Akwesasne Notes*
122	Art Kunkin, *Los Angeles Free Press*
160	George Cohen, *Guardian*
161	*Rising Up Angry*
163	Doug Hosteller
169	Peg Averill, *Liberation News Service*
172	*Women in Vietnam*
177	John Cantor, *Nuestra Lucha*
178	*Liberation News Service*
190	Victor Arnautoff, *On the Drumhead*
191	*Ori News Service*
192	Martha Bunim, *Guardian*
193	Laurie Lujan
194	Nyamavu, *Congress of Afrikan People*
195	George Cohen, *Guardian*
198	Victor Arnautoff, *On the Drumhead*
218	Steve Bohrer, *Strike*
231	Laurie Lujan

In the case of some graphics the source is unknown to us. Still others come from historical books, police publications, commercial newspapers, etc.

We wish to especially thank Vanguard, Foundation For National Progress, and CSPC for their financial assistance.

NOTES

DATE DUE

MAR 24 '89			